THE UNFOLDING SELF

THE UNFOLDING SELF

PSYCHOSYNTHESIS AND COUNSELING

Molly Young Brown

illustrations by Betsy James

PSYCHOSYNTHESIS PRESS
Los Angeles, California

First printing 1983
Second printing 1985
Third printing 1989
Fourth printing, 1992

Book Design by M. Gong

Library of Congress Catalog Number: 83-61449
ISBN 0-9611444-0-8

Psychosynthesis Press
1330 Lincoln Avenue Suite 303
San Rafael CA 94901

Distributed by:
Psychosynthesis Distribution
2561 Tioga Way
San Jose CA 95124

and

Bookpeople
2929 Fifth Street
Berkeley CA 94710

This book is printed on recycled paper.

For my parents, John and Emma Lou Young,
who provided such a loving beginning to my unfolding,
and who continue to support it today.

CONTENTS

LIST OF EXERCISES

PREFACE

The world is unfolding around us in ways that are both disturbing and exciting. On the one hand there is disintegration and disaster, even the threat of extinction through nuclear war. On the other hand, there is a movement toward synthesis, cooperation, and fulfillment in many areas of human endeavor. Actually, these are two sides of the same coin; both reflect an evolutionary paradigm shift, a phenomenon discussed at length in Marilyn Ferguson's *The Aquarian Conspiracy*. It is a shift to a full recognition of our interdependence with everyone and everything else on this planet. Many institutions and traditions, including psychology, are being challenged by this paradigm shift; those that are obsolete, ineffective, or destructive to emerging values will not survive. This process may look like disaster, for change rarely comes without pain. Yet the very breakdown of old models and ways gives rise to hope and a renewal of vision.

We are challenged by change to develop an evolutionary psychology to help us become the kind of people required by the times. Our psychology can help us to become increasingly aware of our vast potentials and to bring them into service in the world; it can help us develop and balance all the aspects of the human personality: intellect, emotion, body, intuition and imagination. An evolutionary psychology can facilitate courage and patience, wisdom and compassion, qualities needed in a time of paradigm shift and planetary crisis.

This book offers a contribution to evolutionary psychology. It is for counselors and therapists who want to challenge their clients to become what they have the potential to be, to move into their creative power and wisdom. It is for professionals who are not satisfied with short-term problem-solving or helping people adjust to life as it has been. As life is changing, so must we help our clients rise to new levels of health to meet it. The psychosynthesis approach to counseling and therapy is a powerful catalyst for this end.

Psychosynthesis at this time encompasses a fairly coherent body of concepts and methods and has come to be identified in many people's minds with one or another of those constructs. In this book, however, the word 'psychosynthesis' is rarely capitalized because it is considered not so much the proper name of a school or theory as it is a synonym for human growth. Psychosynthesis refers to the ongoing synthesis of the psyche, a process which transcends specific models and methods. Facilitating that process is what really matters; we shall discard the models and methods—the forms—when they no longer serve the spirit of human evolution.

Psychosynthesis methods and models are useful in education and for personal growth, and have application in almost every arena of life. This book is focused, however, on the individual psychosynthesis session, a period of one to two hours devoted to the 'psychosynthesis' of a particular individual. In other words, it is focused on individual counseling or psychotherapy using psychosynthesis approaches. This is a guidebook, offering maps, helpful hints, and conditioning exercise gleaned from the study of psychosynthesis which has integrated the wisdom of many guides and travelers on life's journey. It offers a perspective on the essential being and motivation of the individual traveler, a model of human growth, some principles of the process of growth, and ways of applying those principles. It suggests methods and discusses the mechanics of individual sessions. It explores the implications and uses of all these with specific kinds of problems and intermediate goals. Three transcripts in the appendix illustrate some of the principles and methods in sample sessions.

I invite you to participate in this book. I invite you to interact with the material, seeking your own truth and understanding alongside mine. There are exercises suggested from time to time; please try them out as a means of self-exploration and for experiencing more deeply what psychosynthesis is and how it works. Psychosynthesis is an affirmation of the power and wisdom inherent in each person, within the self of each of us. I hope my sharing of my truth will support you in more fully discovering and sharing yours. Psychosynthesis will continue to grow with contributions from all of us committed to an evolutionary psychology. As the founder of psychosynthesis, Roberto Assagioli, has said, "Let us realize the contribution we can make to the creation of a new civilization characterized by an harmonious integration and cooperation, pervaded by the spirit of synthesis." (1976, p. 9)

PREFACE TO THE FOURTH PRINTING

In the nearly ten years since *The Unfolding Self* was published, the world has undergone amazing, alarming, and inspiring changes. The Cold War has ended, the Soviet Union has dissolved, and the threat of nuclear war abated. At the same time, we have become increasingly aware of many mortal dangers to our planetary life support system, created by human abuse. Increasingly, we are called upon to rapidly and dramatically transform ourselves and our ways of living on Earth. Psychosynthesis continues to support this transformation in many countries and cultures, through individual counseling and therapy, in education and organizational development, and in religion, including the developing field of spiritual direction.

Psychosynthesis theory and practice have continued to evolve in the last ten years. The unfolding process of each person, group, and community has come to be increasingly respected, with the result that many psychosynthesis practitioners rely less on formal structures and techniques, and more on presence. If I were to write *The Unfolding Self* today, I would no doubt make some changes to reflect this evolution. Nevertheless, the basic principles are still valid and powerful; for this reason, I have not undertaken a major revision of the book. I believe it continues to serve well as an introduction and guide to psychosynthesis in counseling and psychotherapy.

This printing does include one major revision: the presentation of the Identification Exercise in Chapter 2. John Firman's critique of psychosynthesis in his privately published book, *"I" and Self: Revisioning Psychosynthesis,*[1] pointed out the implied dualism of the original form of this "classic" exercise; I became sufficiently uncomfortable with it that I chose to revise it for the fourth printing.

The other major change is the size; the larger format increases print size, in response to many comments I received about the previous printings. I hope you find it easier on the eyes to read.

Reader response to *The Unfolding Self* has warmed my heart and soul through the years. I look forward to continuing the dialogue as, working together, we bring our capacities into fuller service for the human family and our planetary home.

April, 1992

---

[1] Available from John Firman, 459 Hawthorne Avenue, Palo Alto CA 94301

ABOUT THE EXERCISES

One of the most basic principles of psychosynthesis and many other modern approaches to human growth, is that we learn best by doing. For this reason, I have included exercises throughout the book so that the reader may *experience* the principles and processes under discussion, not just read about them. Although I know it is often difficult to interrupt the flow of reading to do exercises, I encourage you to use them in some way as you study the concepts shared here. It may be helpful to record the exercise directions on audiotape and play them back for yourself, so that you can concentrate on your experience, with eyes closed. Many of the exercises, such as the *Identification Exercise,* may prove more useful with repetition.

It is difficult to credit the sources of these exercises, because many of them have been developed and shared by so many psychosynthesis practitioners that their origins are untraceable. Even exercises I have developed myself, or in conjunction with my colleagues Walter Polt and Susan Farley, are based on principles and ideas gleaned from many sources. In some cases, I have indicated the source of an exercise along with it. To clarify the origins of the others, however, the following acknowledgements should be made:

Exercises which were developed jointly by Walter Polt and me in our training program include: *Exploring Purpose, An Ideal Guide, Natural Imagery, The Process of Psychosynthesis,* and *Experiences of the Will. Who is Aware?* was first introduced to me by Harry Sloan, and *The Evening Review* by Susan and James Vargiu, but I believe they both belong in the same category as *The Wise Person*; they have been a part of the psychosynthesis tradition for so many years that I do not know who should receive the credit for their development.

ACKNOWLEDGMENTS

I have many people to thank for their help in creating this book. Betsy James' illustrations bring vitality and dimension to the book. Susan Farley's patient and thorough editing assured that the book says what I meant it to say. Marilyn Gong designed the book with care and quality. Suggestions and support have come from Doug Russell, Anne Maiden, Hank Maiden, and Elena Maulsby. Walter Polt, my colleague in InterMountain Associates for Psychosynthesis, and Jim Brown, my husband and colleague, were unflagging in their belief in and support of the project.

I want also to express my gratitude for my teachers: Roberto Assagioli, Lenore Lefer, Harry Sloan, John Firman, Anne Yeomans, Tom Yeomans, Anne Maiden, Jim Vargiu, and Walter Polt, as well as those who have taught me by sharing their growth and struggles in counseling. My sons, Gregory and Cassidy, have taught me by demonstrating psychosynthesis principles in their lives and growth; they also supported my work on the book by respecting my writing time and taking up the slack in the household.

I also want to thank the colleagues who encouraged me through conversations and letters. They include Jim Fadiman, Piero Ferrucci, Martha Crampton, Barbara Sachs, Peter Roche de Coppens, Jacqueline Small, Tracy Marks, Deanne Newman, Fairley Barnes, and many other friends who I hope know of my gratitude.

As I prepare some minor revisions prior to reprinting the book in January, 1989, I want to make special mention of Harry Sloan, who died in March, 1988, after a long struggle with cancer. He is the guide in the third session which appears at the end of the book (Transcript C). He offered loving presence in his guiding, and exuberant and often irreverent humor in his teaching. I will always be grateful for knowing and working with him.

The soul walks not upon a line,
neither does it grow like a reed.
The soul unfolds itself, like a lotus
of countless petals.

(*Gibran*, The Prophet, *1960*)

THE UNFOLDING SELF

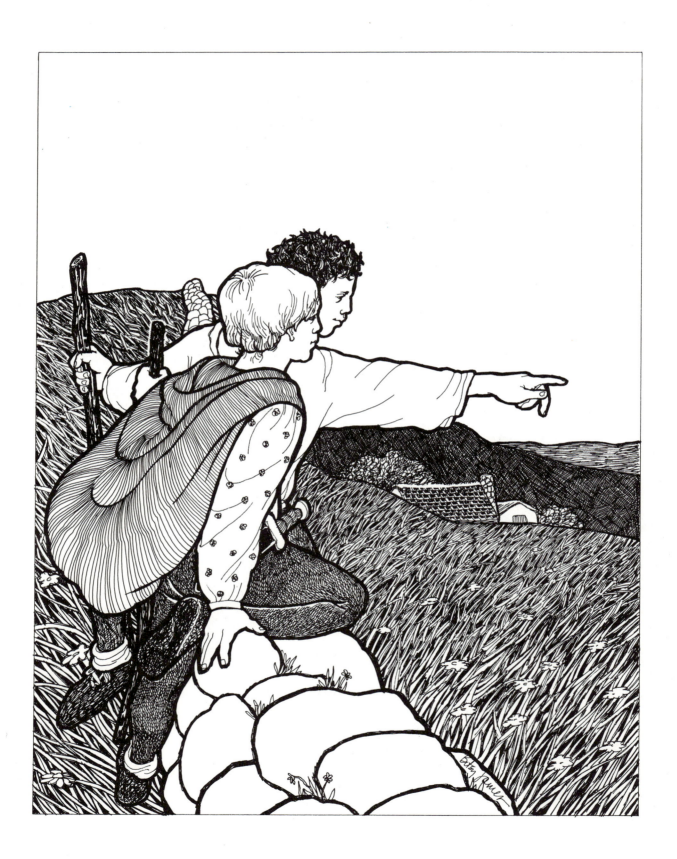

1

PSYCHOSYNTHESIS AND THE ART
OF GUIDING

From a still wider and more comprehensive point of view, universal life itself appears to us as a struggle between multiplicity and unity—a labor and an aspiration towards union. We seem to sense that—whether we conceive it as a divine Being or as cosmic energy—the Spirit working upon and within all creation is shaping it into order, harmony, and beauty, uniting all beings (some willing but the majority as yet blind and rebellious) with each other through links of love, achieving—slowly and silently, but powerfully and irresistibly—the Supreme Synthesis. (Assagioli, 1976 p. 31)

Roberto Assagioli (1888-1974) began exploring psychosynthesis early in this century, formulating his first thoughts on the subject in his doctoral thesis in 1910. By the middle of the century he had developed a model for this natural process of life—the universal principal of synthesis as it manifests in the individual and in relationships among people. Psychosynthesis "is first and foremost a dynamic, even a dramatic conception of our psychological life, which it portrays as a constant interplay and conflict between many different and contrasting forces and a unifying center which ever tends to control, harmonize and use them" (Assagioli, 1976, p. 30). Psychosynthesis is a synonym for human growth, the ongoing process of integrating all the parts, aspects, and energies of the individual into a harmonious, powerful whole. Like most 'natural' processes, this one can be enhanced and facilitated by awareness, understanding, and specific techniques.

Applying the principle of synthesis to his work, Dr. Assagioli drew upon the wisdom of many psychological and philosophical traditions, including psychoanalysis, Jungian psychology and existential psychology, as well as Buddhism, Yoga, and some elements of Christian esoteric study. Assagioli asserted that a human psychology cannot be complete without including the so-called spiritual dimension, our relationship to the cosmos and to our highest ideals. While he drew on the perspectives of religion and philosophy, he did not identify his work with any single belief system. "Psychosynthesis does not aim nor attempt to give a metaphysical nor a theological explanation of the great Mystery—it leads to the door, but stops there" (Assagioli, 1976, pp. 6-7).

3

With the publication of his book, *Psychosynthesis-A Manual of Principles and Techniques* in 1965, psychosynthesis became known throughout the world and attracted many students, especially in the United States, who were seeking to integrate their search for meaning with their interest in human psychology. Many people went to Italy to study with Dr. Assagioli until his death in 1974. He encouraged his students to continue the work wherever they were, expanding the pool of resources—models and methods—while remaining true to their own visions. Centers began to spring up in the United States and Canada as well as Holland, England, France, Greece, and of course in Assagioli's native Italy. Training programs were offered and in the process, the body of knowledge of psychosynthesis grew. Assagioli was able to seed a movement which has grown freely and with remarkably little dogma and constricting structure.

THE ART OF GUIDING

Many practitioners of psychosynthesis use the term 'guiding' to refer to what they do in individual counseling or therapy sessions. Guiding is an art, creatively bringing together all the resources of the personality, of knowledge, and of training and experience to facilitate the psychosynthesis of the client. Guiding from the psychosynthesis perspective has much in common with other approaches, yet goes beyond the limited goals of many. The vision and purpose of psychosynthesis guiding makes possible its unique and powerful contribution to the evolutionary psychology so needed in our changing times. This vision is reflected in the use of the term 'guide' and in the whole approach to individual work.

WHY CALL IT 'GUIDING'?

It is easy to imagine that counseling (or guiding) is as old as mankind, although its forms have varied greatly. We have probably always sought help from each other and tried to help one another with life's problems. Only recently has this practice been formalized into psychotherapy and counseling. On the simplest level, the counselor's purpose seems to be to help people feel better, function better, get along with others, and realize their potentials. A counselor's personal motives may include a sense of doing something worthwhile, compassion for others, and the desire to serve. The choice to be a counselor may stem from the knowledge that as humans we share a common destiny and interest, so that in helping another person to a better life, we advance our common weal. In Buddhism, this third motive is expressed in the tradition of the 'Bodhisattva' who, after enlightenment, chooses to return to help others develop spiritually, for no one can be fully liberated until all humanity has found enlightenment. Although few counselors and therapists would claim to be bodhisattvas, many of us would align ourselves with the goal of advancing the health and potentials of humanity.

While the ultimate purpose of counseling may encompass the welfare of the species, we are concerned here with bringing to life the fullest potential of the *individual*. This is a natural, on-going process; it is not something which needs to be imposed on anyone. The purpose of counseling is simply to cooperate with and enhance this inner direction. Hence it seems more precise to call the process 'guiding' and the practitioner 'guide' to indicate that the purpose is to guide life 'travelers' in finding their own paths and directions. These are the terms commonly used by psychosynthesis practitioners. 'Therapist' can suggest the diagnosis and treatment of sickness, and 'counselor' may imply giving advice, because many practitioners perform those functions exclusively. A guide, on the other hand, is someone who is familiar with the terrain of personal development, who knows some of the hazards and precautions, and who lovingly offers this knowledge and skill to the traveler. A guide does not, however, presume to know what is ultimately right for the traveler, who must finally make his or her own choices. As Bugental describes it, "the traveler seeks sure guidance, guarantees of safe passage, but the guide offers only the suppositions of experience—valuable experience, but always experience other than those of this particular road on this unique day." (1978, pp. 62-3).

Although I use the terms 'guide' and 'guiding' throughout this book, I am not comfortable with using the rather metaphoric term 'traveler.' Instead, I refer to that half of the relationship as the 'client.' I prefer 'client' to 'patient' because the latter suggests one who is ill and consults a practitioner to get well. The process of psychosynthesis is healthy, even though it may entail periods of suffering and distress. I think we will all be more at peace when we view life's difficulties as natural and potentially growth-engendering, instead of labeling them as illnesses to be cured by some outside agent.

So we have a guide and a client entering into a relationship to further the psychosynthesis of the client—and that of the guide as well. This relationship is at the heart of guiding; to illustrate, let me share my own experience as a client at a time before I was a counselor myself.

Several years ago I found myself at a crossroads in my life. I was in distress and went looking for a counselor. I knew I wanted someone who would not get caught up in my confusion or games, who could be lovingly objective about what was going on with me. I also knew I wanted someone who wouldn't impose upon me some preconceived notions about me and my problems, or some standard process for me to go through. I wanted someone to help me work out my own solutions, keeping me on the track, yet patiently waiting for me to do what I needed to do in my own time and manner. I was lucky; I found someone who was able to be with me in these ways. In the year's work with her, I found a new life direction and freed myself from many old patterns which had held me back.

My counselor had qualities many of us want in our guides. She listened well; she accepted everything I shared, including things I felt ashamed of. She let me know in her manner that she trusted me fully to cope with my life and supported my creative steps toward doing so. She suggested methods for working with issues during sessions, such as Gestalt chair work or imagery. She was also open to working in ways I suggested. She shared her insights about my process without imposing them on me. She also shared models and perspectives which helped my mind cooperate with the growth process. I felt she was there at my service during our counseling hour. I felt she loved and respected me as a person and in no way held me beneath herself. We met as equals in the counseling hour, in the service of my growth.

I think it is important to note that my counselor was not versed in formal psychosynthesis. The qualities of a good guide are not exclusively in the province of psychosynthesis, although it is difficult to be a psychosynthesis guide without them. It is difficult to be any kind of guide without them.

As Carl Rogers (1978) and many others have noted, *who* we are as counselors or guides matters much more than the techniques or methods we use. Who we are includes all aspects of ourselves as people, including the philosophical perspectives and methods we choose to use. The process of learning and perfecting our craft as guides is not only a process of learning theory and techniques; it is a process of submitting ourselves to self-discovery about who we really are and can become, about our talents and qualities, about our essential purposes in life and in guiding, and about our own next steps in growth. (See Chapter 4 for more on this topic.)

THE PURPOSE OF GUIDING

Basic to any meaningful activity is its purpose, the underlying motivating force which can pour forth in myriad strategies and forms. Without a clear sense of purpose, we often become caught up in the *form* itself, mistaking the means for the end. We forget *why* we're doing something and our work becomes mechanical and hackneyed. In guiding as in other aspects of life, recalling our purpose can enliven and sustain us, even in times of stagnation or apparent regression. We remember what it's all about, and the rough times become more tolerable.

There are many levels of purpose. The deepest and most fundamental usually provides the widest range of options from which to choose. It also provides a touchstone for evaluating our choices and over-all progress. Unfortunately, we are sometimes content with a superficial purpose which fails to relate our work to a larger whole.

The following exercise is intended to help you clarify and deepen your own sense of purpose.

EXERCISE: EXPLORING PURPOSE

Take a few minutes to get comfortable and relaxed. If it helps, close your eyes and allow your feelings and thoughts to become quiet and receptive. When you feel ready, open your eyes and read the questions below, taking each inside for contemplation. Allow your answers to come in the form of words, imagery, or 'impressions'. You may want to make a note of each response before going on to the next question. Now take a few moments to ready yourself . . .

What is my purpose in guiding, as a friend or as a professional? . . .

And what is the purpose of that? . . .

And what is the purpose of that? . . .

And what is the purpose of that? . . .

Continue in this manner until you find a sense of purpose which seems to have the greatest meaning and usefulness to your work . . .

You may want to write a clear, concise statement of that deepest purpose in your journal before reading on.

(This exercise can also be done with a partner who asks the question about purpose over and over again, allowing the other to respond each time.)

"Zen in its essence is the art of seeing into the nature of one's being, and it points the way from bondage to freedom. We can say that Zen liberates all the energies properly and naturally stored in each of us, which are in ordinary circumstances cramped and distorted so that they find no adequate channel for activity. . . . It is the object of Zen, therefore, to save us from going crazy or being crippled. This is what I mean by freedom, giving free play to all the creative and benevolent impulses lying in our hearts."
(Suzuki, 1949, pp. 9-10)

Therapies and counseling methods have developed to meet different needs and therefore often seem to work toward different purposes. Yet the various approaches are all related to a larger purpose (whether their founders and practitioners know it or not) and they all have a potential contribution to make to human evolution. Ken Wilber explores the relationships among various approaches in *The Spectrum of Consciousness* (1977). He offers a model of consciousness which includes various levels, each of which requires appropriate therapeutic techniques. Each level expresses a basic dualism or split in the mind of the individual, a distortion of the unified consciousness of universal Mind. Each therapeutic approach, then, has evolved to help heal a specific split, whether it be between a part of one's personality and the whole, or between mind and body, or between self and environment. These approaches share a common purpose: "They reverse the process of dualism by helping the individual contact alienated and projected aspects, reintegrate them, and thus 'heal,' 'make whole,' and 'unify,' that level. This process results in 'cure,' 'growth,' or 'healing,' for the simple reason that the individual has, in effect, broadened or expanded his sense of self-identity" (p. 279). As the dualistic split at each level is healed, the individual's consciousness moves to the next deeper level and the next dualism in a continual process of becoming more whole, closer to perceiving his or her essential unity with universal Mind. (Wilber arranges his spectrum from unitive Mind *up* toward greater and greater distortion. In his scheme, higher consciousness is deeper!)

Guiding which includes the whole person, body and soul, seems vital at all levels of consciousness. Wilber points out that "while therapists of one level recognize all the levels *above* their own (that is, farther from universal Mind), they view any level deeper than their own as being of a pathological character and so are quick to explain it away with a diagnostic fury" (p. 191). For example, therapists accustomed to working with repressed sexuality may interpret a spiritual crisis in their old familiar sexual terms, especially if the therapists themselves are not open to their own spiritual yearnings. There is real danger in the indiscriminate use of a single therapeutic approach for all symptoms and for similar symptoms originating from different levels of consciousness. If we begin at the ground of deepest purpose—the realization of the whole person, body, mind, and soul—we are less likely to misinterpret a deeper state of consciousness as pathological or to apply an inappropriate therapeutic technique based on such misinterpretation.

Self-Realization

Assagioli conceives of the central purpose of psychosynthesis as "the harmonization and integration into one functioning whole of all the qualities and functions of the individual" (1976, p. 7), or, in a word, 'self-realization.' Realization implies a potential 'something' to be realized or brought into life. Psychosynthesis shifts focus away from pathology and towards discovering the tremendous potential which lies, largely dormant, within each individual. Our greatest joy comes from tapping and using this potential in creative activity. Each person has a unique set of gifts, a special vision, talent, or quality. In addition, we all have in common a great many talents and qualities which we can develop *together* and use more effectively in creating a better world. The purpose of guiding in individual psychosynthesis work may be stated in this way: to help individuals to discover, experience, and put into expression their unique and universal potentials.

"Great men, as every schoolboy knows, have greeted their moments of learning with crazy joy." (G. Leanord, 1968)

The process of realizing potential has many levels. It does not serve the individual to impose a preconceived vision of his or her potential and how it is to be expressed. We need to recognize and accept each client at whatever level of consciousness he or she is, with whatever talents and problems, and assist in that person's next step. Thus our immediate purpose may be to change a maladaptive behavior pattern or work through grief or anger. And what would be the point in doing this if more of the individual's potential were not freed in the process?

Some Dangers in Goal Setting

There are many legitimate immediate goals in counseling and therapy ranging from 'changing behavior to fit the demands of the world in order to survive' to 'overcoming writer's block' to 'integrating spiritual experience into daily life.' 'Changing behavior to fit the world's demands' is an example, however, of a goal which is sometimes imposed inappropriately. If the counselor is working from a model of pathology, he or she may interpret behavior which is not within the norms of the society as a sign of neurosis or psychosis, when the client's real need is to accept and understand a transcendent, creative, or transpersonal experience and to integrate it into daily life. R.D. Laing and Ken Wilber are two of many writers who have been concerned with the tendency of social groups to label difference as insanity or sin. Often someone whose ideas appear insane to society is close to a new paradigm which represents the next step in a whole field of knowledge. History is replete with examples of this; some of the most significant scientific discoveries were branded heresy by the learned societies and by the common belief of their time. Galileo was one of the most outstanding victims of this phenomenon. Psychologists, counselors, teachers, and other guides are not exempt from being limited by the norms of their society, and may inappropriately, even destructively, impose them on their clients.

Our present world situation, with its overshadowing threat of nuclear holocaust, creates a unique challenge in this area of goals and social norms. Alan Nelson, writing on "The Profession's Role in Peace Facilitation," (1983) notes that awareness of this situation brings "fear, anxiety, despair, hopelessness, depression," and other psychological symptoms. He points out:

> Who wouldn't like to find a psychotherapist so good they could make things right with the world? But what a pitfall for the therapist, trying to adjust persons to either an illusory "normality" where there are no major problems in the world, or to a normality which is itself almost unbelievably destructive.
>
> Our pain and suffering are largely healthy first reactions to accurate perceptions. As difficult as they are they *cannot* helpfully be diagnosed or treated as individual pathology . . .
>
> It is therefore important *not* to pathologize accurate perceptions or understandable reactions to our crises, both for the integrity of the person and for the survival of the species.

Similarly, we have the problem of a large number of people, possibly even the majority in this country, evidencing the psychological symptom of denial in the face of this terrifying reality. If denial is the social norm, how can we use social norms to gauge a person's health or to set appropriate goals in therapy? It seems we must draw upon a wider perspective than the norm, a perspective that includes the terrifying problems of our times as well as the awesome potentials.

There is also the danger of psychological snobbery in choosing goals for clients in terms of levels of consciousness or motivation. We may decide that some clients are somehow better or higher than others, and only they deserve certain forms of therapy. Clearly we must work with people in terms they can understand and use, *and* we must continually see people in their full light as psycho-spiritual beings.

Four basic principles which are explored in depth in this book can serve as guidelines to avoid these dangers. They apply to work with people at all levels of consciousness and motivation. First, we regard all individuals as whole persons, taking into account their strengths and potentials as well as their problems. This helps prevent our energizing the maladaptive aspects unduly. Secondly, we work with disidentification from separate parts and identification with larger wholes. This enables individuals to make choices beneficial to their real needs and potentials. Third, we evoke the individual's own will to make these choices and follow through on them, facilitating independence and self-responsibility. Finally, and probably most important, we strive to be fully present ourselves, so that we have access to the wisdom of our feelings,

"A teacher or a culture doesn't create a human being. It doesn't implant within him the ability to love, or to be curious, or to philosophize, or to symbolize, or to be creative. Rather, it permits or fosters or encourages or helps what exists in embryo to become real and actual."
(Maslow, 1968, p. 161)

"The traditional distinctions between 'sick' patients coming to a psychiatrist to be made normal, and prepared students seeking a teacher in order to become enlightened is today breaking down."
(Rama, Ballentine, and Ajaya, *Yoga and Psychotherapy* 1976, pp. 177-178)

mind, body, imagination, and intuition—so that our own potential for transcendence broadens our perspective in every aspect of our work.

People do not fall into separate, distinct classes of problems and therapy, try as we might to make them. Medical doctors are increasingly aware that diagnosis of disease must include an understanding of the whole person. People are all engaged in a process of gradual growth and awakening, from the catatonic to the pragmatist to the mystic. Growth operates on a continuum and the basic principles of growth are the same at any level. Psychosynthesis stands on these principles and applies them to all kinds of therapeutic and teaching situations, providing a framework for choosing appropriate techniques.

THE ART OF GUIDING: A SYNTHESIS OF MANY TRADITIONS

Psychosynthesis combines many traditions, Eastern and Western, in a careful synthesis, seeking basic universal wisdom about the realization of human potential. There is much agreement among these traditions and approaches about the purpose of what they do. The existentialists, like Carl Rogers and James Bugental, seek to facilitate the development of the 'fully functioning person,' an individual who is integrated in mind and body and who moves to the fullest realization of his or her personal potential. The transpersonal psychologists like Abraham Maslow and Carl Jung, and the Eastern teachers, write of transcendence, of identification with universal Being, and the pursuit of pure Truth. On an essential level, there is no conflict between these two points of view. Realization of one's potentials can be considered to include the transpersonal realm, while the integration and actualization of the personality are essential steps toward expression of transpersonal potentials.

"The goal of psychosynthesis could be described as bridging spirit and matter, as creating a world of form at the personality level which is fully expressive of the person's spiritual being" (Crampton, 1977, pp. 20-21). The process of working toward self-realization includes awareness (knowledge and awakening) and will (responsibility, freedom, self-determination). We push back the limits on our capacity for guiding this process as we expand our concepts of human potential and of the essential nature of the person. It is here that psychosynthesis makes special contributions to evolutionary psychology, offering its perspectives on our essential nature, and on the process of individual growth and evolution, and providing models which are derived from that perspective.

"Transcendence refers to the very highest and most inclusive or holistic levels of human consciousness, behaving and relating, as ends rather than as means, to other species, to nature, and to the cosmos."
(Maslow, 1971, p. 279)

2

A MODEL OF HUMAN GROWTH

Psychosynthesis brings the matter to a point of extreme simplicity, seeing the self as the most elementary and distinctive part of our being—in other words, its core. This core is of an entirely different nature from all the elements (physical sensations, feelings, thoughts and so on) that make up our personality. As a consequence, it can act as a unifying center, directing those elements and bring them into the unity of an organic wholeness. (Ferrucci, 1982, p. 16)

How do people realize themselves? What is the 'self' that they realize? At the heart of philosophy and psychology lies the question of the essential nature of the human being. Can we guide one another without some sense of what we are all about? The models we hold about the nature of the person, both in general and in relation to a particular individual, have profound effects on our goals and our interventions. Psychosynthesis models are positive and growth-oriented; they often prompt guides to develop original methods rather than limiting them to a set of standard procedures. The models themselves are open to adaptation and change as we learn more about people.

Our hypotheses and models are helpful; they give us a starting place from which to explore and develop our work. Yet they are only approximations, educated guesses about the vast mystery of our being. As we approach any psychological model or theory, let us retain a strong sense of this mystery, lest we become dogmatic and close our minds to the ever-new discoveries of living.

Psychosynthesis models describe the nature of the self, the will, and the unconscious. They are concerned with the relationship of the various personality functions to each other and to the self, and the relationship of the self to the universal. They articulate human motivations from pure survival to transcendence and service, and the dimensions of human growth towards greater effectiveness and expanded meaning. These models have shed some light on the mystery of our being. Because they are oriented toward health and potential rather than pathology, they are valuable guides in work with others and with our own evolution.

Assagioli noticed a recurring theme in Eastern and Western philosophy regarding the existence of a *self,* an integrating center which *is* the essential individual, underlying roles, behaviors, feelings, thoughts, physical manifestations, even gender. The *self* is a center of pure

11

awareness and of intentionality, or *will*. It is from this center that we make the choices which determine our life direction, style, and form. Assagioli placed this concept at the center of psychosynthesis thought and practice.

Assagioli emphasized, however, the experiential nature of the 'self,' which is far more significant and important than any logical formulation. The *concept* is an attempt to account for the *experience* of people who are (at times) able to remain 'centered' in the face of external hardship and internal distress. This experience is of *being*, unshaken by changes in the body, feelings, or mind, always conscious and capable of choice. It is this experience which we attempt to facilitate in guiding.

The Identification Exercise is used in psychosynthesis to help people gain more clarity about the nature of the 'self.' Going through the exercise at this point may help our discussion of the self to be more grounded in immediate experience.

IDENTIFICATION EXERCISE

This exercise is a method of letting go of limiting ideas about oneself and finding a deep sense of who one really is. Through this process, we can gain freedom and the power of choice to be fully who we are. We can use with appreciation and power our body, feelings, and mind, rather than being controlled by their ever-changing conditions.

Sit in a comfortable position, relax your body, and allow your breathing to become slow and deep. Read each paragraph slowly and then close your eyes and pay attention to your inner responses.

I have a body, and I value my body. I experience the sensations of my body through different conditions of health and sickness, activity and rest, vigor and tiredness. My body is my precious instrument of experience and of action and so I treat it well and seek to keep it in good health. My body affects and expresses who I am, but it is not my self. I have a body, but I am not only a body.

I have emotions, and I value my emotions. My feelings are countless, contradictory, and changing, yet while they change I know I always remain "I", my self. I remain myself in times of hope or despair, in joy or pain, in a state of irritation or calm. Since I can observe and understand my emotions, and then increasingly embrace and direct them, I know that they are not my self. My emotions affect and express who I am, but I am not only my emotions.

I have a thinking mind, and I value my thinking mind. It is a primary tool of discovery and expression, constantly changing with new ideas, beliefs, knowledge, and experience. My mind is not the essence of my being, however, because I remain essentially my self through all my mind's changes. My mind affects and expresses who I am, yet does not determine who I am. I have a thinking mind, and I am not only my mind.

I have a body, emotions, and a thinking mind, and yet I am not only these. Then who or what am I? I am a center of consciousness and will, distinct but not separate from my body, feelings and mind. I am "I", capable of observing, harmonizing, and making choices about my life, my attitudes and actions. I am the one who is aware, the one who chooses.

Take time to honor your experience in this exercise in all its facets, pleasant and unpleasant.   Then you may want to make some notes about your experience in your journal before continuing.   (Adapted by the author from an exercise by Roberto Assagioli, incorporating ideas from John Firman and James Brown.)

Perhaps you can recall other experiences of being a self, although you may not have put the word *self* on them.   Perhaps you have sensed two aspects of that experience, a quiet awareness and an active will.   In an interview with Sam Keen, Assagioli described the self in this way:

> At the heart of the self there is both an active and a passive element, an agent and a spectator.   Self-consciousness involves our being a witness—a pure, objective, loving witness—to what is happening within and without.   In this sense, the self is not a dynamic in itself but is a point of witness, a spectator, an observer who watches the flow.   But there is another part of the inner self—the will-er or directing agent— that actively intervenes to orchestrate the various functions and energies of the personality, to make commitments and to instigate action in the external world.   So, at the center of the self, there is a unity of ... will and love, action and observation.   (Assagioli in Keen, 1974)

Let's distinguish 'self' from 'ego' as it is commonly conceived.   Ego may imply pride, selfishness, concern with personal glory and aggrandizement.   The self is without qualities. It is pure awareness, without content; the source of the energy of intention, choice, or will. It is closer to Jung's concept of ego than to Freud's.

We need to distinguish as well between disidentification from our ever-changing sensations, feelings, and thoughts, and separating from or disowning our body, feelings, and mind.   The self is immanent in our moment to moment experiencing of body, feelings, and mind, and when we disidentify from them and identify with the self, we more fully experience and own all the aspects of our physical and psychological being.

Moreover, the self is present whether or not we are feeling particularly "centered" or "whole."   We may not be aware of being a self when we are identified with a passing feeling or belief, but the self is always present.   Feeling "centered" may more often put us in touch with the self, but sometimes we discover the self in the midst of despair and disintegration.

The concept of the self profoundly affects the way in which we approach guiding.   We see ourselves cooperating with the self and working to evoke the client's identification with the self (as is described in later chapters).   This process is emphasized far more than the content of the client's issues or even the psychological problems.   Knowing the self is there gives the guide support and courage with even the most resistant and confused client.

PERSONAL SELF AND HIGHER SELF

The self is understood to be a manifestation of a Higher Self, an energetic source which is rarely experienced directly.   Yet most Eastern and transpersonal psychologies point to its reality.   "This Self is above, and unaffected by, the flow of the mind-stream or by bodily conditions" (Assagioli, 1976, p. 19).   The Self is reflected in the personal self which is more accessible to direct experience.

There are not really two selves, two independent and separate entities. The self is one; it manifests in different degrees of awareness and self-realization. The reflection appears to be self-existent, but has in reality no autonomous substantiality. It is, in other words, not a new and different light but a projection of its luminous source. (Assagioli, 1976, p. 20)

The self with a lower case 's' is used in psychosynthesis to refer to the personal center. The Self with an upper case 'S' refers to the luminous source, the Higher or Transpersonal Self. Self-expression or Self-realization refers to the expression of the Self through the personality, with the personal self acting as administrative agent. We always have the choice as personalities to resist this expression; this is what often leads to problems which bring people into therapy or counseling. Guiding is the process of helping one another rediscover and 'tune into' the expression of the Higher Self.

The relationship of the self to the Higher Self is shown in Assagioli's oval diagram below, a model of individual consciousness. At the center is the personal self, descended, as it were, from the Higher Self at the top of the oval. The Higher Self at once partakes of individual consciousness (the oval) and of universal consciousness (outside the oval). This is shown by the rays extending into the oval and above it. The Higher Self is a synthesis of individual and universal. That is why it is also called the Transpersonal Self; it transcends the personal.

> **"It feels as if one were being drawn inward toward a center of great luminosity, yet to fly straight into it would be like a moth darting into a flame or the earth hurtling itself into the center of the sun. So one moves around the center instead, close enough to see the brightness, to feel the warmth, but maintaining the orbital tensions, a dynamic relationship of a small finite being to a source of light and energy that has no limits.**
>
> **"The small finite being is, of course, the "ego," the "I" of which each one of us is aware. The mysterious "non-ego" or . . . the "not-I," is termed by Jung the "self" . . . . It is that center of being which the ego circumambulates."**
> **(Singer, 1973, pp.271-272)**

Figure 1 — Oval Diagram

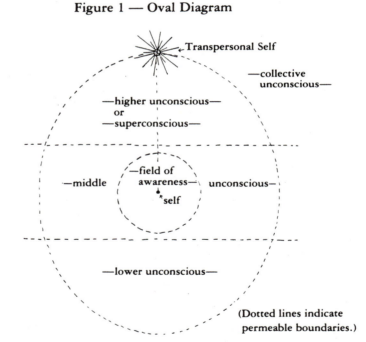

The *will* is "the most direct expression of the self" (Assagioli, 1974, p. 113) and this is true for both the personal self and the Higher Self. "Just as there is a personal will . . . so there is a Transpersonal Will, which is an expression of the Transpersonal Self and operates from the superconscious levels of the psyche" (p. 113). Transpersonal Will is the "will to transcend personality limitations through union with someone or something greater and higher

. . . the union of will and love" (p. 116). Aligning the personal will with the Transpersonal Will often brings an experience of power and release. We may feel a 'pull' or 'call' from a 'higher power.' The original meaning of 'vocation' suggests this experience; *to call forth*. The Transpersonal Will calls forth from the personality through the personal will those abilities and skills needed to express the Self more fully in the world. It is the agent for Self-realization, our central purpose in guiding. (This experience is discussed more fully in Chapter 8, "Spiritual Awakening and Transformation.")

BEYOND THE SELF

The Self is thought to be an individual expression of a larger Whole, called among other names Universal Being. This paradigm is in harmony with Eastern conceptions of reality and with some theories about the nature of consciousness and reality now on the frontiers of Western scientific thought. The holographic model of the universe suggested in the work of Karl Pribram and David Bohm is one such theory. Any section of the photographic holograph will reproduce the whole image; Pribram and Bohm suggest that any 'section' of reality may contain the pattern of the whole. The Self, then, might be said to be a hologram of Universal Being. The Self is the interface between the part (the individual) and the whole (Universal Being). It is through the Self that the individual is in union with fellow humans and with the whole of creation. At rare moments in life we may experience this sense of oneness and unity for ourselves. Our recognition of this reality allows us to validate these experiences in our clients.

LEVELS OF CONSCIOUSNESS

The oval diagram also charts the fields of consciousness in the individual. The unconscious is understood to have three levels: the lower unconscious, corresponding to Freud's unconscious arena of repressed desires and traumas, fundamental drives, and elementary psychological activities which direct the life of the body; the middle unconscious as a neutral area of recently forgotten and easily recalled experience, similar to what Freud called the preconscious; and the higher unconscious or superconscious, which is in closest relationship to the Higher Self. Here lies our creativity, intuition, promptings to love, compassion, and service, our highest values and inspirations, our spiritual energies and emerging growth patterns. The superconscious is the repository of our highest potential. In the midst of the middle unconscious is a circle representing the immediate field of awareness at any given time, with the self at the center. The lines between these areas are dotted, indicating their permeability either way. Even the outside oval is permeable as material from all levels of the collective unconscious moves into our unconscious and we send out our thoughts and feelings into the collective.

Awareness, acceptance, and integration of material from the higher unconscious is as vital to our personal development as is processing material from the lower unconscious; in fact, the 'repression of the sublime' can have as severe consequences as the repression of sexuality and aggression from the lower unconscious (Haronian, 1967). Rather than being merely a victim of desires, conditioned responses, and unconscious drives, the individual has the capacity to be the orchestrator of his or her own life, one who can both bring into actualization the tremendous potentials stored in the superconscious and direct and integrate the energies and patterns of the lower unconscious. In guiding, we need to be prepared to explore both realms.

PERSONALITY FUNCTIONS AND THE WILL

The relationship of the various functions of the personality to the self and the will is illustrated in the star diagram (Assagioli, 1974). In explaining the diagram, Assagioli writes:

> The will has been placed at the center of the diagram in direct contact with the conscious *I*, or personal self, to show the close connection between them. *Through* the will, the *I* acts on the other psychological functions, regulating and directing them. The diagram is oversimplified, like all diagrams, but it helps to give prominence to the central position of the will. (1974, pp. 12-13)

As you study the diagram, take a moment to focus on each of these personality functions within yourself: desire-impulse, sensation, emotion, thought, imagination, intuition. We have often failed to recognize imagination and intuition as distinct functions in our culture; identifying them as such seems to give them more power and usefulness. It may be nearly impossible to separate any of these functions, for all influence and use each another. This is dramatically summarized in Assagioli's psychological laws listed below. They describe how each psychological function responds to changes in others: physical conditions respond to images, ideas and emotions; emotions respond to images, ideas and physical conditions and acts; images and ideas are evoked by emotions and by physical postures and movements. All of these are in turn affected by unconscious drives and desires.

Figure 2 — Star Diagram

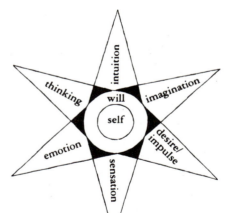

It is the will, the primary function of the self, which integrates, harmonizes, and directs these personality functions towards self-realization. We can enter the system, so to speak, through any modality to effect change. We can choose a change in imagery, emotion, or posture, for example, to introduce a new behavior pattern and attitude, using whichever modality is most amenable to direction at the time. Psychosynthesis guiding aims to develop and train the will to bring the personality functions into effective relationship with one another. As they are balanced and harmonized, they can be used to express superconscious qualities and carry out the purposes of the Higher Self.

———— ASSAGIOLI'S PSYCHOLOGICAL LAWS ————

I. Images or mental pictures and ideas tend to produce the physical conditions and the external acts that correspond to them.

II. Attitudes, movements, and actions tend to evoke corresponding images and ideas; these, in turn, (according to the next law) evoke or intensify corresponding emotions and feelings.

III. Ideas and images tend to awaken emotions and feelings that correspond to them.

IV. Emotions and impressions tend to awaken and intensify ideas and images that correspond to or are associated with them.

V. Needs, urges, drives, and desires tend to arouse corresponding images, ideas, and emotions.

VI. Attention, interest, affirmations, and repetitions reinforce the ideas, images, and psychological formulations on which they are centered.

VII. Repetition of actions intensifies the urge to further reiteration and renders their execution easier and better, until they come to be performed unconsciously.

VIII. All the various functions, and their manifold combinations in complexes and subpersonalities, adopt means of achieving their aims without our awareness, and independently of, and even against, our conscious will.

IX. Urges, drives, desires, and emotions tend and demand to be expressed.

X. The psychological energies can find expression: (1) directly (discharge/catharsis), (2) indirectly through symbolic action, and (3) through a process of transmutation.

(Assagioli, *The Act of Will*, 1974, pp. 51-65. The reader is urged to read these pages for a more thorough explication of the laws and their effects on our lives.)

SURVIVAL AND SELF-EXPRESSION

The psychosynthesis model of the individual is of a Self, or luminous source, manifesting through a personal self, through the many functions of the personality. The Self is consciousness acting and creating through the *will*, whether at the transpersonal level or the personality level in the world. The purpose of life is basically to find forms for expressing the qualities emanating from the Self, which is itself without quality, just as pure white light passes through a prism to form rainbows.

In order for the individual to express the Self, the organism must first survive physically, and the personality must survive in terms of mental and emotional stability and in relationship to the society around. Unfortunately, survival often becomes an end in itself and the behaviors at one time necessary for survival persist long after the adverse conditions have passed. Survival behavior becomes the goal, rather than a means for providing an environment for Self-expression.

Maslow's hierarchy of needs (1954, pp. 80-92) is a familiar model for exploring the progression from survival to Self-expression. One rendering of this model is shown in the following illustration. At the bottom are the basic physiological needs for food, sleep, elimination, and so forth. Next are the safety needs, for relative stability, order, and security (including shelter). Moving more into the emotional realm are the belonging and love needs, for family and friends. Next, the personality as a whole has needs for self-esteem, for respect and recognition.

At the top of the hierarchy are self-actualization needs, to develop and use one's capacities. If we capitalize the Self in Self-actualization, we could say that these needs are for Self-expression, through the capacities of the personality. That is why the top of the vessel is open. The satisfaction of the other needs provides a foundation for Self-expression to pour out in service to the world.

Figure 4 — Maslow's Hierarchy of Needs

As we satisfy each level of needs, the next higher level emerges so that we really never are satisfied, once and for all. Discontent motivates us to satisfy ever more complex needs until we reach the open- ended level of self-actualization. We never become 'self-actualized,' only 'self-actualizing.' And we must continue to meet our lower level needs, to make sure that our foundation of psycho-physical health is strong.

Subpersonalities

In conscious work on our personal growth, we often encounter constellations of behavior, feelings, and thought which are left over from a time they were needed for survival, to meet lower level needs. Although they no longer perform that function, they are loyally continuing on. They are like the Japanese marine who was discovered on a remote island in the Pacific several years after the end of World War II. Unaware that the war was over, he had continued to obey his orders. He was hailed as a hero and brought home with honors for his loyalty and service.

These constellations of behavior, feelings, and thought are called subpersonalities in psychosynthesis. They, too, need to be recognized for the service they are attempting to perform. Many of them are still useful in some situations; others, however, actually sabotage the very need they were designed to fulfill. For example, a little girl develops a cute, flirtatious subpersonality to win approval from her relatives, to satisfy her belonging needs. As she grows to womanhood and continues to act from this subpersonality, her opportunities to establish mature relationships are limited. Still, this subpersonality persists, loyal to the cause. Now it has become an atavistic survival pattern which prevents the expression of other qualities in her life.

When the initial purpose of a subpersonality is recognized and honored, it is often possible to reclaim the purpose and energy while letting go of the role or form. Other, more appropriate ways of meeting the need can be found. The Japanese marine was brought home from his island and no doubt found a new role for himself in society. The qualities of value in that subpersonality can be reintegrated into the personality as a whole, perhaps balancing qualities in other, previously conflicting, subpersonalities. (Methods for working with subpersonalities are included in Chapters 3 and 5.)

Many of us carry a survival subpersonality or two around with us, parts of us which never quite believe that we are going to 'make it.' The following exercise can help us become more aware of these patterns within.

EXERCISE: SEEKING A LOYAL SOLDIER

Take a few minutes to find a relaxed and comfortable position. Close your eyes and just be aware of your breathing . . .

Now begin to review your daily life over the past few weeks. Start with today and move backwards until you find a time or times when you felt afraid or anxious or constricted in some way. Perhaps it was about money, or a relationship, or your job, or some other aspect of your life. Choose a time when you were not in any immediate physical danger . . .

Allow yourself to relive this experience. Recall your feelings, your thoughts, your physical sensations and responses. . . . How does the world look from here? How do you feel about your own abilities? What actions are you tempted to take? . . .

Now in your imagination step away from yourself in the situation you have just recalled. See yourself as someone else looking at the situation might see you, with all the feelings, thoughts, reactions you experienced. Observe without judgment, just seeing who is there, what subpersonality you were identified with in the situation . . .

Notice what this subpersonality is trying to do for you. Ask it what it is trying to do and really listen to what it has to say . . .

Find a way to communicate your appreciation for its loyal service to you. Let this subpersonality know you are grateful for its attempts to take care of you.

Now consider how this subpersonality limits you when it's in charge. Notice its blinders, its limiting beliefs about you or the world . . . Perhaps you can sense what it really needs, what qualities or energies it needs to be more effective for you . . . Are you willing to give it what it needs? Imagine doing so symbolically. Notice how it responds . . .

Before returning to your reading, take a moment to make any agreements you might need to better integrate this loyal soldier into your personality. When you are finished you may wish to write about the experience and any agreements in your journal.

My survival subpersonality usually comes up as a worrying voice, typically focused on money issues. Our survival subpersonalities serve a useful function, keeping us alert and clear about our basic needs and our responsibility to meet them. But they can also limit our creative work in the world, if we become identified with their rather myopic perspective. We always have the choice to move beyond this perspective.

Acting from survival-for-its-own-sake has certain common characteristics. We tend to be fearful, overly cautious, and pessimistic. We tend to dislike change and avoid taking risks. We become identified with the survival of the *means* of Self-expression (our bodies and personalities) and forget what it's all here for. Our ability to clearly perceive what is around us is clouded by projections, fears, and distortions. We tend to *react* through habit, often with inappropriate and indiscriminate force. We are like a trapped and snarling animal which may bite the hand of its rescuer.

Perhaps the most painful aspect of survival-only consciousness is that we cut ourselves off from purpose and meaning for our lives. It all dries up, leaving us without joy and without inspiration. The experience of meaninglessness may push us to ask the question, "What's it all about?" We begin to look beyond survival and seek a larger meaning for our lives.

We move towards Self-expression. We become able to see 'what is' more clearly, with discrimination. We respond more easily and subtly, from conscious choice rather than habit. We are more self-determining, living our lives with purpose and choice. And best of all, we begin to share our special gifts and qualities with our family, communities, and the larger world.

What is the experience of living from Self-expression? Take a few minutes to recall times when you were creative, productive, 'in the flow,' or whatever terms capture that experience for you. How did you feel? What qualities did you bring into your daily life and work? What did you discover about yourself?

The experience of living from Self-expression is unique to each person because each of us has a unique pattern of qualities and capabilities. This pattern seems to be inborn, although the circumstances of life affect it and may either enhance or suppress its manifesting in behavior. Self-discovery or 'finding out who you really are' means uncovering this pattern. When someone else recognizes even a part of our pattern and tells us, we usually feel deeply touched. Something within us knows this is our truth.

Living from Self-expression allows us to have clear values and to set priorities in how we spend our time and energy, because we know what is really important to us. We find it easy to work; our energy is high and relaxed; we can surpass what we thought were boundaries in concentration and endurance. We follow 'the path of heart' as don Juan called it (Castaneda, 1968). We live mindfully, choosing consciously and comfortably, trusting ourselves. When feelings come up, we pay attention to their source and inquire into their message for us. We are not concerned with their 'appropriateness;' we accept them as they are. Yet we can remain free from the undue influence of fear, self-doubt, and discouragement. We are able to see a broader picture in which temporary set-backs are of less significance. We can feel compassion and forgiveness for those parts of ourselves which fear, flounder, worry, and crave, and we can take care of their needs without turning from our chosen path.

It is in moving from survival to Self-expression that we often need the help and support of teachers and guides. A guide can help us to perceive more honestly the dynamics of subpersonalities and to transform their energies. A guide can help us discover our in-born qualities and capacities and find ways to bring them into expression in our life and work.

TWO DIMENSIONS OF GROWTH

Human growth can be said to occur in two dimensions: the personal and the transpersonal dimensions. The personal dimension is concerned with the meaning and integration of our personal existence, with the experience of being significant and effective in the world. The personal dimension of growth has been emphasized in Western culture. We value being strong, intelligent, integrated, self-motivated, pragmatic, efficient, and effective, having a 'well-rounded' personality. Most of us have ample room for growth along the personal dimension. Maslow's list of self-actualizers includes many people who have developed well along the personal dimension.

The transpersonal dimension of growth is less acknowledged in our culture, but no less essential to human fulfillment. As we grow in this dimension, we consider questions of ultimate, universal meaning; we seek the meaning and purpose of a larger reality. The transpersonal dimension may include religious study, prayer, meditation and other spiritual practices intended to strengthen the contact with the Universal or the Divine. It also includes intellectual musings on a high level, such as the theoretical scientist's concern with the ultimate nature of matter and energy. It includes artistic and creative expressions of all kinds. It is important not to limit our understanding of the transpersonal dimension solely to the common religious forms which express it. Assagioli makes a clear distinction between the " 'existential religious or spiritual experience'; that is, the direct experience of spiritual realities" and the "theological or metaphysical *formulations* of such experience and the *institutions* which have been founded" (1976, pp. 194-195).

We could consider the interpersonal to be a third dimension of human growth. Rather than creating a three-dimensional model, however, we can include the interpersonal within the other two dimensions. Development along the personal dimension includes the mastering of basic social skills—the courtesy, communication and friendliness which allow us to function together. These skills are vital; without them we suffer from isolation, stress, and confused and destructive relationships. As we develop along the transpersonal dimension, we discover our basic interdependency, our essential union with one another. We discover and respond to an inner drive to serve and support one another. Without these qualities, our relationships would be superficial, manipulative and unsatisfying. Full and balanced human growth along both dimensions means fulfilling interpersonal relationships within our families, our circles of friends, and our communities.

In Figure 5 (adapted from Firman and Vargiu's comprehensive article on the two dimensions of growth, 1977), personal development is represented on the horizontal axis and trans-

Figure 5 — Two Dimensions of Growth

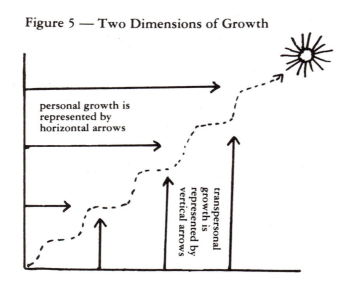

personal growth is represented by horizontal arrows

transpersonal growth is represented by vertical arrows

personal growth on the vertical axis. The Higher Self appears as a star in the upper right corner, the point at which individuality (the personal dimension) and universality (the transpersonal) unite. Ideally, growth includes both dimensions, as indicated by the dotted line. Of course, it is never straight, at times moving primarily horizontally, at other times more abruptly vertically. This integrative path is the path of Maslow's "transcending self-actualizer."

Often, however, an individual grows primarily within one dimension, to the neglect of the other. In Western culture, this is usually the personal dimension emphasizing success, effectiveness, and pragmatic values. People growing exclusively in this dimension tend to be materialistic, goal-oriented, and without much concern for human values or the greater good of humanity.

In recent years, however, there has been a subculture of young people who have developed primarily along the transpersonal dimension, who have had mystical experiences (often through the use of hallucinogenic drugs) but have not developed their ability to function in the world. These people tend to speak in generalities, espouse various religious cults, and yet are unable to communicate their vision to others or manifest it in useful ways in the world. They are often viewed with scorn by the larger society, and their gifts are lost to us.

Both these extremes tend to be viewed in stereotypes: the ruthless businessman with ulcers and the spaced-out hippy or cult follower. Unfortunately, projecting such stereotypes serves to insulate us from discovering those tendencies within ourselves, and from grappling with the conflict they suggest.

When people have neglected one or the other dimension for a period of time in their lives, a crisis eventually occurs, brought on by an external event with which they are unprepared to cope, or by increasing inner distress. If a person neglects the transpersonal dimension, an 'existential' crisis may occur in mid-life, when one has achieved most of one's goals and gained recognition and prestige for personal accomplishments. Gradually or suddenly, the questions begin to nag: What's it all about? Is this all there is to life? So what? What's missing? Vitality and meaning seep out of previously enjoyed activities. The sufferer experiences apathy, fear, and despair.

What has happened is that the 'I' has become identified totally with the personality. It thinks that's all it is. What is needed is an opening to relationship with a larger reality, an expansion of the meaning of personal existence and closer identification with the Higher Self. The individual must consciously disidentify from his or her personality and from the achievements and abilities that have earned approbation and a sense of worth. This does not mean to reject them, only to see them as something one *has*, rather than something one *is*. The Identification Exercise can help this process. Then one can open one's awareness to nature, to beauty, to other people, and to other realms of experience, through contemplation, meditation, reflection, service, or artistic expression. It is extremely helpful to have an understanding guide and companion in this process.

When an individual has become overly identified with the superconscious over a period of time, a 'crisis of duality' may occur. One may have become enchanted by the color and form of superconscious experience: by religious ritual and trappings; by the feeling of unity and harmony induced through prayer, meditation, and fasting, or hallucinogenic drugs; by artistic fervor or abstract philosophical thought. Gradually, however, as in the existential crisis, one becomes disenchanted. Somehow, the ultimate union is never quite reached, but dances elusively just beyond grasp. The individual may experience depression and increasing difficulty in recreating the ecstatic experience. It is as if the goal so long sought is not the true Higher Self at all, but rather a reflection as in a mirror, with the distortions mirrors often create.

As in the existential crisis, the individual needs development along the neglected dimension. This does not mean giving up the transcendent visions and values, but rather consciously and methodically finding ways of expressing them in the everyday world. One may need to engage in 'worldly' activities previously scorned, such as going to school or dressing according to social standards. One must grapple with feelings of alienation and awkwardness, of guilt, uncertainty, and self-doubt. Holding the purpose in mind of building a bridge between one's transcendent visions and the common world of humanity can affirm one's choice in the face of these feelings. Here again a guide can support and help expand the transition.

When we integrate both the personal and the transpersonal dimensions of life and growth, there are at least four identifiable characteristics in our life and work. These are: (1) the capacity for responsibility and choice in the moment and in life as a whole; (2) true preference for living in accordance with one's purpose and regarding as less valuable those aspects of life which detract or conflict; (3) the capacity to accept the limitations of one's life and responsibilities and a willingness to be in a world just *as it is*; and (4) a sense of having a destiny, a meaning to live, an overall purpose in life.

These are the basic conceptions of human growth upon which psychosynthesis guiding is based. In the following chapters, we will explore how guiding techniques and attitudes can facilitate the two dimensions of growth, the integration of both lower and higher unconscious, and the fuller expression of the Higher Self through the personality in all its functions.

"For me there is only the traveling on paths that have heart, on any path that may have heart. There I travel, and the only worthwhile challenge is to traverse its full length. And there I travel looking, looking, breathlessly." - don Juan (Castaneda, 1968, p. 118 and frontispiece)

3

DISCOVERING THE SELF

The factors that contributed to my growth were many — finding someone who understood me, exploring the unconscious, awakening my latent love . . . but one star is brightest among all: the self. I found the source of livingness inside me, something I didn't even know existed. (from Ferrucci, 1982, p. 60)

From time to time, in the midst of life, in the midst of a session, we remember, for a moment, who we are. 'I am myself' is a strong and powerful statement when spoken from the heart. When I know I am a self, a center of awareness and consciousness, a center of choice and will, my life takes shape around me and I am at peace. The rest of the work of integration, resolution of conflicts, life choices, and opening to superconscious qualities occurs almost spontaneously. I know that my life is up to me.

What more can we ask of a particular session than that it facilitate the experience of being a self? Growth and transformation follow naturally from that experience. A psychosynthesis session offers clients the opportunity to discover a little more about who they essentially are, to taste the experience of being a self beneath roles, subpersonalities, and partial identifications. No matter what other work is done in a session, the central purpose is always to experience being a willing, loving, aware self.

The self is sought within the context of whatever issues concern the client at the time of the session. It is not an abstract process any more than life is. We work with the challenges life brings us each day and discover our power and love within that interaction. We work with the issues brought to each session to discover again the self within. Although the processes of self-discovery and self-identification are similar in most sessions, each person's experience of these processes is unique each time. Perhaps we must approach the center of the circle from every point on the circumference before we really know where the center is. Each issue and challenge in our lives is another point on the circumference.

AWARENESS AND CHOICE

Both facets of the experience of self are valuable in a session: awareness and choice. Awareness can take the form of intellectual insight or experiential awareness, or both. Feelings, patterns, relationships, attitudes, and memories which remain unconscious seem to be largely outside our control; they can affect our behavior in unpleasant ways. The need to release this material from the unconscious is recognized by most depth and analytic psychologies.

There is a striking difference, however, between intellectual awareness or insight *about* something, and the direct conscious experience of it with and without words and concepts attached. Again, the greater value of the latter kind of experiential awareness is largely accepted. There is growing recognition, too, of the value of symbolic awareness, the clothing of our psychological dynamics in dreams, imagery, internal and external symbols. If we realize that words and concepts are a form of imagery, we can see that opening to a wider range of imagery will increase the power and depth of our awareness. In psychosynthesis guiding, we share methods for increasing all levels of awareness; we do not impose our own models and symbols of what is going on.

Yet we are not after awareness just for its own sake. As we become more aware, as we learn to observe without judgment, we become more closely identified with the self. We move into that subtle state of being aware of awareness, becoming aware of that which is aware, the self. This is the heart and soul of psychosynthesis work, to discover (and rediscover and rediscover) the center of awareness, the self.

The following exercise focuses on the awareness of being aware.

EXERCISE: WHO IS AWARE?

Take a few moments to observe your body. What position is it in? . . . How is it moving? . . . Where is it comfortable and uncomfortable? . . . Check out the further reaches of your body: Your big toe, the top of your head, the small of your back. . . Feel your breathing in your throat and chest. . . Sense your heartbeat, your digestive processes. . . As you continue this scan, ask yourself gently: Who is aware?

Now inquire as to your emotional state. What are you feeling? . . . What are the feelings attached to various sensations in your body? . . . Open yourself to the subtle nameless feelings as well as the obvious emotions. . . If it is helpful, recall your feelings during earlier events of the day or week, feelings you may still have traces of within you. . . Now, once again, ask yourself gently: Who is aware? Who is aware of my feelings?

For the next few minutes, notice what you are thinking. Watch or listen to your thoughts go by. . . Notice how your thoughts follow one another, how your mind focuses or wanders. . . When you realize you have gone on a mental trip, notice where you went and what brought you back. . . Ask: Who is aware? Who is aware of my thinking? . . .

Turn your attention now to the room you are in. Notice the temperature of the air, the smells, the sounds, the texture and feel of your chair. . . What is the quality of the light? . . . What colors do you see? . . . Allow your awareness to expand beyond the room to the whole building and beyond. . . Continue to expand your sense of what is there, into the neighborhood, the community, the countryside. . . Pay attention to the sky. . . and to the earth beneath you. . . Can you sense the distance to the stars? . . . Notice yourself in the midst of all this. . . Who is aware? . . . Who is aware of the stars and the space and of you in the midst? . . . Who is aware? . . .

Give yourself plenty of time to experience whatever is happening. . . Then write some notes in your journal if you like, before continuing.

In a sense, the content of awareness is less important than the experience of awareness itself. Within a session, we can focus on anything that comes up—feelings, thoughts, reactions, impulses—and then we can draw attention back to the source of that awareness. The experience of being aware is an experience of clarity, power, and peace. We are in touch with the *self* in its awareness aspect, *being* the one who is aware of the passing contents of our lives.

The experience of the self may also come through making a choice, *being a will-er*, and focusing attention on that experience. When we become conscious of the choices we are making, we acknowledge that we are creatures of will. We discover our self in its will aspect and identify with that inner core of being which is the capacity to act intentionally. Psychosynthesis guiding makes the experience of choosing more vivid and conscious, thus enhancing the sense of self.

In the following excerpt from a session transcript, the client has discovered two conflicting subpersonalities and worked with their needs and strengths to balance and harmonize them within himself. A definite transformation has occurred with the two of them. The guide (G) then facilitates the client's (C) realization of what he has done and of his power to do.

G: Who transformed them?

C: Well, there's this other *I* here (laughs). *I* transformed them. They did it themselves. No, I'm confused with that. There's a sense in me that says *I* did and those are parts of me.

G: Can you experience that? Is that a real experience or is it just a thought?

C: It's a thought, but I guess the thought was preceded by an experience.

G: Okay.

C: There's a consciousness that these are parts of me and they are me, but there's a bigger center. Especially when I went to look at both of them. . . . When I was neither one of them, I felt like *I* transformed them.

The client experienced an 'I' which was identified with neither subpersonality and felt the power to transform the parts of his personality. This was an experience of a 'bigger center,' of the will, the self.

There are many opportunities within most sessions to point to the experience of 'being a will.' Specific methods will be discussed in detail in Chapter 7. Choices the client is already making in life can be explored and made explicit. Guided imagery often offers choices to be made symbolically which later carry over to the client's life. The process of identification and disidentification discussed below involves the will. Every time we make a clear choice and focus our awareness on that act, we experience our selfhood. This is why working with the will is central to psychosynthesis guiding.

IDENTIFICATION AND DISIDENTIFICATION

The process of identification lies at the heart of the process of growth at all levels. If the purpose of psychosynthesis guiding is to help us experience who we are, then who we think we are becomes an important issue. Who we think we are means how we identify ourselves, what parts or subpersonalities we have identified with. Who and what we identify with either limits us or challenges us to expand our capacities. Growth may be defined as a process of

"It's a journey that has taken us from primary identification with our psyche, on to an identification with our souls, then to an identification with God, and ultimately beyond identification." (Ram Dass, 1977, p. 17)

disidentifying from past limited perceptions of ourselves and the world and identifying with new, more inclusive and integrating ones. We need to identify with each new stage in order to truly own it and integrate it into our functioning, and then we need once more to let it go, in order to move on to the next. "We are dominated by everything with which our self becomes identified. We can dominate and control everything from which we disidentify ourselves." (Assagioli, 1976, p. 22) When we are identified with one or another subpersonality, with our mind or emotional nature, or with our body, we are victims of a single worldview and self image, and subject to shifts and changes stimulated by outside events and internal confusion. When we are able to disidentify from these parts of ourselves, we free the 'I' and are able to choose our perspective and behavior from a broader range of possibilities. In the process, we move closer to identification with the self and with its source, the Higher Self. We can use our personalities as vehicles for Self-expression instead of being caught up in melodrama. The twin processes of disidentification from parts of the personality and identification with the self (and ultimately the Higher Self) are crucial to psychosynthesis.

Disidentification can also be accomplished sometimes by first *identifying* strongly with a part. Identification, when made consciously and deliberately, can help develop awareness and understanding through acceptance of the various parts of ourselves. Gestalt therapy techniques help the client identify with various parts of the body, with troublesome symptoms, or with figures in dreams, and from this vantage point to dialogue with the central identity or ego. (This central identity is usually not the self, but rather another dominant subpersonality.) This allows clients to empathize with the parts of themselves which have been denied or repressed, to discover the needs of those parts and their value to the whole person. Progoff (1975) suggests a similar practice in his Intensive Journal where one writes out dialogues with various parts of the body, with various personality aspects, or with people in one's life.

Disidentification occurs when we can step away and look back at a part of ourselves, at a behavior pattern, at a constellation of feelings and thoughts, or even at our personality as a whole. Disidentification has to do with the *stepping away from*; identification has to do with *where we step to*. It may require two or more of such steppings-away before we step *into* identification with the self, but each step moves us nearer to that experience and also confirms our ability to do it. Each time I disidentify from any part of myself and do so consciously, I learn of my power of choice. I experience my will.

Identification and disidentification occur in three stages described by Carter-Harr (1975). In the first stage, "the process of identification is unconscious and largely beyond our control. Our identification is with one or another personality element (such as a feeling, a subpersonality, a role) and will change responding to the pressure and demands of inner and outer conditions much more than to our desires and aims" (pp. 62-3). In the second stage, we become aware of our identifications and develop the ability to choose to shift our identification from one personality element to another. This gives a greater range of expression. On the heels of this experience comes the third stage, when we learn to disidentify from all personality elements and identify with the self, "our true center of identity and awareness." Now, "we not only have the experience of personal identity and individuality, we can also be most objectively aware of our psychological life and our interactions in the world, and can therefore guide our actions and development with the greatest effectiveness" (p. 63). Eventually, this fuller life leads to increasing identification with the Transpersonal Self. We experience universality and at the same time, our sense of identity and individuality is enhanced. "Individuality and universality blend into the true experience of Being" (p. 90).

SUBPERSONALITIES

Most commonly in psychosynthesis sessions, the work centers on disidentification from subpersonalities, those crystallizations of thoughts, feelings, physical attitudes, and behaviors discussed in Chapter 2.

Subpersonalities are "structured constellations or agglomerates of attitudes, drives, habit patterns, logical elements which are organized in adaptation to forces in the internal and external environment" (Crampton, 1977). In other words, they are learned responses to our legitimate needs: survival needs, needs for love and acceptance, needs for self-actualization and transcendence. These needs are valid and can be met in conscious, self-responsible ways. Unfortunately, by allowing a reactive subpersonality to do the work, we also tie up a lot of energy and operate inefficiently. Sometimes the subpersonality pattern only reinforces the need, rather than truly meeting it. Subpersonalities are similar to the ego states described in transactional analysis (Berne, 1967), or to the complexes described in psychoanalysis.

When we work with subpersonalities in a session, we provide an opportunity for the person to release and transform the subpersonality patterns and, in the process, discover the personal self. Often the first step is to identify with the experience of the subpersonality, to focus on and feel what that is like. An excerpt from Transcript A illustrates this step. (The client is C; the guide G.)

C: (asking herself) What needs to happen in this session today? What do I need to find out? (pause) I just had this feeling that somehow I am pushing it, and I am not opening up enough to really hear what it is that I need to hear.

G: Would you be willing to go into that "pushing it" experience?

C: Uh-hum.

G: Allow yourself to really exaggerate that pushing.

C: I feel like I am pushing this rock, this huge boulder, and it is not going anywhere, and then it changed to a whole group of people.

G: How do you experience that with your body?

C: It's just like (grunts). Really a lot of effort, but it is not working. An obstacle or something is there.

G: Are there any particular words that accompany that experience, what you're saying to them as you're trying to push them, push this group?

C: Well, I get like, "move," but that is not strong enough. It is not really that. It is almost like I am pushing them to give me space.

The guide continues to facilitate exploration of the experience, both of pushing and later of being the group. In the process, much is learned about two subpersonalities: the Pusher and the People. As the client identifies with each in turn, she experiences each more fully. At the same time, she disidentifies from each in turn and experiences the self who transcends both.

Another step, which may come first or second, is to actively disidentify from the subpersonality, to step away internally. This may be suggested by the guide's referring to an experience as belonging to a part of the client. An example from the same transcript, a little further along:

C: Am I pushing them away because I don't want them to judge me or see me? I don't know.

G: Part of you is doing the pushing now. . .

Another example of disidentification is in Transcript B. The client has been identifying with the figure of a stone statue and also with its wings. The guide suggests:

G: Does it feel like it would be useful to move to yet another perspective at this point?

C: Uh-huh.

G: I would like to suggest that you become the pond.

C: Interesting, I am really sinking into it. The mass despair or something (as the statue).

G: It's okay.

C: Okay. I'll become the pond. I mean, this is all the 'me' that I adopted after those early visions. It is interesting.

G: The stone?

C: Uh-huh. (long pause) I don't know as the pond. I'm looking at this drama that is going on, on the banks.

G: On your banks.

C: Yes.

As soon as the guide suggests identifying with the pond, the client notices that she, as the statue, has been sinking into despair. She becomes aware of how identified she is in general with the statue. Finally she is able to disidentify from the statue as she identifies with the pond.

Disidentification may also be more obvious. When a client expresses a feeling, the guide may evoke an image for that feeling ("What is that like, that feeling of shakiness?" or "See if there is any image for that feeling of wanting to fight, maybe a symbol for it.") As soon as an image is suggested, the client can be guided into dialogue with the image, automatically from a disidentified place. Clients may be asked to locate a feeling in the body and dialogue with that physical part of themselves. I often suggest that a client move to another chair or stand up beside me and look back at the subpersonality which has just been expressed, telling me what he or she sees and feels about that part.

From a disidentified perspective, the individual can perceive both the valid purpose of the subpersonality and its ineffective or destructive pattern. Sometimes, rather than moving into the self, people move into a second, conflicting subpersonality. After some practice identifying with one and then the other, the suggestion can be made to step into a third position and look at the two parts. Usually, this enables the person to be an Observer, a fairly centered perspective.

Now the person can experience being a *self* and taking responsibility for the conflicting *parts*. Now understanding and integration are possible, for the self can choose to meet the needs and use the energy and value of the subpersonalities. There is no need to repress or deny them. The self can have compassion and appreciation for them without any longer giving them control.

When we resist disidentifying from a subpersonality, the importance of that subpersonality and the degree of our overall identification with it is underlined. A helpful guide will persevere, offering the opportunity to disidentify in different ways, perhaps even pointing out the pattern and asking for the client's advice. By doing this, the guide at least is speaking to the self of the client, seeing more than the subpersonality in the person. It is crucial that the guide recognize the existence of the true self of the client underneath the temporary subpersonality facade.

Sometimes disidentification from a subpersonality goes too far, in a manner of speaking. People become identified with a second, conflicting subpersonality and actively reject the first. We have all had the experience of wanting to kill off or throw out some behavior pattern or feeling that seems to just get in our way: apparent laziness, anger or hatred, helplessness, impatience, a sharp tongue, silliness. On some occasions it may be important to work with the judgmental subpersonality that wants to do the killing; at other times it is more important to convey acceptance and appreciation to the subpersonality under assault.

A method from Neuro-Linguistic Programming can be used here. I focus my eyes on a place where the subpersonality seems to be in the client's awareness (to the left or right, above or below) and speak directly to it: "I want you to know that I appreciate what you are trying to do for John. He really wants to get rid of you right now but I can see you're hanging in there in spite of all that. You are really trying to help him even if he doesn't know it. I'm on your side. I'm glad you're there!" Many times I have seen people break into tears of relief at this, much to the consternation of their predominant subpersonality. In that moment they identify with the rejected part, disidentify from the rejecting part, and all kinds of awareness floods in. They can then move into a disidentified Observer position and accept both subpersonalities.

This method is demonstrated in the following excerpt from Transcript B:

G: I want to speak for a moment to the statue; to the rock, to the stone. And I just want you, the stone, to know that I think you still have something very valuable to offer. And I really am determined to help that be discovered. There is something that you have to offer that has to do with humanity, with being a person, with being human, being whole. And the bird would like to fly away and leave that behind. And the pond would like to seep away and leave that behind. And yet somehow there is still something there. There is something that refuses to go away. You are something that refuses to go away and demands to be included.

C: I appreciate the vote of confidence. I don't know. Maybe it's too late for me. I mean really, I was a person. I was a kid and that's when I knew what it was about then, and I think about it and it's been so long . . .

G: Since you became a statue.

C: Yeah, well I had to. I had to protect the bird. It's been so long. I've just been a statue for too long.

G: But you don't have to protect the bird any more.

C: I don't know how to move any more. I can't move. I'm just totally rigid.

G: So you were a person and then you became a statue to protect the bird.

C: Yeah. I was a kid you see and then I discovered I had this bird on my hands and . . .

When the guide expresses support and appreciation for the statue, the client is able to finally see its value since childhood: to protect the bird.

When we disidentify from a subpersonality, even slightly, we become aware of its attributes, its world view, its style of behavior, and its emotional patterns, so that it can be recognized from within. Dialogue can often accomplish this, either through guided imagery or Gestalt work. In this way, the energies of the subpersonality can be freed and made available to the self. We can begin to exercise choice over inner and outer reactions and behaviors.

Each subpersonality has at its core a valuable quality and a valid need. In order to uncover this need and quality, three questions can be addressed, directly or indirectly, in the course of a session:

1. What does the subpersonality want? (evoking the emotional interpretation of what is needed)

2. What does it really need? (moving deeper to discover what is missing in this distortion, what it needs for balance and wholeness)

3. What does it have to offer? (including positive attributes of the subpersonality and evoking the underlying quality)

Sometimes it is useful to address these questions from the point of view of the subpersonality, having it speak for itself. At other times, it may be better to ask these questions while observing the subpersonality from another point of identity. Usually we are more than willing to meet the need of the subpersonality once it is known, and to appreciate the quality that is made available without distortion. In fact, this transformative process is often accompanied by feelings of great release, relief, and joy.

Once I explored a love-starved subpersonality which tended to make me demanding and pesky for attention and affection, especially with my husband. When I explored the need, I discovered a deep urge for connection, for realizing the essential unity between myself and others. Immediately, I felt the tension and discomfort of this pattern drain away. I could validate this need which was to find expression for a valuable *quality*, one which would *enhance* my relationships, not inhibit them. I have found I can stop and evoke this quality when I feel myself becoming 'grabby.' I can then approach the other person *knowing* our deep connection and be flexible about expressing it in a way that feels appropriate to both of us.

Work with subpersonalities often includes the relationship between two or more of them, as noted above. Generally, we tend to identify more with one and resist or repress the other. As we are able to disidentify from each of them and identify with the self, we can help our conflicting subpersonalities to appreciate one another and develop a working relationship. Sometimes subpersonalities will merge into a synthesis, forming a new, more balanced and useful way of responding to life.

For example, a young man might see himself as a responsible, hard-working person, intent on establishing himself in his profession. This would be his dominant subpersonality. Yet from time to time he 'flips out,' usually with help from alcohol or pot. He identifies with an opposite subpersonality, one who is totally abandoned to play and self-indulgence and who doesn't seem to care what anyone else thinks of him. As this young man becomes aware of these opposing subpersonalities, he discovers *he* is neither of them and can appreciate their qualities: responsibility on the one hand, and playfulness on the other. In time he balances these two qualities in his life and they merge. He can now laugh and relax while on the job and he can responsibly temper the excesses he used to find necessary when at play. He has synthesized these needs and qualities within himself.

Each time we transform subpersonalities in this way, we experience the essential and natural process of psychosynthesis and we experience the loving, willing self. (Vargiu's excellent discussion of subpersonality work appears in *Synthesis 1*, 1974.)

THE INTEGRATION OF THE PERSONALITY

As we experience the self and the will and begin to develop our capacity to disidentify and transform parts of ourselves, the direction of sessions can turn more to the integration of the personality functions of body, feelings, and mind. Most of us identify with and develop disproportionately one or another of these aspects of our personality. We may think we are our minds, or feel we are our emotions. Athletes and dancers sometimes identify themselves with their bodies.

Whichever aspect we identify with, the other aspects are generally distrusted and ignored, or manipulated by the dominant part. Mentally identified people may, for example, take care of their bodies, in a very logical or mechanical way, not really listening to the body's own messages about what they really need. Emotionally identified people may allow their feelings to make them ill. Mentally identified people may be slightly contemptuous of their feelings; emotionally identified people tend to distrust their minds and prefer to deal with issues 'on a gut level.' Yet even a mentally identified person is controlled by feelings, for they unconsciously affect the way we think about things, if they are not heeded directly. In fact, each of the three aspects—body, feelings, and mind—finds ways of influencing our behavior, often in unconscious conflict with our dominant, identified function.

It may be of value to recall the Identification Exercise from Chapter 2. You may want to review it now, going through the process again. From which of the three did you find it easy to disidentify, saying "I *have* this part but *I am not* this part"? Which did you find most difficult? This may be the aspect of your personality you tend to identify with. You may want to observe this for awhile—and you may find some resistance to observing it!

Psychosynthesis proceeds as we gradually disidentify from the predominant aspect and develop a balance of all three, so that mind, feelings, and body are all available together for the expression of our life purposes. We may need to recognize the value of neglected aspects and find ways of bringing these energies more fully into play—and work. Highly intellectual people may need to appreciate and respond to their feelings, while emotional people may need to discover and develop their minds. Of course, this is a never-ending process; as we move along the spiral of growth, we continually discover and integrate new depths and powers of our personality aspects.

When I was first introduced to the Identification Exercise by Jim and Susan Vargiu in 1971, I found the idea of 'I am not my mind' positively shocking. The thought filled me with fear. Emotions were easy to disidentify from; I wasn't really sure what they were anyway, or of what value. My mind was another thing. I remember the first time I discovered how valuable it was to disidentify from my mind. I had made an error in judgment about our car, an expensive mistake we could ill afford at the time. I was devastated with despair and self-judgments of failure. At some point I remembered the Identification Exercise and went through it. I realized, then, that although my mind had made an error through insufficient information, *I* was not wrong, or bad, or stupid. Somehow that was of great comfort and enabled me to forgive myself (or my self to forgive my mind) and make the best of the situation.

By identifying with the observing self, we can make a more realistic assessment of ourselves and our situation, permitting more effective and creative behavior.
(Diekman, 1982, p. 108)

Later it was a revelation to me to discover that some people were actually identified with those strange phenomena called feelings. I discovered why I had felt conflict with some people, or had been unable to understand them. They were emotionally identified while I was mentally identified. Gradually, as I developed my emotional aspect and brought it more into consciousness, I was better able to understand people with an emotional orientation and to share my mental orientation more effectively with them. For me, at least, disidentifying from my mind and discovering my self enabled me to be more in harmony with others.

In psychosynthesis sessions, it is helpful to be aware of the client's identification and to evoke the development of neglected aspects. This process enables the client to direct and harmonize his or her functioning through the will, and also to have fuller use of all the capacities of the personality. There are some rules of thumb regarding emotional and mental identification when, as is often the case, clients begin sessions in great distress, experiencing feelings of anger or fear. The mentally identified client will tend to analyze the feelings, typically saying, "I don't understand why I feel this way." This person needs to be encouraged to experience the feelings more fully (and will often skillfully resist doing so). Gestalt techniques, movement, and Reichian methods may help. On the other hand, the emotionally identified person may come into a session drowned in feelings, pulling emotionally at the guide, with an attitude of helplessness and despair. This person's mind needs to be evoked and strengthened, through questions about value and purpose. He or she needs to experience choice in relation to feelings, to know it is possible to step away from them and still be real and alive. Identifying with the neglected aspect temporarily may help to disidentify from the dominant part. Both the neglected aspect and the dominant aspect may be balanced and harmonized in ways similar to working with conflicting subpersonalities.

Our central purpose remains the discovery of the self; we work with subpersonalities and personality functions from that center. The self is capable of observing what is needed and of willing the appropriate action. No one else can better know what is right for us.

STAYING WITH EXPERIENCE

The information we need for identifying our imbalances and our blocks to effectiveness are present within our moment-to-moment experience. We expand our knowledge of ourselves by *experiencing* our experiences. I don't know if anyone has found a way to verbalize this in prose without jargon. There is a phenomenon here to be described, however; we are not just making up words. It is the essential phenomenon of consciousness; moment-to-moment experience.

Many of the things we do in our daily lives seem to be ways of moving away from this essential experiencing: talking *about* it, conceptualizing it, repressing or denying it, and distracting or sedating ourselves in various ways. When we stop avoiding our experience, however, when we *really*, really pay attention, something transformational often occurs. We *understand it, from the inside*. We see it in its larger context. We perceive the motivations, fears, hopes, associations moving through it. We begin to sense how it grows, how it shapes our behavior. We discover how experience builds on itself, establishing feedback loops, reinforcing and extinguishing itself. There is a change in our knowledge of who we are and in our power of choice. The way we talk about our experience becomes fuller and evokes similar experience in others.

One of the best ways we can support each other's growth is to help each other stay with our experience, expanding and intensifying our awareness of it from moment to moment. The basic technique of active listening, feeding back to others the feelings we hear them communicating, is effective because it helps focus experiencing. Many of the methods discussed in Chapter 5 contribute to the intensification of experience. A guide may persistently encourage a client to stay with whatever he or she is feeling, thinking, sensing, perceiving, and imagining. Especially for clients who have done a lot of inner work, this may be the best approach.

THE CHOICE TO BE A SELF

To experience choice is to experience being a self, a self who is the one really conducting the session. It is extremely important, therefore, that the client be aware of the process of the session and make choices about where it goes. That's what it's all about.

Granted that some people are more accustomed to observing themselves and taking responsibility than others, we still attempt to offer maximum responsibility for the conduct of the session to the individual. Not only does the experience of choice in the session lead the individual to the experience of self, but it also provides opportunities to discover and follow inner direction and wisdom in growth. This inner direction, whose source is the Higher Self, is available in the superconscious if we are open to its promptings. The guide is a *guide*, not the director of the session; self-responsibility for the individual is the foundation of the work and the only way it can harmoniously progress in his or her best interests.

Choice can be offered at the beginning of a session by a request that the client indicate a direction or purpose for the work. The guide can also offer specific choices about emphasis or the relative importance of the various issues presented as the session progresses. For example, a guide might say: "Okay. I think there's a couple different directions we could go. One would be to explore the situation itself as an example of this process. The other would be to look directly at the parts that seem to be in conflict. What seems best to you?" The guide would convey through this offering of choice that the direction of the session is up to the client who in turn experiences his power of choice.

The content of the choice is important, yet it remains secondary to the act of choosing itself and the empowerment of the individual that occurs through choice.

Beneath all significant choices we make about our lives and growth is *the choice to be a self*, and the choice to be true to ourselves. Perhaps you have experienced moments of this choice, realizing that you alone are responsible for your fate, and that you alone can choose who you are to be and what you are to do. My experiences of this sort include feelings of near terror at the aloneness along with joy at the freedom. It's up to me *and* I am up to it; I have the resources within me to survive, cope, and create.

From this stark moment of responsibility and selfhood, it is a short step to another level of opening and awareness. Having identified as a personal self, I move toward identification with the Higher Self. I am also part of a greater whole, connected to everything around me, and receiving sustenance and guidance from it all the time. I have only to open to it. I alone am responsible and I do not have to do it alone. I can choose to co-create reality in harmony with all the other co-creative forces and beings of the planet.

When clients experience this choice of selfhood, the guide is challenged to be there also. The roles of guide and client are transcended and we become what we really were all along anyway: two people co-creating our world together, helping one another, learning from one another. There is really nothing else the guide needs to do except blend with what is happening, and make his or her own choice to be a self who is part of a greater whole.

While the trumpets of heaven swell in the background, my pragmatic subpersonality insists that I temper my previous statement with 'a little reality.' We rarely experience fully the choice to be a self, and such experiences are usually fleeting, quickly deluged by feelings and old thought-forms which are not big enough to contain the experience. In sessions, therefore, it is almost always possible to enlarge such experiences, to deepen them, and to ground them in imagery and choices about daily life. I have often felt inclined to stop with a nice peak experience during a session, and then realized there were more steps to take. When I see such possibilities, I may ask, "Do you want to take another step? Are you willing to go a little further with this?" It is astonishing to me just how vast such an experience can be, and though I may be tempted to stop when I've reached *my* presumed limits, the client may be ready for more. So when I said above, "There is really nothing else the guide *needs* to do," I did not mean to imply that there is nothing more *to* do. We can always deepen and widen our awareness; we can always move to yet another level of consciousness and choice.

As David Spangler (1976, p. 51) says, "We live in an ocean of communication, filtering most of it away and leaving only that which fits the limits of our accepted identities." This ocean of communication is all the relationships and interconnections and knowledge available to us, and is part of us all the time. When we are identified with parts of ourselves, with one or another way of perceiving or processing information, with one or another subpersonality, we are limited in the communication we take in, filtering or blocking out the rest. When we are identified with the self, the personal center of awareness and will which is linked to the Higher Self, we can transcend our blocks and filters. We can be in contact with the ocean all at once, as well as selecting aspects to respond to and synthesize into new forms. As we discover and identify with the self, we discover and open to ever widening potentials for ourselves and for our planetary home.

Part of the ocean of communication is within our personalities themselves; within our subpersonality patterns, our feelings, our thoughts, our physical responses and structure. In seeking to discover and be ourselves, we include all of these aspects, using their qualities, energies, and forms to live and learn and work in the world. We do not need to reject them or separate ourselves from them. We do need to recognize that they are only parts of us, and that we are centers of choice and awareness who can actively participate in our own destinies. Receptivity to the resources and sustenance of the world begins with receptivity to the resources we have developed within our personalities. The task of discovering the self includes the discovery of the personality as well, and the claiming of this valuable vehicle for Self-expression.

To facilitate the discovery of the self in a session as guides, we must begin from some degree of self-identification ourselves. Guiding challenges me to become more attuned to my self and to respond from that center. The next chapter explores the guide's challenge in being a self in sessions, a state of being I call 'Presence.'

4

THE GUIDE'S PRESENCE: BEING A SELF

He had the remarkable capacity to reach through the layers of self-doubt, of anxiety and tension, of fears and insecurities, of false pride, to reach through these false identifications to the very core of a person—to one's essence—and recognize and greet and affirm it. He seemed to be able to see through the pain and the chaos of those who came to him, to their positive and creative inner core, and say to them, both with and without words, "This is who you are." We have often said he spoke to the highest in us and we rose to meet him. (Anne Yeomans writing about Roberto Assagioli, 1976.)

Have you ever experienced a special quality in another person who supported and listened to you in a time of crisis or decision? The other person seemed to be fully with you, yet allowed you to be just who you are and to work through in your own way the problems before you. By really *being* there, body, mind, and soul, the other person helped you to discover your own inner resources and to move closer to a sense of self and choice.

It is this subtle quality of *presence* which seems to make a profound difference in the effectiveness of counseling. It is the awareness of our own selfhood and the willingness to share ourselves with the other person. Presence includes concentration, the focusing of our full attention on the process at hand, including our own responses. It includes the paradox of non-attachment, allowing the other person's searching and growth to unfold as it may. Presence includes the conscious choice of our perceptions, models, and beliefs, as they affect our ability to see and hear another's reality. Presence taps into wisdom and intuition—inner knowing in all its forms. Presence means opening to one's highest qualities, such as clarity, love, compassion, joy, and radiance. Presence requires trust, openness, empathy, and acceptance. Presence is a deep commitment to the service of another's growth.

The following exercise may help you experience the power of qualities of presence.

EXERCISE: AN IDEAL GUIDE

Take a few minutes now to find a comfortable, alert position and to relax. Close your eyes and pay attention to your inner experience. Then open your eyes, read a sentence or two, and take it back inside for contemplation. . .

Imagine now that you are in an emotional crisis or are facing a difficult and important decision. Perhaps you can remember such a time in the recent past and can relive the experience. Be *in* that experience now. . .

Recall or imagine how your body feels, what kinds of postures or movements express your inner situation. . . . What are your feelings? . . . What are your thoughts? . . . How is your mind working? . . . How does the world in general look to you from this perspective? . . . Take time to fully experience this.

Now imagine that you have a companion with you, someone whom you trust and feel completely comfortable with, even in this trying time. Allow a sense of this person to grow in your imagination. . . .

What are the qualities of this person with whom you choose to share your turmoil and distress? . . . How does he or she respond to you? What if anything is said? What does he or she communicate without words? . . .

Allow yourself to fully experience this person's presence, making any changes in the image that you need in order to be completely comfortable. . . .

If you are willing to take another step, imagine that you *are* this perfect companion, that those qualities are yours. You may look back at the person in crisis and experience what feelings and thoughts you have in relation to him or her. . . .

You may want to say something to the person in crisis about how you, the companion, see him or her, or about your willingness and attitude in being there. . . .

Take time to allow this experience its full impact. . . .

Imagine bringing these qualities and attitudes into your relationships with others, especially those in whom you would like to facilitate growth. . . .

When you feel ready, open your eyes. You may want to take a few notes in your journal about the qualities of your perfect companion. These notes will be helpful in comparing your experience with others'.

THE WHOLE PERSON

The "therapist is a rather free individual, functioning as a person with all his feelings and fantasies as well as his wits." (Jourard, 1964, p. 63)

Any relationship which aims at facilitating deep personal change needs the involvement of the whole persons of the participants. We need to open up to all our resources—mental, emotional, intuitive, sensory, and instinctive—and allow them to respond fully and appropriately to the other person. As guides, we use our personalities as instruments for gathering information, for reflecting what we see and surmise, for expressing what we know. To do so with only part of our whole personality makes our work more difficult and less effective, a disservice to ourselves as well as our clients.

Feelings

Being present with our whole personalities means monitoring our own emotional process as it occurs from moment to moment while we are with another. During an individual session, if the guide feels frustrated, excited, anxious, eager, reluctant, or depressed, something is happening which evokes these feelings. They need to be included in the whole field of awareness, to be used as information about what is taking place. Feelings are sensors. The guide experiences urgings, listens to them without immediately accepting their apparent messages, and then interprets and questions what it is the feelings are responding to. On one occasion observing a session, I felt surges of pity and a desire to comfort and hold the client. These feelings were an energetic response to subliminal cues from her and were worth heeding. However, it was not appropriate to embrace her, even if I had been the guide. What my mind could tell me by interpreting my feelings was that this was a 'heart' issue, that she needed to embrace, comfort, and love herself. By including my own emotional response in my awareness, I was able to understand the process more subtly and deeply.

Similarly, feelings can be used to energize and support a client's work when they are expressed through voice tones, body language, and communicated in the guide's overall demeanor. Expressions of awe and wonder can help counteract the cultural habits of cynicism and repression which are sometimes evoked by a mystic experience or a moment of deep contact with the Self or with another person. Even the expression of a guide's feelings of anger or hurt can be helpful to a client in some instances. My ideal as a guide is to be fully myself, present to the other person, and to choose how and when to express parts of myself as they can facilitate the other's awareness, choice, and growth.

Body

Probably our most basic contact with others is through our bodies, in our physical being-in-the-world. Our bodies are what the other person sees and touches, the medium for expressing the other aspects of our personalities. Full presence rests upon physical and energetic presence; a willingness to touch and be touched, and a readiness to experience our own physical responses and to learn from them. We are willing to be seen by our clients, instead of hiding at the head of a couch or behind a desk. We are willing to touch and embrace our clients as fellow human beings as long as such simple affection serves them and does not induce dependency. We can even bring our physical presence into telephone conversation, in our voice tones and breath.

We can also use our physical responses to learn more about the other individual in the same way as we use our emotional responses. Areas of tension and holding in someone's body will often generate a sympathetic tension in our own bodies. We can literally sense where that person is in pain or is energized. On the other hand, we can model relaxation and openness in the way we sit and move. By paying attention to our breathing and our balance, we open ourselves more fully to what is emerging in a session.

Mind

Is it obvious that full presence includes the guide's mind as well? Many therapeutic approaches such as psychoanalysis have focused on the intellect and its power to analyze, interpret, and draw conclusions. Other approaches have reacted to this emphasis and have instead tended to focus almost exclusively on feelings or the body. No matter what the technique, however, if one is to be fully oneself in a therapeutic session, the mind cannot be excluded or derogated. In the observation mentioned above, when I felt an urge to embrace the client, I needed my mind to explore the implications of my feelings, to understand what they were responding to, and to look at the appropriateness and helpfulness of alternative actions I might take. The mind is engaged as a partner, a tool, interwoven with emotion, imagination, and intuition; together these help the guide to respond with precision to the client's need.

It is probably true that we have used the mind in an unbalanced way in Western technological society. We have tended to allow it to set up 'logical' belief systems and conceptual structures which we then use to determine our decisions. When the mind is used as an equal partner with other personality functions under the direction of the will, it moves into a new role. It clarifies, evaluates, and figures out how to put into expression the information arising from the intuition-imagination-feelings-sensation blend. In this new role it functions best if it continually frees itself of unconscious and untested assumptions, and of theories which are inadequate representations of reality.

To use our minds in a balancing way when guiding, we must continually evaluate our own theories and assumptions. We must open our perception to what is occurring in the moment and with the particular individual we are guiding, and allow our observations to influence our previously established mental constructs. Imagination and intuition contribute to this interplay, expanding the linear thinking mode with non-linear consciousness. We use our constructs then as frames for regarding issues and events, trying out different ones until we find one that 'fits'—intuitively and pragmatically. We try out different theoretical and philosophical frames for a client's dilemma until we find one that guides our facilitation of growth. This process can take place within minutes in a session, and also over a whole series of sessions. I think this use of the mind is different from therapeutic approaches which overlay a single construct, theory, or method and attempt to help the client only through that frame.

Imagination

Imagination is a rich source of information about the process occurring in a session, often carrying intuitive visions into consciousness. Images may arise in response to our meditating on the needs and potentials of a given client, before a session. They may arise in response to our questioning ourselves about a feeling or sensation experienced in the course of a session. Sometimes images will occur spontaneously, offering a new perspective or dimension. At other times it is useful to pause, even in the midst of an interaction, ask an inner question, and allow the answer to come through the imagination.

When a client is working with imagery, either spontaneous or guided, we can use our imaginations to tune into the imagery, bringing ourselves right into the other's inner process. I picture the client's reported visualization in my own mind and use my kinesthetic and auditory imagination to experience whatever the other person reports feeling or hearing. I modify my version of the imagery as the other shares more details or changes. This seems to enliven the individual's imagery as he or she senses my participation in it and allows my responses to emerge from a whole and intuitive understanding.

Intuition and the Superconscious

Closely related to imagination is intuition, which Assagioli and Jung both classify as a distinct psychological function. Assagioli says of intuition:

> *Intuition* is a higher form of vision. Etymologically, it is related
> to vision and means to 'see within' (*in-tueri*). At its highest, it can be
> equated with a *direct supra-rational comprehension* of the nature of reality,
> of its essence. It thus differs from what is commonly called 'intuition'
> (hunches, psychic impressions, presentiments concerning people and
> events). (1974, pp. 225-6; emphasis mine)

This function plays a vital role in guiding. Through intuition, we can comprehend another's deep needs and emerging potential and respond accordingly. "Awakening intuition enables one to see the choices available" (Vaughan, 1979, p. 4). Because intuition is non-linear and involves perceiving a whole pattern all at once, it allows us to see more of the choices available for our responses and interventions. It frees us for more fluid involvement in another's process.

Intuition can be developed and used in guiding and in other creative activities. Vaughan describes several methods and exercises in her book *Awakening Intuition* (1979). Meditation is probably the most universally recommended method because the practice trains the mind in concentration and receptivity to supra-rational understanding. Meditation also connects the individual with the transpersonal realm. Meditation just prior to a session, or even briefly in the midst of one, can tune up the guide's receptivity to intuition.

My image of using intuition in guiding is that I hold many threads of a fabric in my hands at any given moment. I must sense which threads to hold loosely and which to follow with intensity. Intuition helps me choose in a way which rational analysis simply cannot match. The rational process alone is for me too linear, too slow, too cumbersome, for the moment-to-moment subtlety of a session. Intuition comes to me through all my inner senses. I listen to my intuition; I taste and feel of it, using my rational mind to compare its message to past experience, principles, and observations. If nothing contradicts the message, I form a hypothesis and ask an open-ended question to test it out. I observe the client's response, both verbal and non-verbal, to discover the accuracy of the hypothesis and the appropriateness of exploring it at that time.

For example, I might pick up cues from a client that her issue in some way involves her relationship with her mother. I might simply ask her about her mother, telling her that our relationship with our parents often affects our lives in subtle ways. Or I might ask her to allow an image to come to mind for the energy or quality she is experiencing and privately notice whether it might represent her mother. Sometimes that image will actually be of the mother. I might ask her to dialogue with her mother, either as she is now, or from the point of view of herself as a little girl (usually in a specific situation recalled at the time). From the client's response to whichever question I use, I can usually tell whether or not my hunch is correct. If it is, we can pursue this thread of exploration. Sometimes, however, the client resists, going blank or refusing to follow my suggestions. This might indicate that I'm on the wrong track or that the client is not yet ready to confront this issue. I would then feel my way to a more gradual approach, or postpone it altogether until a later session.

As guides sharing our whole selves with our clients, we share our highest qualities as well as our everyday personalities. Intuition, love, compassion, and other qualities which reside in our higher unconscious are as valuable to a client's growth as our thoughts, feelings, and physical presence. Optimally, we learn to open to, trust, and use them all.

GENUINENESS AND WORK ON ONESELF

Carl Rogers has emphasized the importance of wholeness and genuineness in the counseling relationship. Among the essential qualities of a good counselor, the first is:

> . . . genuineness, realness-congruence. The more the therapist is herself in the relationship, putting up no professional facade, the greater is the likelihood that the client will change and grow in a constructive manner. It means that the therapist is openly being with the feelings and attitudes that are flowing within the moment. (1978, p. 9)

Such genuineness requires dedicated self-awareness, courage, and honesty. It requires constant work on our part as guides, to further our own growth and wholeness. Being a whole

"The capacity of the therapist for compassion, empathy, love and acceptance is of crucial importance in determining the level of the final outcome. The client learns to respond as the therapist responds, learns to listen to him/herself as the therapist listens. The more evolved and aware and open the therapist is, the more space the client is given for growth within the therapeutic relationship. This is just another way of saying that any psychotherapy is only as high as the psychotherapist." (Vaughan-Clark, 1977, p. 80) person is a process, not an end point, and all of us who intend to help others in a counseling or guiding capacity need to be deeply dedicated to our own growing self-awareness.

Often a guide's response to a client or to a client's situation becomes the focus of the guide's own session at another time. It seems that the very issues a guide is facing personally come up again and again during sessions with clients. This may be because we are more sensitive to those issues that are alive for us, or it may be that similar issues confront members of a community at the same time. The phenomenon Jung called synchronicity may also be at play here, "a peculiar interdependence of objective events among themselves as well as with the subjective 'psychic' states of the observer or observers" (Jung, 1950, p. xxiv). Once, working with a client who was torn between her sense of service to God and her desire to have a rich personal and sexual life, I discovered that I, too, needed to synthesize this apparent polarity into 'juicy service.' In working with these issues on our own, we serve our clients as well as ourselves. More than once a conflict within myself has been dramatically changed by work with a client who had exemplified the conflict for me.

I think it is a professional responsibility for any therapist, counselor, or guide, to include activities enhancing personal awareness as a regular practice in his or her life. These may include therapy, meditation, personal journals, artistic and spiritual pursuits, classes and workshops. It is more than a case of preventing intrusions of our own unresolved conflicts into our clients' work; it is the challenge of constantly expanding our potential as whole, aware, growing persons and allowing this whole person to be present to our clients, friends, and family.

"The quality of the helping relationship, based on unconditional love and close attunement to the client, is the indispensable context without which techniques are mere mechanical gimmicks which will lack true healing power. The level of the guide's personal integration is a crucial element which determines the amount of clarity and love he/she is able to bring to the traveler on the Path." (Crampton, 1977, p. 50)

NON-ATTACHMENT

Paradoxically, presence rests on non-attachment, the letting go of preconceptions about what ought to occur and of the desire for some kind of measurable success. The challenge is to be involved without getting entangled, to keep one's understanding and perceptions of the process broad rather than narrowed down to one small aspect or point of view. Working for a particular outcome may help structure the session, but attachment to achieving that outcome may subvert some other more appropriate process and result.

June Singer (1973) writes of her lesson in non-attachment:

> My training analyst. . . shocked me one day by saying, "You are not supposed to want the patient to get well!"
>
> At first I could not quite believe this, for I surely did not understand her meaning. But gradually as it sank in I was able to see that if I acted out of my desire to heal the patient, I was setting myself up as the miracle worker. I would be doing it for my own satisfaction, for the joy of success. . . . My own needs would be in the foreground then, and the patient's needs would revert to the secondary position. Besides, the possibility for healing lies in the psyche of the patient. . . . If I, as analyst, impose my concepts of the direction into which the analysis should go and what the outcome should be, I am doing violence to the potential unity of the patient's psyche. (p. 25).

For this reason, it is essential for guides to be aware of their own needs and biases, and to free themselves from their influence as much as possible.

Similar dynamics are involved when the guide must deal with a personal response to the client or to a client's situation, such as feeling angry about the way a client has been treated. Although the anger is honest and may need to be shared, it is another kind of attachment which can interfere with the client's growth in therapy. It is another issue for the guide's personal work outside the session.

Involvement together with non-attachment seems to be a contradiction or at least a paradox. How can we really be *with* someone and yet not care what happens (or at least not let our caring get in the way)? A synthesis of these two attitudes arises from a wider view which trusts the essential unity of life and the unfolding of the individual's growth. From our limited human perspective we do not know if any one outcome is preferable to another. Releasing our clients to their destinies, releases them to take full responsibility for themselves. The client is free because the guide is not imposing his or her idea of what is supposed to happen.

Using a model suggested by Assagioli (1974) for balancing and synthesizing opposites, we can illustrate the synthesis of detachment and involvement with a triangle. The base of the triangle represents the apparent polarity; finding a point along that axis would be a compromise, losing something of each pole in order to avoid conflict. To find the point of synthesis, we must move to a higher, more encompassing perspective. At this point, the full potential of each pole can be realized without conflict.

Figure 6 —
Synthesis Triangle

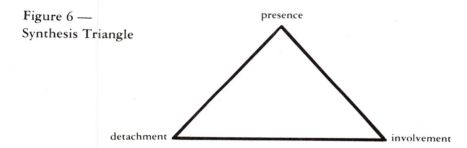

Non-attachment to outcome is possible when the guide knows and trusts that dilemmas and choices are evolutionary stages toward each client's self-realization.

Transference and Countertransference

It is significant that such important concepts as these are never mentioned in the basic psychosynthesis books. I believe it reflects an essential difference in assumptions about the counseling/psychotherapeutic/guiding process. No psychosynthesis guide would deny that transference and countertransference occur, although other terminology may be used for aspects of these dynamics. Much of what I have said about non-attachment and work on oneself refers to monitoring countertransference and preventing its intruding into the relationship. The whole process of disidentification and self-identification helps release both guide and client from the tyranny of transference. Inner conflicts are resolved *within* the client as much as possible, through imagery and inner dialogue, so it is not so necessary to work them out in the relationship between client and guide. Self-responsibility and choice are strongly encouraged and supported. I believe there is far less burn-out among psychosynthesis guides for this reason.

An image comes to mind which illustrates how non-attachment and disidentification on the part of the guide can release the need for working directly with transference. An aikido master can effortlessly guide all attacks on by, so that he never has to throw up hard defenses or really expend much energy at all. At the same time, his attitude toward his attacker can be loving and connected; in fact, he blends with the energy of his attacker in order to guide it on by. In the same way, we can learn to blend with and redirect the energy of a client's projections and transference so that they don't 'stick' to us, drain us, wound us, or complicate our lives. They can go on by, and circle back around to their origin within the client.

ACCEPTANCE AND RESPECT

"The second attitude of importance in creating a climate for change is acceptance, or caring or prizing—unconditional positive regard. It means that when the therapist is experiencing a positive, acceptant attitude toward whatever the client *is* at the moment, therapeutic movement or change is more likely . . . . It is a nonpossessive caring. The therapist prizes the client in a total rather than a conditional way."
(Rogers, 1978, p. 12)

Non-attachment is possible when we truly accept and respect our clients *just as they are*, from moment to moment. We are not attached to changing them, nor to having them stay the way they are. We accept them in their totality, which includes their potential for growth as well as their inhibitions and problems. When we fully accept people, we are able to be with them without holding back any part of ourselves out of distaste or judgment. This is not to say that we have to *like* all our clients all the time; we can accept our own dislikes and preferences with the knowledge that these feelings, too, are part of a process and do not reflect the totality of our beings. We *can own and disidentify* from our personal feelings and hold a larger perspective of caring.

Acceptance is the first step in transformation. As long as we refuse to accept our feelings, needs, limitations, and potentials, we react to them or repress them. To bring these aspects into awareness, we must create a safe internal environment by accepting ourselves, *just as we are*. This kind of acceptance is not resignation. It is a positive embrace of what is and what is potential, within ourselves and in our external environment. Acceptance precedes full awareness and further choice.

Our challenge as guides, then, is to accept ourselves, in the moment, just as we are, and our clients as fellow human beings, just as they are. In doing so, we bring the quality and energy of acceptance into the relationship which in turn evokes self-acceptance within the client. Fear and self-hatred subside, awareness and power increase, and transformation begins.

CONCEPTS AND BELIEFS

The set of ideas and concepts with which we approach a session has a strong effect on our capacity for acceptance, non-attachment, and overall presence. We can approach each session with belief in the individual's capacity to understand his or her life, to make choices, and to transcend apparent limitations. We think, in effect, "Here is a person who has the capacity to solve his or her own problems, whose problems are not the result of mere inadequacy, but challenges that lie in the way for a purpose." This attitude and conceptual framework has profound effects on the way we look, act, gesture, wait, and question, and on our access to intuition. These in turn communicate a whole context to the other person and profoundly affect the work of the session. When the focus is on the problem, on the pathology, and the purpose of counseling is to somehow relieve the symptoms and solve the problem, understanding and growth are severely limited. Frances Vaughan-Clark (1977) states bluntly, "A therapist operating in a theoretical context that does not include the transpersonal is necessarily limiting the potential growth of the client" (p. 71). This limited understanding and expectation is communicated through subtle non-verbal cues and by the emphasis and direction of questions and responses. The focus of the client's work will probably be on short-range goals, on faults and defects. The immediate problems may be solved, but the underlying growth patterns will probably not be significantly enhanced.

Concepts, models, visions, and even perceptions can be chosen and nurtured in oneself. We can choose ways of perceiving others that allow us to respond positively and helpfully. As guides we can choose to hold in mind the biggest possible picture of our clients and the meaning of their dilemmas; in doing so, we create a context for optimal growth. The wonderful side effect of this is that we are modeling at the same time we are facilitating, modeling the possibility of choice in how clients look at others and themselves. This possibility of choice opens doors to new approaches to problems and to life. We no longer limit our growth with constricting views of what is possible and who we can become.

CONCENTRATION AND EMPATHY

There is another choice involved in presence; the choice to concentrate on the client during the session. This may seem obvious, but the concentration required is intense and needs conscious commitment and practice. It requires the choice to disallow intrusive personal thoughts and feelings that do not concern the relationship with the client. As guides, we make our mental, emotional, and physical energies available to the process that is occurring. It is a here-and-now kind of consciousness; although an awareness of time passing may be maintained, that, too, is in the service of the other person. When thoughts stray, we bring them back to the client; our feelings respond to the individual rather than to outside concerns. When personal feelings are aroused by the interaction with the other person, they are included; that is part of the process. Feelings and thoughts from the guide's life outside, however, are set aside by commitment and choice. This is not unlike the concentration of meditation.

How is it possible to concentrate so fully on someone else and still be congruent with one's own feelings and needs? The psychosynthesis model of the person indicates that we are many-faceted; it is not incongruent to choose which facet of ourselves to bring into consciousness at any given moment. Our relationships with clients are as real as any other part of our lives. While client and guide are together, that relationship is the chosen and important reality of the hour. As guides, we are not only people who have this or that problem in private life, who have this or that worry or concern. We are people who choose to move away from distracting feelings and thoughts and toward other feelings and thoughts, equally real, thereby expressing that part of ourselves which guides and serves others. True congruence is being a self, a center of awareness and choice.

Once again appears the double effect of subtle modeling while facilitating. By focus and concentration, by the choice to be fully present for the client, the guide models the capacity inherent in everyone to disidentify from one narrow aspect of one's life and to identify with the center of awareness and will, the self. This does not happen without work! Ram Dass (1977) has said repeatedly that working with others means working on oneself. To be present with a client in this focused manner, we must work on ourselves with piercing honesty and vulnerability, discovering subpersonalities, exploring what creates consciousness and awareness and what distracts and numbs, coming ever closer to inner knowledge of personality, self, and Higher Self.

Haronian's description of an effective relationship between therapist and client suggests potential depths of concentration and empathy:

> To meet at the interface of I and Thou means that each member of the pair is willingly and consciously as close to the other as possible; so close that for each person, the subject-object dichotomy is blurred and more or less dissolved. Ego (selfish) needs are not operative. At this point, one self meets the other, and these disinterested aspects of each individual merge for a moment in a sense of union. . . . In the moment of relationship, there is a sense of community of interest. (1975, pp. 33-34)

"The third facilitative aspect of the relationship is empathetic understanding. This means that the therapist senses accurately the feelings and personal meanings that are being experienced by the client and communicates this understanding to the client. . . .

Being empathetic involves a choice on the part of the therapist as to what she will pay attention to, namely the inner world of the client as that individual perceives it." (Rogers, 1978, p. 14)

BIFOCAL VISION

Presence rests on the recognition that guide and client are two Selves sitting and working together. A unification of these two people's awareness occurs, so that both are approaching the mystery of the client's unfolding with love, respect, responsiveness, and discernment. The guide models this attitude and sustains it by committing his or her whole self to the session. The guide calls upon his or her highest functioning—intuition, wisdom, compassion, emotional response, and physical expression—and places them at the service of the other person's Self.

Guiding ultimately occurs within the individual; the best guide is the individual's own higher Self. Guiding is the process of aligning with the client's Self by holding an awareness of one's own Self and cooperating with what emerges from that source. Crampton emphasizes this principle:

> It is assumed that the real guide of a psychosynthesis interview is the client's higher Self and that the Self, at any particular time, is directing the person's attention in certain directions. With this in mind, the external guide, whose role is to support the client's inner process, is attentive to what seems to 'want to happen' in the session.
>
> The psychosynthesist will seek to have that bifocal vision which enables one to see the client simultaneously as a personality and as a higher Self. We need to be aware of the problems and weaknesses that exist at the personality level as well as to sense the person's strengths, both actual and potential. If we can remember that a creative life force and transpersonal qualities are seeking to manifest through the personality, however distorted it may be, we will tend to evoke the client's highest potentials and enable him or her to contact the hidden sources of wisdom, strength, and direction which lie within. The guide who believes, and who can help the client to discover, that the truth lies within is giving the greatest of all gifts to that person. (1977, p. 50)

BEING MY SELF AS A GUIDE

Because guiding is an intensely personal process, I want to share my personal experiences and commitment as a guide. The most basic and difficult aspect of guiding for me is really knowing and accepting what it means to be a guide. To truly guide another's journey to Self is a sacred undertaking and must be approached with humility and commitment. I must be willing to put my personality out on the battlefield, to make myself available as a vehicle for the process unfolding before me. I must choose to be present with my heart and mind and soul; anything less will short-circuit the process, and it will be another superficial encounter about living rather than an exchange of life itself.

For me, this means being willing to be uncomfortable, to be the temporary recipient of anger or rebellion, to be seen not as a pal but as someone who sees something that my clients may not yet see. It means being able to be fully and serenely present to others' pain, anger, embarrassment, and self-pity without giving in to the urge to make them feel better in the moment. My desire to be liked by my clients, to be one of the gang, often interferes with this intention. The false modesty which denies my wisdom and power often coaxes me to doubt my right to be firm and urges me to give in to my client's resistance. My lack of faith in people themselves may tempt me to do the work for them, to 'help' them, to lend them my will inappropriately. The antidote to all these tendencies is to ask myself what it is that the people who are my clients need from me. Invariably the answer is that they need firmness, clarity, direction, wisdom, and unconditional love. They can seek casual friendship and comfort for their subpersonalities elsewhere. I do not help them by reinforcing dependency on me for these. I experience this in my own work as a client; from my guide, I want and need truth and the evocation of my highest potentials. It is a strong temptation as a guide just to make my clients feel better in the moment. I understand why doctors hand out tranquilizers to patients in emotional distress. It requires faith and a willingness to sustain my own pain and discomfort to do what is truly needed.

When I am willing to be uncomfortable when it serves another's process, I model disidentification from feelings; I model choosing in the face of pain and distress. I must be present, then, with my discomfort, sharing it openly on occasion, with the clear choice not to allow it to control me. I do not try to appear as some sort of emotionless guru; that would be simply playing out a subpersonality of no value to the client. The ability to tolerate this kind of discomfort is sustained by faith in the client's ability to grow and in my own wisdom and clarity. It must come from my commitment to the service of another's growth. It comes from alignment with my deepest sense of Self.

I must continually choose to put service above my desire to be a 'good guide,' my desire to have the emotional payoff of a 'good session.' This may mean being willing to go to a dead end, knowing it is probably a dead end, in order for a client to experience that and choose a new direction. Ultimately, it means being willing to risk losing a client rather than struggling to please in a manner which does not serve his or her purpose.

Through the process of guiding, I discover myself; I discover the special gifts and qualities which are expressions of my Self. The qualities which I appreciate in myself are power, clarity, and love. I understand now that in my very presence is power; I do not need to push my clients or carry them along. There is tremendous power in silence, in waiting with love and trust. My interventions are most effective when they come from a clarity about what is occurring and when they intend to evoke clarity in clients. Throughout a session, I direct love toward my client, trusting, confident, serene and caring love, communicated in gesture, voice, and facial expression. These are the qualities I bring to guiding and they are far more important than any techniques or methods. When I share these qualities, I share the best of myself.

PRESENCE

In this exploration of the aspects of presence in counseling and guiding, I have included many qualities which are often considered as separate from presence. In addition to the inclusion of the whole person of the guide—body, feelings, mind, imagination, and intuition—I suggest that non-attachment, acceptance and respect, expansive, inclusive concepts and beliefs, concentration and empathy, and a bifocal vision which sees both the personality and the potential of a client, are all part of full and facilitative presence. This kind of presence is within reach with intention, honesty, and practice. However, as I write these words, I think of the many times I am not in touch with this kind of presence, when I forget these principles and try to operate on skill and personality alone. I get confused and identified with my own subpersonalities as we all do. The challenge is to forgive ourselves our lapses and to continue to work with ourselves and each other to learn to live our full potential as guides and as people.

5

THE INDIVIDUAL SESSION:
METHODS AND TECHNIQUES

It is one of the beauties of psychosynthesis that it is not a closed system with rigid, crystallized methods. It provides an open structure that can integrate effective methods from other disciplines and leaves room for the creativity of the practitioner. (Crampton, 1977, p. 39)

In my experience, the *forms* of the work are of less importance than a vision of *purpose*, an understanding of the *process* of growth, and an appreciation of the power of *presence*. These principles can be integrated into many different forms of therapeutic and education at work. However, psychosynthesis guiding does tend to use certain methods and procedures, because they have proven to be effective in evoking human potential. So, if my readers are not hopelessly lost in the lofty realms of abstraction, I will attempt to bring things back down to earth and describe typical (if there can be such a thing) individual psychosynthesis work in concrete terms.

To an objective observer, what would an individual session of psychosynthesis guiding look like? Many of the external characteristics are the same as other forms of therapy and counseling. Guide and client usually sit facing one another directly, either in chairs or on cushions on the floor, depending on their preferences and the context in which the session occurs. The client often sits on a couch or on the floor so that there is room to move or lie down. Occasionally, there may be observers for the session, people training to be guides, other members of a workshop, or friends or family invited by the client. These people are invited to support the work of the session with their attention and energy and may be used in the client's work when appropriate.

In the best of environments, the furnishings are simple and the room is quiet. All this is conducive but not essential to focused work. Some guides conduct sessions out of doors. I have been guided on an airplane when I began sharing my inner experience with my traveling companion, a skilled guide.

51

BEGINNING A SESSION

Silence

Sessions may begin with a period of silence which provides an opportunity for client and guide alike to center attention and energy on the session and put aside distracting thoughts and feelings. This may be done as a silent meditation if the client is comfortable with this form, or the guide may suggest simply, "Let's close our eyes and just be aware of breathing for a few moments, in order to relax before beginning." The guide may open to imagery and intuition regarding the client's need and direction in the session. The client may become more aware of what is happening inside and what he or she wants to work on during the session; this sometimes turns out to be different from the agenda previously planned.

When we each feel ready, we open our eyes and the session begins. The client usually starts by sharing aspects of recent experiences, concerns, or problems. Immediate emotional and physical experience also provides a good starting point.

Focusing On An Issue

" The power of human consciousness is great indeed, but it can be made totally ineffectual by objectifying a life concern as though it were an arithmetic problem or an intellectual puzzle. If the client, beginning to be aware of a genuine life concern makes a problem to be solved of that concern, then the client loses access to the truly creative depths of consciousness."
(Bugental, 1978, p. 87)

As the client talks, a central theme, issue, or dynamic will move into the foreground. We discover that no matter what the chosen agenda of the session, the issues and concerns we need to confront tend to emerge and become part of the agenda. We may begin a session with two or three widely disparate concerns and discover, in the end, that all have been included in the course of the session. The focus of the session provides the grist for the mill, the content through which the patterns of thought and feeling can be brought into awareness and transformed. Just as the events and figures in dreams represent our inner reality and process, so do the events and perceptions of our waking world. We create the problems we need in order to grow. The task, then, is not to solve a problem or treat a symptom, but to use the life concern as the focus of our inner exploration and unfolding awareness and choice.

The first few pages of Transcript A in the Appendix illustrate this process of focusing on an issue. The client discusses at some length recent experiences affecting her vocational plans and the indecision, confusion, and sense of comparative inadequacy which she experiences around this concern. She finally concludes: "Well, it is all kind of a mumble jumble." To help her focus and clarify, the guide asks:

G: What is the strongest experience? What is the strongest feeling in this whole mumble jumble?

C: (Pause) Well, it is this feeling of 'them' and 'me' and the strongest right now is me. That's where I feel I am going to get my answers of what I need for myself—the image that I had of that healing witch or whatever she was. And just continuing to work through my process and all that other stuff. It only exists in my mind, so to say. I am making up a lot of it in terms of my comparisons with other people.

G: When you said you have the experience of 'me,' what is that experience? What is that experiencing?

C: Well, how I am working on myself and going through the training and having acupuncture done and exploring my dreams. I feel that is the route I am going to continue on. My confidence and strength will come more and more as I understand.

G: I heard you say "route that I will continue on" and I thought of the kind of 'root' that a plant has. Then I realized that's not what you said.

C: Oh, yeah! Hum?!

G: The 'root' of myself instead of the path that I'm following. . . .

C: Yes, I like that, because that's what it's like.

G: Would you be willing to consult that root and see what needs to happen today in our session?

C: Uh-hum. (long pause, several hums) What needs to happen in this session today? What do I need to find out? (pause) I just had this kind of feeling that somehow I am pushing it, and I am not opening up enough to really hear what it is that I need to hear.

The guide emphasizes feelings and experience in an attempt to help the client connect with the underlying dynamics of her vocational quandary. Because the client's responses are vague and unfocused, when an image suggests itself, the guide uses it immediately. Here the guide trusts her intuition and the known maturity of the client enough to share her alternative image of 'root.' This seems to fit for the client and is then used to elicit the client's inner wisdom about the purpose and direction of the session. The underlying issue of "pushing it" and "not opening enough to hear" emerges. This is the dynamic which becomes the focus of the session.

As the concern emerges, the guide needs to clarify it, making sure that he or she understands it as the client does. Choices can be offered to the client about emphasis and about methods to use to explore the concern. The guide will be guided by intuition and experience in selecting approaches to use which are congruent with the client's concern and overall needs.

CHOOSING METHODS AND TECHNIQUES

The methods chosen for a session may be dialogue, guided imagery, drawing, movement, Gestalt techniques, dreamwork, cathartic methods, and combinations of these. Methods are chosen primarily on the basis of the client's needs and the purposes of the session, as well as according to the client's readiness and preferences, and the guide's preferences and style. That which will evoke the client's fullest experience of self is the method sought.

There are a great many techniques employed in psychosynthesis, as we find that no one technique fits all purposes or all persons. Some clients may work very well with certain techniques and not well with others. This depends both upon the psychological type and the level of development. A therapist who wishes to be fully responsive to the needs of a particular client must therefore be able to use a variety of approaches. It is important to bear in mind as well that new methods and techniques are constantly being developed in psychosynthesis. It holds to the principle that techniques are made to fit the person rather than the person being made to fit the techniques. Often the most effective approach is one that the guide develops on the spur of the moment to meet the needs of a particular situation. (Crampton, 1977, p.39)

Methods and techniques evolve as each guide creates new ways of facilitating awareness and choice, often intuitively, in response to a particular client's need, or from the guide's own work on him/herself. Each of us tends to develop a comfortable style of working which includes certain techniques which express our own qualities and personality. We tend to attract those clients who can best respond to our particular style. There is a problem, however, with our apparently inevitable human tendency to become attached to form. Methods and techniques are only *forms* and if we become concerned with them to the detriment of the purpose and spirit behind them, we may forget that change occurs mostly through relationship, presence, and love.

With these precautions in mind, we will survey methods commonly used in psychosynthesis work.

DIALOGUE

Dialogue between client and guide is probably the most basic and familiar form of guiding. Rogers' client-centered therapy is a model for this approach: feedback and 'active listening' to feelings remains an essential tool for clarification, deepening exploration, and validation of the moment-to-moment process of the client. Bugental refers to the "inner search therapies" in which interventions facilitate the inner searching of the client by pointing to resistances, clarifying and modeling non-judgmental and non-analytical observation. This basic approach is quite powerful in facilitating awareness and often allows integration and choices to occur spontaneously. As an adjunct to other methods, dialogue provides an opportunity to discuss the implications of the work, to look at questions to be explored between sessions or in future sessions, and to seek ways of applying what has been learned. In such discussions, however, the focus remains as always on the client's inner process and experience. The beginning pages of Transcripts A and B illustrate dialogue.

There is some difference of opinion in psychotherapy circles about the use of active methods where the guide makes specific suggestions about how to conduct the inner search. Bugental (1965), for example, believes that active methods run the risk of contaminating the client's own stream of awareness with the guide's intrusions. He also requires a minimum of 250 contacts with a client before thoroughgoing results are achieved. In psychosynthesis, and in other eclectic therapies, however, long-lasting results may occur rapidly, sometimes even in the first session. Leuner (1969), a pioneer in the use of guided imagery, states that his approach yields positive, lasting results in an average of 40 hours.

Active methods can teach clients new ways of exploring their inner worlds which they might take years to discover on their own. They bring the guide's wisdom and intuition more actively into the process in the service of the client, an additional force for growth which must be balanced against the danger of contamination which concerns Bugental. The guide's own point of view colors interventions no matter what the method used; in active methods, it may simply be more obvious and therefore less subversive of the client's own process. In my own experience as a client—as well as a guide—I have found guiding which went beyond the basic dialogue extremely helpful in bringing forth new patterns which were ready to emerge, challenging me to make clear choices and take responsibility for my life, and unblocking the obstacles to fuller realization of my potential. Active methods provide means for moving beyond transference as a major tool for therapy. They are most effective with people who are willing to take active responsibility for their own learning and growth.

On the other hand, active methods can be used manipulatively to induce a kind of glamorized, dramatic 'change,' especially in the setting of a group or workshop. Behaviors of pseudo-openness, inappropriate self-revelation, and catharsis can become the norm of a group without real inner change occurring. An active method, like dialogue, is dependent on the skill and sensitivity of the guide and on attunement with the individual's emerging process.

On the border between dialogue and active methods are two recently developed therapeutic approaches: Gendlin's 'focusing' (1978) and Bandler and Grinder's Neuro-linguistic Programming (NLP). Gendlin studied a number of people who seemed to profit from therapy and discovered their common ability to focus on their inward experience of a problem and discover its existential essence. He believes this process can be taught and so has broken it down into steps which he describes and illustrates in his book. 'Focusing' can be taught to clients; I have recommended that many read the book and try out the steps on their own and in sessions.

NLP emphasizes the effect of language on human reality and focuses on discovering the impoverished models of the world and of self which are expressed in the client's linguistic structures. These models can then be expanded by questions, challenges, and clarification. Their methods seem particularly applicable to freeing people from restrictive dichotomies of reality, from polarized views which prevent choice along a spectrum of possibilities. NLP methods also uncover conflicting subpersonalities through observation of incongruities among the client's 'paramessages;' that is, between the various modes of verbal and non-verbal communication. NLP is a powerful technology of therapy which can sharpen a guide's awareness of the client's process and help the guide tailor interventions to the client's modalities of perception and expression. This 'metatherapy' uncovers polarities and moves toward a broader, integrative model of reality.

There has been some abuse of NLP techniques for, like any technology, it can be used for manipulation as well as transformation. NLP has become a kind of pop therapy which may encourage people to use the techniques more for their own image enhancement than for the client's benefit. Using the methods within the perspectives of psychosynthesis mitigates against manipulation and places the work within a larger context of personal and spiritual growth. The conscious choice of the client to utilize a particular method for a purpose guards against the guide's taking on an image as a superstar who performs mysterious transformations upon the client. The guide's presence, humility and acknowledgment of the client's Higher Self as the true 'therapist' will also assure the methods are used appropriately. I mention both NLP and 'focusing' here as a recommendation for further study by the reader, whether for personal or professional applications.

GESTALT THERAPY

Another system of methods often incorporated into psychosynthesis work is Gestalt therapy as developed by Fritz Perls (1969) and his students. Although psychosynthesis principles differ in some ways from the implicit principles of Gestalt therapy, many Gestalt techniques work will within a psychosynthesis framework. One primary difference is that Gestalt therapy sees the self as a shifting point of identity, rather than as a center of awareness and will. On the other hand, gestalt therapy encourages disidentification from the parts of oneself in order to re-own them and bring them back into the whole (gestalt), a purpose highly valued in psychosynthesis. In one technique, for example, the individual acts out a dialogue between the central 'I' and parts of the personality or of the body, such as hands, feet, heart, stomach, or whatever is showing symptoms of distress. Often an empty chair is assigned a role, such as a parent, spouse, or other person in relationship to the client. The client's perception of the other person is assumed to be largely a projection of his or her own unconscious aspects. The client then plays both roles by moving from one chair to the other and speaking from each perspective.

Within a psychosynthesis framework, such dialogues are seen as exchanges between two subpersonalities, the dominant one with which the client is mostly identified, and the one projected onto the extra chair. Although some resolution and cooperation may be worked out between them, the client may not experience being a self or a will who can choose between various responses and subpersonalities. In order to evoke this experience, the psychosynthesis guide may suggest that the client stand in yet a third position and look back at the two chairs and the subpersonalities or parts they represent. From this perspective, the individual may see the needs and values of both parts objectively and without judgment and can direct their integration and harmonization. If this third position turns out to be yet another conflicting part, a fourth position can be taken, or another approach may need to be tried. The guide may suggest an image of light streaming down on all parts or of a wise person coming to assist. In this way, Gestalt approaches are often combined with imagery, a method to be explored more fully below.

If the reader is not familiar with Gestalt therapy, further study may be quite valuable in expanding the techniques and methods available for guiding oneself and others. The bibliography at the end of this chapter lists several good sources.

DREAMWORK

Dream analysis has been used since Freud as a therapeutic tool. Dreams have long been seen as containing wisdom from our unconscious and from the spirit world beyond our normal consciousness. Because our reality is determined by our inner experience, dreams are extremely important to the natural, on-going process of growth we call psychosynthesis. We can facilitate their transformative power by bringing them more into consciousness in our waking life and acknowledging their significance. Retelling dreams and recording them in a dream journal helps make them more a part of our waking reality, and guides often encourage clients to write down and share their dreams even if nothing more is formally done with them.

Gestalt techniques of dreamwork can extend this, especially when dealing with unpleasant or recurring dreams whose messages are difficult to discover. The individual identifies with various figures in the dream and speaks from their perspectives. ("I am a fire burning up my house. I am hot and roaring and angry!") This differs from a cognitive analysis in that one tries on the various parts of oneself that are reflected in the dream, and experiences their existential reality and interaction within oneself. Insight and transformation may occur spontaneously when this is done.

In psychosynthesis work, dreams are often used as the beginning of imagery exploration. The individual relaxes and focuses within and then allows the dream to continue in imagery, replaying the dream as it occurred and going on from where it ended or trying out an alternative turn of events. Within this waking dream, the guide may suggest dialogue with various figures and alternative ways of getting to know and befriend fearful or antagonistic figures. In this way, a nightmare may be transformed into a reunion with repressed and valuable energies.

GUIDED IMAGERY

Imagery has been central to psychosynthesis work since its inception, yet psychosynthesis should not be identified with imagery, as it sometimes has been. Imagery is one very important tool in psychosynthesis work, but it is only a tool. It is congruent with psychosynthesis concepts of the creativity of the unconscious and of the role of intuition and imagination as psychological functions on a par with thinking, feeling, and sensation. Methods using imagery abound and invite further study, as do most of the methods mentioned here. The following discussion only outlines the principles and suggests a few of the many techniques available. The bibliography at the end of the chapter suggests additional reading.

Imagery can be experienced through all of the senses: sight, hearing, body movement, even smell and taste. The first three are most common and often combined. Although many imagery methods emphasize visualization, it is important to use the other modalities both for people who have trouble visualizing and to enrich the visual experience.

Both mind and feelings participate in imagery; even the body participates, visibly or on a subliminal level. Perhaps this is why profound changes often occur through symbolic action and discovery. It is not even necessary to cognitively understand imagery; like dreaming, its effects can be transformational without interpretation. Indeed, too intellectual an approach can sap the life from the process.

Consider for a moment how much our lives are already unconsciously influenced by imagery pouring from television, films, radio, and magazines. One way we can defend ourselves against inundation is by noticing the symbols used, their associations, and the intended effects. We can make choices about our responses and screen ourselves from imagery which is destructive. The current fad of horror movies provides us all with the choice not to see them; to keep our consciousness less cluttered by images of insanity, evil, viciousness, and meaningless suffering. By the same token, we can seek out and use positive imagery from media, art, our own dreams, and therapeutic work. We can choose to use these images in such a way as to inspire and lift our consciousness.

We can live our imagery consciously and with choice. Assagioli's laws quoted in Chapter 3 indicate how imagery affects our thinking, our feelings, our physical states, and even our outward reality. It is probably impossible not to work with imagery in therapy; guided imagery simply focuses and makes more conscious the whole process.

When using imagery in a session, I call upon my own imagination and intuition. It is a challenging process. My own past experience with symbols may be helpful, as well as what I know of archetypes and universal symbols. But all this background information must be applied with care, for many individuals have unique responses to certain symbols, tangential or even opposite to the common responses. There is often strong resistance to the real meaning of an image, mirroring the repression which has gone on before—repression of the sublime as well as of basic drives. The resistance must be honored and allowed to loosen or dissolve gradually. My inner excitement at the appearance of a strong positive image, if expressed, may be helpful in supporting the client, or it may confuse the process and evoke resistance. It seems most helpful when I can observe and participate in the client's imagery within my own imagination, asking for details and clarification when my version is incomplete, being willing to change my version quickly whenever it seems to conflict with the client's, yet holding the possibility that my version contains some truth as yet unseen by the client. Careful open-ended questions can often ferret this out. And of course it is a matter of experience and training; the more I work with other people's imagery, the more I am able to accurately 'tune in' and respond in helpful ways.

Many people need training to use imagery as a therapeutic tool for themselves. Most of us have been told at one time or another that something was 'just your imagination,' with emphasis and scorn placed on the word 'just.' We have been taught to mistrust our imagination as something alien to rational thought and sensible living. So we have ignored, suppressed, or felt vaguely guilty about our natural on-going imagery. Sometimes imagery *is* misused, when

"Active imagination is, more than anything else, an attitude toward the unconcious. It cannot be said to be a *technique* or even a *method* of coming to terms with the unconscious, because it is a different experience for each person who is able to use it. The common feature of all varieties of active imagination is its dependence upon a view of the unconscious that recognizes its contents as containing innate structures (archetypes) which inevitably define the potentialities and the limitations of the personality." (Singer, 1973, p. 343)

"We sin against the imagination whenever we ask an image for its meaning, requiring that images be translated into concepts." (Hillman, 1975, p. 39)

we allow ourselves to constantly 'trip out' in fantasies of how things might be, avoiding confrontation of difficulties, and avoiding choice and responsibility. I hope it is manifestly clear that imagery guided by consciousness and choice is a force for responsible and healthy engagement in life, not an escape.

Whatever the reasons, many people do not consciously experience imagery, nor recognize that their inner experience truly is in the form of imagery. Often they do not visualize, and mistake that for an inability to use imagery. Such individuals need to have their modalities of imagery, usually auditory and/or kinesthetic, honored. When they accept and use these modalities consciously, the visual modality often develops, too.

How can we help people develop their imaginative faculties? First, by paying keen attention to the natural imagery which we use all the time. For practice, try this simple exercise.

EXERCISE: NATURAL IMAGERY

Write a paragraph or two about a major life concern of yours, or a recent experience, focusing on feelings, impressions and thoughts. Write about the experience or concern in terms of how you experience it rather than how it might be analyzed from the outside. It is best to do this without reading the next paragraph of instructions.

Now go back and read what you have written. Notice and circle any similes, metaphors or other images you used. Notice figures of speech you may normally take for granted. Notice also the primary modality of your images: visual, auditory, or kinesthetic. You may be surprised at how full of imagery your spontaneous writing is.

You can also do this with another person, asking him or her to describe a concern or event. You jot down any images that occur and share them with the person afterwards.

When I notice the natural imagery in a person's speech, I can reinforce and expand it without even talking about imagery *per se*. Often people will describe an emotion in terms of physical sensation and imagery, such as "I have a knot in my stomach." Questions which might be used to expand this imagery would be: How big is the knot? What does it feel like it's made of? What's tied up in there? If the knot could talk, what might it want to say to you?

We can train ourselves to use imagery more freely by listening to non-vocal music, usually classical, and observing the free flow of imagery which occurs. Free drawing with colors also helps; without previous conception of what we want to draw, we let our hands and eyes be guided by the unconscious. June Singer (1973) used finger paints because people seem less inhibited in this medium. These methods are based on the assumption that we all have imagery within us; we need only provide outlets for its expression and give ourselves permission to enjoy and trust it.

Working with imagery is not essential to psychosynthesis. In some cases, it may be important to use other methods at first, until the person feels more comfortable with feelings and with material from the unconscious. In other cases, it might be important to develop the individual's rational mind and de-emphasize an imagination prone to escapist fantasies. In this case, reintegration of the imagination would be an essential later step.

The simplest use of imagery is within a dialogue when the guide asks the client to suggest a symbol or image for an experience. Sometimes this occurs spontaneously, the client saying something like, "I feel like I have rocks in my head." When an image is suggested, either spontaneously or in response to a question, it can be flushed out, explored, experienced through different modalities, and enlivened by attention and care. A conversation can be set up with it, or it can simply be given a voice and allowed to have its say. If it expresses a need, that need can be met symbolically, and the image allowed to change in response. It can be worked with as a subpersonality as described in Chapter 3.

Inner dialogue between subpersonalities is often accomplished through imagery. The client discovers images for one and then another conflicting subpersonality and imagines them talking with one another. The client may take one role and then the other, or observe from a third perspective. Often the images of the subpersonalities change in the process, becoming more powerful and integrated.

The use of imagery in this manner is one reason why transference is de-emphasized in psychosynthesis work. Transference occurs with the symbolic figures so it does not need to enter so much into the relationship with the guide. Because of the central purpose of evoking and developing the individual's own will and self, transference and dependence on the guide is considered to be counter-productive in most cases. When transference is onto symbolic figures, resolution can occur more quickly because the guide's personality responses are less likely to confuse and complicate the process. The individual is able to work out conflicts between subpersonalities without having to project one or both of them onto the guide.

The guided daydream or fantasy is a more elaborate use of imagery within a session. In this form, the guide usually begins with some relaxation and focusing suggestions and then mentions a setting for the imagery, often a meadow. The individual imagines being in that setting and describes the scene to the guide. The guide offers suggestions as events unfold, using archetypal symbols or those unique to the individual to evoke either transpersonal energies or patterns from the lower unconscious which need to be addressed.

"In the directed daydream, the transference is generally expressed toward a symbolic character in the story." (Desoille, 1966, p. 25)

Often daydreams include imagery of movement in the vertical dimension. Ascent may bring on images "which become increasingly luminous and which express a sense of calm, of serenity, and ultimately of joy—in effect, the open and generous feelings" (Desoille, 1966, p. 2). Descent, on the other hand, tends to evoke somber images which may be unpleasant or distressing. Climbing a mountain often means contacting one's higher wisdom or sense of transcendence while going down into a cave or under the ocean may mean contact with repressed figures and energies from the lower unconscious. Leuner (1969) may suggest that clients explore a brook, symbolizing psychic energy, upstream to the source, or downstream to its expression in the world.

Leuner also suggests other thematic symbols within a guided imagery session: a meadow (a neutral symbol for where one is now), a mountain (for ascent and transformation), a house (for the personality), a close friend or relative, sexual images, a lion (for aggression), an admired person (ego ideal), a forest or cave (for the repressed unconscious), and a swamp creature (for a repressed subpersonality). When fearful figures appear in a daydream, he may suggest confrontation, feeding them, reconciliation through touching, or, in rare cases, exhausting and killing. He also suggests drinking or bathing in magic fluids to strengthen and provide an experience of purification. These symbols and symbolic actions are extremely helpful in working with resistance, for often an issue which would be difficult to face in normal consciousness can be worked through in the 'disguise' of imagery.

Drawing and other forms of art expression are used frequently in psychosynthesis work. In addition to the free drawing suggested above, drawings can be used in response to specific questions addressed to the unconscious. The individual is guided to find a relaxed and restful position, eyes closed, and to discover within a quiet, receptive place. When the question is asked, the individual is encouraged to simply wait and watch for any images in any modality which arise in response. These images are observed and translated into a form which can be at least partially captured on paper. If nothing occurs, the individual may want to randomly select colors and begin to draw freely, without plan. After the drawing is complete, the individual may write or talk about feelings, associations, and impressions which come up in response to the drawing. The four questions outlined in the next chapter in the section on "Cycles of a Session" may be used separately or together in a drawing exercise.

Drawing may also be used to record important images or scenes from guided daydreams or other imagery experiences. Some individuals find drawing a useful medium for work between sessions and may bring drawings into a session to share a concern they want to address. When I studied with Dr. Assagioli, he suggested that I do a free drawing each morning and then write about my response to it. These drawings were then shared with him in our sessions together and used as the basis of theoretical points as well as personal process.

Evocative Words and Affirmations

Words are images, too, and many words evoke imagery within us. James Hillman (1975) writes of the "therapeutic incantatory power of words," supporting the Eastern practice of reciting mantra in meditation. A common psychosynthesis method based on this principle of words uses 'evocative words' to bring qualities such as love, joy, clarity, or strength into one's life. The individual repeats the key word as a mantra, or makes a small sign of the word and places it where it is frequently seen (on the refrigerator door, the dashboard of the car, over a desk). The word chosen often emerges from an imagery session. The individual experiences associated imagery each time the word is encountered and repeated, strengthening its unconscious effects on thought patterns, feelings, and behavior.

Affirmations use similar principles although they tend to be more concrete and cognitive. Affirmations are statements we make to affirm our choices and intentions. They vary in form, as statements of choice ("I choose to be patient with my children"), or statements in the present tense of how we intend to be ("I am slender and energetic.") Affirmations are often supported by imagery, as we picture ourselves bringing in the desired quality into various situations typical of daily life. A drawing of an image of the desired quality is a form of affirmation and can be displayed at home to remind us of our intention non-verbally. Assagioli's first psychological law is the basis of these methods of change: "Images or mental pictures and ideas tend to produce the physical conditions and the external acts that correspond to them" (1974, p. 51).

Imagery and affirmations are valuable in the training of the will. For example, individuals may make clear choices within a daydream (e.g., rearranging the house they are exploring, or responding to a figure) which are symbolic of choices within their ordinary life and consciousness. When we are deeply involved in imagery, we are in fact making real choices which we will carry through in ordinary life. Moreover, in imagery we can experience the act of choosing precisely and richly and discover, therefore, the self and the will.

MEDITATION

Meditation is often used in psychosynthesis work, both in and outside of sessions. Meditation in this context is not tied to any particular religious practice, but rather refers to the whole spectrum of practices of silent, inner focus which enhance self-awareness, relaxation, and centeredness. Like imagery, meditation allows us to become more aware of intuitive wisdom, and, like imagery, often requires training and experience. Some people will embrace meditation enthusiastically and may already practice a form of it. Others will be chary, fearing a religious intention or finding such non-rational use of the mind threatening. The word itself may evoke some of these responses, so other terms can be used: relaxation exercise, a time to quietly collect our thoughts, a few moments to pause and see what needs to happen. A guide may meditate before and during a session, no matter whether the method is introduced to the client. Taking time to sit in silence at the beginning of a session, or at a confused time during the session, is a good introduction to the value of meditation.

The reader may already practice a form of meditation and can explore its use within a session. Some guidebooks to meditation are referenced at the end of the chapter. Most forms can be adapted to use in sessions although more structured and demanding forms should probably be avoided at first unless the client is already practicing one.

Assagioli worked with meditation in some depth, often instructing his clients and students in specific methods. Most commonly, he shared a form he called 'creative meditation' based on some practices of Raja Yoga and focused on a seed thought or quality. This form has three stages: reflective, receptive, and creative. After clearing the mind and feelings of distractions, one begins to think about the seed thought, bringing into mind all that is already known about the idea or can be integrated from previous experience. This is the reflective stage when one reflects upon the subject. Then follows the receptive stage, when one allows all this reflection to settle into the background and simply waits receptively for new insight to come. In the creative stage, one considers how the new insight and understanding from the previous stages can be expressed in daily life and work, and imagines vividly carrying out whatever choices are made. For a more detailed discussion of creative meditation, see Appendix Two in Assagioli's *The Act of Will* (1974).

Meditation is central both to identification with the Higher Self and to the development of the will. One of the challenges of meditation is learning to direct the mind and feelings through choice, rather than allowing them to wander and react the way we do most of the time. Meditation allows us to practice non-judgmental self-observation and to experience compassion and firmness toward our rebellious subpersonalities, feelings, desires, and thoughts. Because of all this, meditation is an extremely useful tool in guiding when used appropriately to the individual's readiness and needs.

JOURNAL KEEPING

One of the principles of psychosynthesis guiding which I most appreciate is that we are each responsible for our own on-going growth. This growth is coherent and meaningful, and as we begin to perceive that, we can better cooperate with the process. Keeping a journal is an enormous aid in our understanding of the unfolding of our daily lives, and in participating actively in it. A journal allows us to see patterns and their development over time as well as focusing our attention on a daily basis on our inner experience. I cannot recommend highly enough that anyone seriously committed to personal growth keep a journal, guides and clients alike.

Ira Progoff's Intensive Journal is an excellent model for comprehensive journal keeping. Workshops on this form are available as well as books, referenced at the end of the chapter. Some people prefer this sort of organized structure, with different sections for different purposes, such as relationships, dreams, and theoretical work. Other people, like me, just enter it all as it comes, keeping track only by date. For me the purpose is not reading it later, although I often do so at random, but the *process* of recording my thoughts and feelings as they occur. Somehow writing it down breaks into the cycles of worry and distress that sometimes lock us up, facilitates disidentification, and brings in new perspectives from the superconscious. I also include drawings in my journal; 'writing it down' may occur in a form other than words. Journals are intensely personal; for that reason, I prefer to spend a little money on myself for a hardbound, unlined record book. A good friend, perhaps less materialistic than I, prefers simple spiral notebooks. What does seem important is to have a separate and specific book in which to keep one's journal so that it does not get lost or scattered.

Clients are encouraged to keep a journal and may often bring it to sessions to share significant passages. Clients may make notes in the journal during a session, as questions and insights occur. Many write notes on a session after it, or include transcripts of taped sessions. Insights from creative meditations may be recorded, during and after the actual meditation. A journal is a workbook and record of our self-discovery; just as a scientist keeps notes on his experiments, we can keep notes on our explorations. Keeping a journal can be a major step forward in an individual's willingness to take responsibility for his or her own psychosynthesis.

Assagioli introduced me to a valuable exercise which I include in my journal. He suggested that each day I write a letter to my Higher Self, on whatever topics occur to me at the time. For a long time I kept this up on a daily basis; now I use it in times of need. I have found the act of writing the letter to be extremely useful in itself. Often before I finish, I am writing my own answer to my dilemma or have moved into a new, expanded perspective on the issue. At other times, answers come to me later in unexpected ways: a remark from a friend or stranger, a passage in a book, or an image in a dream. The act of writing the letter seems to open up my receptivity to insight and gives me a sense of having resources beyond my immediate consciousness. I often recommend this method to clients to use on their own.

MOVEMENT

According to Assagioli's second psychological law, "Attitudes, movements, and actions tend to evoke corresponding images and ideas; these, in turn, evoke or intensify corresponding emotions and feelings." Movement can be helpful in a session to capture and express a sense of what is going on within an individual and also to express how that person would really like to be. It can be especially helpful for those who have difficulty verbalizing their experience, or conversely, for those who tend to over-intellectualize. Postures, movements, and non-verbal sounds may express feeling states or existential situations. Exaggeration of a gesture or facial expression often helps clarify a feeling or attitude.

Movement may also be used after another approach has facilitated some insight, understanding, and choice. A person may want to demonstrate and experience a choice with the whole body, moving in an expressive way. This can often deepen one's experience of just how dramatic a change is, when it affects the entire body so obviously. In a manner of speaking, movement is another form of imagery, just as imagery is inner movement. As Assagioli's laws reflect, change occurs in a feedback loop which can be entered at many points, such as movement or imagery. For optimal results, we use several modalities to strengthen awareness and choice.

Many people in the body therapies, whether in movement, dance, bioenergetics, sensory awareness, or structural integration, have used psychosynthesis principles and context to enhance their work and have brought their methodologies to psychosynthesis guiding with dramatic results. More such work needs to be done. I again refer you to the bibliography at the end of the chapter for further study in this field.

CATHARTIC METHODS

When deep emotion blocks an individual's progress, or a person is trapped by mental identification, cathartic methods may be useful. These include a whole spectrum from other therapies: beating on pillows, screaming and yelling, crying, laughing, emphatic gestures, or expressing feelings with the whole body in a dramatic and forceful way. Often such catharsis is the beginning of transformation and is experienced by guide and client alike with a kind of relief in spite of its intensity and discomfort.

It is vital to the integrity of the psychosynthesis process, however, that cathartic methods be used with purpose, that they be chosen consciously with specific ends in mind. ("If I can release this awful hatred, maybe I can experience my love again.") Sometimes it is not possible for the individual to be fully aware of this purpose, but at least it remains within the guide's conscious intention. Cathartic methods are means to an end, not an end in themselves, although some therapists seem to have become enamored of the drama and use them indiscriminately. This can produce an expectation which reinforces the anger, fear, or despair rather than releasing it into transformation. Catharsis can become a way of life for an emotionally identified individual who only feels alive in the midst of it, and who never experiences the ability to choose responses and take responsibility.

In psychosynthesis work, cathartic methods are used under the direction of the self: the person *chooses* to allow the emotions fuller expression and observes the process. This perspective may even deepen the experience of the emotions because the self is in charge and the individual need not fear becoming lost in an abyss of fear, anger or despair. Rather than abandoning oneself to feelings, one chooses to express them, transcending them even as they are given an honored place in one's life.

Often catharsis occurs spontaneously within guided imagery work, when it seems to have an organic appropriateness; it feels right and healthy. It seems important, however, not to react to the emotionality *per se* by stopping the work; we all need to learn how to think, feel, imagine, and intuit all at the same time. So while an individual weeps, the guide may continue to encourage awareness, disidentification, acceptance, and choice through gentle interventions.

HOMEWORK

Psychosynthesis is an on-going process for which the individual must take the major responsibility. What occurs in sessions is only a part of that process; sometimes a boost and intensification, sometimes only a progress report or mileage marker. Many people find it helpful to choose specific homework activities for themselves between sessions, to continue the work on a conscious basis and to ground new insights and choices in practical daily living.

Often the homework emerges from the work of a session quite naturally, with the individual's choice to make specific changes in daily activities. One person's homework was to buy herself a new coat to honor her choice to take better care of her physical body and appearance. People may choose to do daily drawing, writing, or meditating, sometimes on a specific theme. Assagioli's 'creative meditation' may be used, focused on a particular quality the individual wants to bring into life. Journal keeping is usually encouraged. Clients may review the session through notes or audiotape, and may bring a written summary and commentary into the next session. Individuals may consider and write responses to the psychosynthesis questionnaire suggested in Assagioli's *Psychosynthesis* (1976, pp. 78-84). Behavior modification techniques may be used for the purpose of retraining a recalcitrant subpersonality or changing a deeply ingrained habit pattern. Exercise, dance, or movement may be included in the daily routine. Changes may be made in diet or in other health practices. Whatever is done, homework needs to be purposeful and comfortably chosen by the individual to contribute to healthy, natural growth.

One form that homework often takes is reading books suggested by the guide or another person. Many of the books listed at the end of the various chapters here may be useful. Every guide has favorites, both fiction and non-fiction, which have contributed to his or her growth and awakening, and which can be loaned to clients. Books alone can be an intellectual escape from growth, but used in the context of a whole therapeutic process, they can enhance and inspire. People can be encouraged to make journal entries in response to their reading and share these in sessions. Often the figures in fiction or biography enter into the person's personal mythology and enrich imagery work. Gandalf from Tolkien's *Lord of the Rings* has appeared to me as a Wise Person on several occasions. Carlos Castaneda's series of books recounting his experiences with the Yaqui shaman Don Juan have profoundly affected a whole generation and contributed a wealth of imagery and wisdom to our perspectives on the world. Reading stimulates the mind and the imagination and is a valuable part of the growth.

Homework is a focused way of continuing the work of the session and exploring the individual's next step; even if not carried out, it can provide material for the next session. The individual may consider what got in the way, or the nature of the choice to forget or neglect to do it. Not doing homework could be a triumphant choice for a previously submissive or other-directed individual as well as the expression of rebellion or resistance.

Almost any method can be useful in the process of psychosynthesis if it is consciously chosen by the guide and client, and is in harmony with what is already occurring naturally. Rather than being 'eclectic' in methodology, a term which to me implies a grab-bag approach, the guide can seek to *synthesize* the various methods with guidance from the Higher Self of both guide and client.

> Above all and regardless of what techniques may be employed, the psychosynthesis approach will view the person as a totality. A particular intervention may take place at the level of the body or feelings or mind, but the eventual goal will be to integrate all of these dimensions and to include them in a transpersonal perspective. Psychosynthesis seeks to support and to actively nurture the evolutionary process which it sees as moving from fragmentation and separativeness toward wholeness, inclusiveness, and unification. (Crampton, 1977, p. 51)

BIBLIOGRAPHY FOR TECHNIQUES

This bibliography is by no means exhaustive. I have simply listed the books which I have personally found most useful as guides in the various topic areas. They will no doubt lead you to other resources.

Neuro-linguistic Programming (NLP)
Bandler, R. & Grinder, J. *Frogs into princes*. Moab Utah: Real People Press, 1979.
Bandler, R. & Grinder, J. *The structure of magic*, (2 vols.) Palo Alto: Science and Behavior Books, 1975 & 1976.

Focusing
Gendlin, E. *Focusing*. New York: Everest House, 1978.

Gestalt therapy
Perls, F. *Gestalt therapy verbatim*. New York: Bantam, 1971.
Perls, F. *In and out the garbage pail*. New York: Bantam, 1972.

Guided Imagery
Assagioli, R. *The act of will*. New York: Penguin, 1974.
Assagioli, R., *Psychosynthesis*. New York: Penguin, 1976.
de Mille, R. *Put your mother on the ceiling: children's imagination games*. New York: Penguin, 1976.
Edwards, N. *Drawing on the right side of the brain*. Los Angeles: Tarcher, 1980.
Emmons, M. *The inner source*. San Luis Obispo: Impact, 1978.
Ferrucci, P. *What we may be*. Los Angeles: Tarcher, 1982.
Jung, C. G. *Memories, dreams, reflections*. New York: Random House, 1961.
Jung, C. G. *Man and his symbols*. Garden City: Doubleday, 1964.
Osborn, A. F. *Applied imagination*. New York: Charles Scribner's Sons, 1953.
Samuels, M. & Bennett, H. *The well body book*. New York: Random House/Berkeley: Bookworks, 1973.
Samuels, M. & Bennett, H. *Spirit guides*. New York: Random House/Berkeley: Bookworks, 1974.
Samuels, M. & Samuels, N. *Seeing with the mind's eye*. New York: Random House/Berkeley: Bookworks, 1975.
Schutz, W. C. *Joy*. New York: Grove Press, 1967.
Shorr, J. E. *Psycho-imagnation therapy*. New York: Intercontinental Medical Book, 1972.
Thomas, P. *Psychofeedback*. Englewood Cliffs, N.J.: Prentice-Hall, 1979.
Watkins, M. H. *Waking dreams*. New York: Gordon and Breach, 1976.

Meditation
Levine, S. *A gradual awakening*. Garden City: Anchor Press/Doubleday, 1979.
Ram Dass. *Journey of awakening*. New York: Bantam, 1978.
Suzuki, S. *Zen mind, beginner's mind*. New York: Weatherhill, 1970.
Walsh, R. "Initial meditative experiences." *Journal of Transpersonal Psychology*. 9 #2, 1977 and 10, #1, 1978.
The Meditation Group for the New Age publishes a series of booklets on meditation. Write P. O. Box 655, Ojai, Calif. 93023.

Journal-Keeping
Progoff, I. *At a journal workshop*. New York: Dialogue House, 1975.

Body Work
Johnson, D. *The protean body—a Rolfer's view of human flexibility*. New York: Harper & Row, 1977.

6

TWO MAPS FOR THE INDIVIDUAL SESSION

The teacher who walks in the shadow of the temple among his followers, gives not of his wisdom but rather of his faith and his lovingness.

If he is indeed wise, he does not bid you enter the house of his wisdom, but rather leads you to the threshold of your own mind. (Gibran, 1960, p. 56)

Maps are not the territory. We all know that, yet we often forget it. Maps are merely representations drawn from individual experience, measurements, observations, and estimations. Yet we know that maps are useful, for they give us ideas about what to look for, landmarks to notice and gauge our progress by, and a way of planning with some degree of accuracy. I want to share with you some maps of the journey of individual sessions because I find them useful to consult when feeling lost and unsure of where we are and where we need to go. I also totally ignore them when I feel certain within myself of the territory and our journey through it. I invite you to do the same. In sharing these maps, I will refrain from apology for their limitations, but let us remember that they are only maps, sometimes extremely valuable, sometimes almost useless. Like the little girl with the curl in the middle of her forehead, when they are good they are very, very good, and when they are bad, they are horrid!

The first map is of the cycles of a session, the way sessions often move through the levels of consciousness represented in the oval diagram (see p. 6). The second is one we often called 'P-I-P' in my training; it is more a recipe than a map, involving three 'ingredients': purpose, intention, and plan.

THE CYCLES OF A SESSION

One way of mapping the process of a psychosynthesis session is to notice and describe how the realms of lower and higher unconscious are explored and how the source of imagery, thought, and feelings seems to shift from the lower unconscious to the higher unconscious and back. Individual psychosynthesis work generally includes both and the individual's consciousness can be said to move in both directions: 'down' into the lower unconscious to explore blocks, complexes, and inhibiting patterns; and 'up' into the higher unconscious to discover and integrate intuition, creative understanding, and transpersonal qualities such as strength, love, and joy. (This directionality is common but not universal; some people's higher unconscious seems to come from their 'roots' below.) The shifts and changes of these directions make up the cycles of an individual session. If it were possible to mathematically graph a typical session, it might look like the figure below, in which a sine-wave illustrates this cyclical pattern. The wave form passes through two cycles around a midline which would be considered the normal level of consciousness of the individual. The two cycles increase in amplitude (intensity or depth) and duration in time. Each cycle as shown here begins with a downward phase followed by an upward phase of approximately equal amplitude.

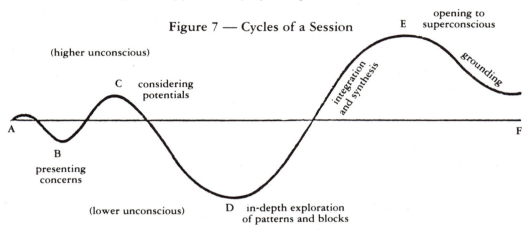

Figure 7 — Cycles of a Session

At the beginning of a session, the client's level of functioning determines the baseline. The client presents an issue or a problem, usually something which has been experienced as unpleasant or undesirable, dipping slightly into the lower unconscious as represented by the first downward phase (B). As the guide and client consider the potentials which the problem is blocking and look at how things might be, the wave moves through the upper phase of the first cycle (C), signifying a short excursion into the superconscious. Then as the client explores the concern and the blocks to the potential through imagery, dialogue, and other experiential techniques, the wave moves into the second cycle of greater amplitude or depth (D), delving into the lower unconscious. When the blocks are worked through and the energies previously held there are released, the session may move upward again into the second phase of the larger cycle (E). Now the individual may open to new awareness of inner potentials residing in the superconscious, experiencing wisdom, joy, compassion, and other qualities needed for a fuller life. The individual may have a peak experience matching in intensity the pain of the previous work in the lower unconscious. During this phase, synthesis of the released energies and of subpersonalities may occur. Finally, the qualities and learnings of the session are brought back into daily life in a creative integration called 'grounding.' The wave returns to a new baseline (F) higher than at the beginning because of the growth the individual has realized during the session.

One significant feature of this model is the first upper cycle (C). Rather than focusing first on the problem, a psychosynthesis guide initially explores the potential, providing purpose and mobilizing intention for the work in the lower unconscious. This process also helps define the real problem: what is really blocking the person's growth at this time. We all carry various neuroses with us but we only need help with those which are blocking our progress toward specific growth steps. A fear of water may not interfere with one's life in the city, but if one is interested in marine biology, one will need to deal with it. And a vision of the goal will motivate the work involved in overcoming the fear.

Another special feature of this model is the second phase of the larger cycle (E) where the person contacts the qualities and patterns *already* residing in the higher unconscious. Nothing needs to be added from the outside, other than specific skills training or information. The qualities may need to be evoked and developed, but they are to be discovered within. "No man can reveal to you aught but that which already lies half asleep in the dawning of your knowledge" (Gibran, 1960, p. 56).

Another way of looking at these cycles is through four questions which demonstrate the basic process of psychosynthesis. I use them as referents during sessions, both internally for my own guidance and explicitly with the client. The following exercise is based on these four questions.

EXERCISE: THE PROCESS OF PSYCHOSYNTHESIS

Have ready four or five sheets of paper, as large as you like, and drawing materials, either oil pastels, colored markers, or crayons. Sit in a comfortable, upright position and close your eyes. Take a few moments to simply breathe and sit, allowing your body to come to rest. . .

Now quietly observe your feelings and your thoughts. Let them be there and let them also come to rest. . .

Now find a quiet place inside where you can be open, receptive, and patient; where you can receive responses from within. Allow yourself to abide in that place as you contemplate the first question. . . .

1. Now ask yourself: "Where am I now in my life?" Allow images, sensations, feelings, thoughts to arise in response . . . simply observe them. . . . When you feel ready, find a way of capturing that response on paper, in colors, shapes, symbols, or pictures. Open your eyes and begin drawing.

When you finish, set that drawing aside and once again close your eyes and quiet your body, feelings, and thoughts. Seek your place of quiet receptivity again. . . .

2. Now ask yourself: "What is emerging in my life now? What is my next step?" Again observe and trust whatever images, sensations, feelings, and thoughts arise. . . . Find a way of representing and recording your response on paper and begin drawing.

When you finish, set the drawing aside and return to your quiet place within. . . .

3. Now ask youself: "What is getting in my way? What is holding me back?" Observe your response and draw.

Set this drawing aside and return to quiet. . . .

4. Now ask yourself: "What do I need to develop in order to take my next step and to move through my block? What quality do I need to develop in my life?" Take your time now to allow images, sensations, and feelings to respond.

Observe, trust, and draw whatever comes. . . .

When you finish, look back at all four drawings and notice whatever is there to see. You may want to write about your response to each drawing, what you felt and thought. You may want to share your drawings with a friend or guide. If one is particularly meaningful to you, put it up on the wall of your home somewhere so it can continue to inspire you.

Now that you have had the opportunity to explore these questions yourself, let's look at them in terms of the cycles of the psychosynthesis process and of an individual session.

1. **Where am I now in my life? (or, Who am I now?)** This question corresponds to the baseline and the first dip into the lower unconscious, for if there are disturbing concerns, they will usually be present in the response. This question allows the person to take a look at and grasp the whole of his or her life, and to begin the work of transformation through self-awareness and acceptance.

2. **What is emerging for me now? or, What is my next step? or, What is my potential at this time?** This question moves into the first upward half cycle, allowing a glimpse or even a larger vision of what is possible for the individual, what is emerging from the unconscious. One or more forms of the question may be used, because it is the directionality that is sought here, not a specific answer to a specific question. The response to this question provides motivation and guidance for the next.

3. **What is getting in the way? What is holding me back? How am I stopping myself?** Again, one or more forms of this question may be used, because we are now seeking the blocks which are buried in the lower unconscious, the patterns, fears, and inhibitions which are blocking the potentials envisioned in the second question. This is the major half cycle which moves into the lower unconscious, focused on the beliefs and subpersonalities which are ripe for transformation.

4. **What do I need to develop in order to take my next step (or realize my potential)?** The qualities needed are sought now and they lie in the higher unconscious, qualities such as courage, strong will or good will, receptivity, freedom, or trust. Drawings made in response to this question are often beautiful, ecstatic, and evocative. Somehow this question seems to take us into the higher unconscious almost automatically, especially following the previous explorations of blocks. Often the quality needed lies dormant within the block. When the quality is discovered and experienced, grounding can occur with the individual considering practical ways of bringing that quality into daily life.

I often use these four questions in workshops and in individual sessions, usually having the participants draw in response to them. In workshops, I always draw a set myself and never fail to find some new insight and value from the experience. As I write this, the second drawing of my last series hangs over my desk, reminding me that my next step is completion (of this book).

These questions can also be used by the guide internally in a session, to check the progress occurring and determine what needs to happen next. They correspond to the cycles and provide a concrete way of recalling and using a rather abstract map. Their use is noted in the session transcripts in the appendix.

Considerations for Application

When someone is depressed or tormented by self-doubt and low aspirations, it may be useful to move into the superconscious first, evoking through the use of imagery some experience of strength, wisdom, or other higher quality. These qualities give the individual support and hope in dealing with the difficult problems blocking the way. Often problems which are the result of a spiritual awakening are revealed and eased by this procedure. The experience of the superconscious and the possibility of a Higher Self set a positive pattern for the whole psychosynthesis process. One woman found deep validation and encouragement from an image of a Wise Old Man she discovered at the top of a mountain during her first session. This image enabled her to feel much needed self-worth and confidence.

Whichever comes first, it seems important that both elements are included in the work, the *lower* to work through blocks and free energies, the *higher* for synthesis and unfolding potentials, even if the cycle extends over more than one session. The two directions balance each other so that the *whole* person moves forward to greater integration with no part left out to create problems later, and no potential remaining unavailable. In addition, the higher unconscious is a source of courage and confidence for work in the lower unconscious. At least a brief excursion into that realm should precede work in the lower unconscious.

As mentioned before, the use of 'lower' and 'higher' to indicate these realms corresponds to most people's sense of direction in imagery. However, it is by no means universal. Two people I have worked with seem to get in touch with transpersonal energies through downward imagery. One explored the bottom of the ocean and discovered a pulse in the ocean floor which seemed to be the very pulse of Being, of the cosmic spaces she then experienced. The other reached a powerful figure of strength and wisdom at the center of the earth. Although the imagery was downward, the work would be placed in the upper part of the cycle, in the realm of the superconscious.

I use this map of the cycles of a session when I am not sure where to move next, or when something seems to be missing about the session as a whole. I check out whether or not we have explored both the lower and the higher unconscious and brought the energies of both more fully into the life of the individual. Also, I notice which came first and ask myself whether that was the most useful order. I may observe that a particular individual resists going into either the lower or the higher unconscious and consider how I can facilitate more opening there. This map also helps me plan from one session to the next and helps me anticipate what may need to happen next. When one session has dwelt mainly in one half of the cycle, the next may need to move into the other. I also use this in being aware of my own process, both personally and as a guide. Do I tend to avoid the higher and relish the lower work? Or do I get lost in the superconscious and forget to ground the insights in daily life? How can I better balance these two essential parts of a whole, cyclical pattern?

Sometimes, consulting the cycle map is not enough to help me understand what is happening in a session and what is needed. Then I turn to the P-I-P recipe to see if I have forgotten an important ingredient.

THE P-I-P RECIPE

Most individual sessions have three ingredients: a *purpose* for the session and for the various steps in the session; the *intention* of client and guide to work towards this purpose; and a *plan* for selecting techniques and choosing interventions. These three are interrelated and reflect each other; if I neglect one, not only will the session as a whole suffer, but the remaining ingredients will not function well by themselves. Why evoke intention if there is no purpose? What good is a plan without the intention to carry it out or without a purpose for its direction? Early in the session, I need to be aware of these three on some level of consciousness; as the session proceeds, I need to check back to see if they need reinforcing or if they have changed.

Purpose

Purpose is as vital to a session as it is to life; it provides meaning and direction, a context within which to make choices and experience oneself. Assagioli (1974) considers purpose to be the first and essential stage in the act of will. He suggests that we examine our motives, sorting out the unconscious drives and urges and the conscious reasons, to discover and choose those most conducive to growth and well-being, the 'highest' motive possible. Purpose encompasses these motives which "carry forward and foster [the] great evolutionary impulse" (p. 146).

I find it useful to think of a purpose as something larger than a goal, for it implies a direction rather than an endpoint. Goals can be seen as way-markers or mileage signs along the path of a purpose. My purpose may be to bring the principles of psychosynthesis into the world; my goal may be to write this book. When I have reached my goal, I have the satisfaction of knowing that I am acting according to my purpose, and I may set myself another goal, this time to conduct certain workshops, or write another book. An understanding of purpose guides the choice of goals in life and in psychosynthesis sessions.

Within a session, we usually have certain goals; they are way-markers for the over-all purpose of the session. The purpose of the session can, in turn, be seen as reflecting a larger purpose in the superconscious of the individual, the life purpose of the individual gradually emerging and finding appropriate expression. The concept of an underlying life purpose can inspire us to open to our potentials and can challenge us to use our capacities in creative and socially constructive ways. When the purpose of an individual session is seen as reflecting and contributing to this larger purpose, guide and client are inspired by the significance of the work and are more likely to bring their full resources to bear. The larger vision energizes the specific, immediate task of freeing up blocks, integrating subpersonalities, or whatever needs to occur.

Often, neither guide nor client is aware of the purpose of a session, although they may have agendas or tentative goals. The purpose may remain in the higher unconscious of the individual until well into the session. It is their task together to discover that purpose and bring it into consciousness. They do not have to assign a purpose from the outside, although they can try out various hypotheses until they find one that seems to be right.

How is this purpose discovered? Often it emerges naturally from the individual's concerns and issues. The guide listens *through* the content presented, waiting to catch the thread of purpose which is there. It may be to free the individual's capacity of choice, to bring more of a certain quality into the individual's life, to develop the capacity to love, to discover a vocation, or to remove blocks to creativity and joy. When the purpose is glimpsed, it can be made explicit in terms which are comfortable to the individual. The guide might say, "It seems to me that you want to work on this problem in order to be able to be more creative (to have a better relationship with your spouse, to be more effective in your work, or whatever). Is that true?"

At other times, it may be appropriate to ask directly, "What do you see as the purpose of this session today? What would you like to see happen here?" The second of the four questions discussed in the previous section is useful: "What's your next step? What seems to be possible for you right now in your life?" The individual's reply may be an explicit statement of purpose or it may require further clarification.

When purpose is not clear, client and guide may find themselves working at cross purposes. The guide may be working in one direction, believing that the purpose is obvious, while the client struggles to move in another. For example, a guide might consider the purpose of a session to be for the client to make peace with leaving his wife while he is seeking a way to reconcile. Although at times the purpose is implicit and need not be verbalized as such, it is

"In considering motivations, then, one is helped by distinguishing between two classes which we may designate respectively as *drives* and *urges*, and *reasons*. Drives and *urges* can be conscious or unconscious and can be generally regarded as spontaneous tendencies which "move" us to tend to do so. *Reasons*, on the other hand, to be really such, must be conscious and have a cognitive, mental aspect. They presuppose a clear vision of the goal, a recognition of its value, and the intention to reach it. One can take a drive or urge, test its rationality, and transform it into a reason."
(Assagioli, 1974, p. 144)

probably better to state the obvious than to think erroneously that there is agreement. Most guides and clients are no better at mind-reading than the rest of the population.

It is helpful to seek the deepest level of purpose that the individual can comfortably comprehend, providing more inspiration within the context of a larger vision. (You may recall the exercise on the purpose of guiding suggested in Chapter 1 and your experience of purpose and motivation in that exercise.) When one person sought help in sticking to a decision to lose weight, we explored the purpose of losing weight and found it to be greater energy, lightness, and health. At another point in that person's growth, it might be useful to explore the purpose of having energy and health, to facilitate awareness of the underlying and supporting life purpose.

It is often helpful to define purpose for exploring specific problems within a session, or for using a particular method. For example, a guide can ask, "What would be the purpose of your really expressing your anger now?" Clarification of purpose helps develop the mind and facilitates disidentification as well as creating a meaningful context for the work.

Intention

"A motive is not a motive if it does not 'move,' if it does not impel toward a goal. And the direction of the motive is given by *intention*" (Assagioli, 1974, p. 140). Intention is the motive *power*, the energetic willingness to work toward a purpose, vision, or mental ideal. Intention is "the mobilization of concern for one's life and the determination to do something about it" (Bugental, 1978, p. 83). Intention is vital to a session where it provides the motivation to learn and grow in a specific area, in spite of resistance from parts of the personality and the discomfort and pain which may lie along the way. It is the principle of *will* integrated into the work of the session.

We cannot assume that intention will be present simply by agreeing on a purpose for a session. Often it must be specifically evoked and strengthened through awareness and conscious choice. Intention is most powerful when it is present both mentally and emotionally. When an individual is emotionally involved, the guide may ask how his or her life might be changed if this problem were solved or this potential realized, thus evoking *mental* intention. If an individual *thinks* a direction is appropriate, the guide may evoke *emotional* intention by asking how he or she feels about life right now, how a particular problem is experienced when it gets in the way, and how it might feel to have the desired changes already part of his or her life. The guide may help the person more deeply experience repressed or ignored emotional effects of a situation. Yearnings toward spiritual or transpersonal qualities and experience also contribute to emotional intentionality if made conscious and validated. Intention exists on all levels of our being, as Maslow has so effectively shown us, and we can call upon any and all of these levels to work towards our purpose in a session.

An excerpt from a Transcript C illustrates the evoking of intention, here from a level of spiritual aspiration.

C: I'm choosing to express my Self and bring that into manifestation, to. . . and that's where. . . I'm having a little trouble now because I know the 'I' isn't supposed to have any qualities and all that stuff, but. . . I experience this sense of power and wisdom and love and compassion, a constellation as being manifestations or, ah, energy that comes from the Self.

G: How important is it to bring that into your life?

"Intentionality is the structure which gives meaning to experience. It is our imaginative participation in the coming day's possibilities, out of which participation comes the awareness of our capacity to form, to mold, to change ourselves, and the day in relation to each other." (May, 1969, p. 80)

C: What does it mean to bring. . .

G: How important is it?

C: It feels. . . that's why I say there's this sense of mustness. . . it feels like it's at center, it feels like it's at center of importance.

G: So, how important is it?

C: It's the central importance, it's *the* meaning.

G: So if you had to choose between the playfulness and, the step on the brink, what would you choose?

C: I know I *have* to choose the expression of my Self, because the other is only a . . . it's like one means, it's like. . . .

G: Are you willing to choose the expression of your Self?

C: Yes.

G: How do you experience yourself when you experience the willingness? The willingness to choose it. . .

C: I feel strong; I feel joyful and I also feel solid.

The guide encourages the client to experience intentionality itself, to experience herself as a willing being.

To evoke intention is to offer an opportunity to the individual's willing *self* to align with the purpose of the session, to choose to cooperate with the changes and growth emerging from the higher unconscious. This is difficult to do if the person is strongly identified with a subpersonality, especially a parental one which is more concerned with 'shoulds' than with possibilities, or a childish one which only wants to rebel. The individual's self needs to be addressed in asking for intention, much like speaking to another adult over the noisy demands of a group of unruly children. ("I know that parts of you are frightened, but are *you* willing to go ahead?") Preliminary guidance in disidentification as discussed in the previous two chapters may be necessary to help an individual experience the self and the will. Several sessions may even be needed to cross this hurdle before the deeper purposes of the work can be addressed.

Often an individual comes into a session with intention to work already mobilized; it is what brought him or her there to begin with. Someone who has worked on personal awareness and growth over a period of time may have developed a general intentionality which is easily brought to bear on a particular session or issue. It never hurts, however, to support and energize this intentionality by talking about it and guiding a deeper experiencing of it.

Intention may be brought to bear in specific choices about how to address a problem within the session. When asked for preference at such times, a client experiences being in charge of the process and intention is mobilized. The choice can be offered: "Does it seem more useful to you to go into your anger or to look at the situation which is stirring it up in you?" Whichever choice the client makes, he or she will participate with more energy than if the choice were not made available. Even if the guide feels strongly about the next step to take, choice can be offered in a general way: "Want to try something? Are you willing to go into this more deeply? Are you willing to take another step with this?" This evokes a general intentionality without focusing on the specific form to be used.

At any point where a client makes a choice about direction, the guide may strengthen and clarify intention by inquiring about the motives for that choice. Whether or not the guide agrees with the choice, it may be helpful to ask *why* that is best, what the individual hopes to learn from that path, or who (what subpersonality) is making that choice. The choice may also be referred back to the purpose: will it move the work in that direction? When someone makes a choice about how to work and understands its antecedents, that intention provides strong support for the work that follows.

Plan

The third important ingredient in the recipe of a psychosynthesis session is plan, the strategy and methods the guide uses to fulfill the purpose of the session. The plan is based on past experience with the client, on intuitive hunches and rational assessments as to what would be most effective, and most importantly, on the individual's expressed preferences and choices. The plan is subject to revision as the session progresses; if one approach doesn't seem effective, another may be tried after the guide makes sure that the purpose is clear and that intention is present.

The form of the work is far less important than commitment, so if purpose is clear and intention aligned, any reasonable plan will usually work if followed with patience and focus. This is why different methodologies may have equally good results even with similar problems. A plan gives coherence to the work and helps keep both guide and client from becoming sidetracked or wandering about in the content. On the other hand, we want to avoid reacting to vagueness and wandering by becoming rigidly attached to a plan. A balance needs to be found between these two extremes. The methods and steps are the forms chosen by guide and client which allow them to put full attention on the quality of the interaction and the unfolding process.

Let me give an example of some plans which might be used to fulfill a particular session's purpose. A woman is seeking to clarify her relationship to God as distinct from her relationship to her church in order to sort out inner values underlying various life choices. She seems to have confused her inner sense of God's urgings with the dictates of her church and needs to distinguish between them. She clearly has strong intention to deal with this difficult issue. One plan would be to have her imagine God in one chair, her church in another, and to dialogue with them. Another would be to conduct such a dialogue through imagery; a full guided fantasy might be used to work with these images, including a journey up a mountain to consult a symbol of higher wisdom. Regressive techniques might help the client work with parental issues underlying this conflict. Yet another approach would be a discussion of her relationship to church and God, how she experiences those relationships, and the value of each, using her mind in an objective manner. The choice of plan would be based on this person's strengths, which qualities or aspects she needs to develop, her sense of appropriateness, and at least partially on the guide's preferences and areas of skill.

A plan may include an awareness of the cycles of a session and ways of assuring that all levels of consciousness and all the resources of the individual are allowed to participate in the process. It may include ways of clarifying purpose and evoking intention. It will probably be concerned with the integration of subpersonalities and of body, feelings, and mind. At its best, it will be dedicated to the over-all purpose of psychosynthesis work, which is to enable the individual to identify with the self, to experience the will, and to contact in his or her own way the energies of the higher unconscious and of the Higher Self.

The plan includes the moment-to-moment choice of interventions based upon the guide's abstractions or working hypotheses. These abstractions include the purpose of the session, what is needed next, what seems to be emerging, and where the process seems to be going. Abstractions may change during the course of a session as more information emerges and as the guide checks their validity by questions, suggestions, and requests for clarification. Thus the plan for interventions must change accordingly.

Abstractions may be more or less conscious. I often experience mine initially in my body or feelings as much as in my mind. With my mind I take in physical and emotional data and formulate it into a coherent abstraction, even if it is one which I cannot, at the time, express in words. When I first began to become conscious of my abstractions as the antecedents of my interventions, part of me resisted the attempt, fearing I would become a logical automaton, excluding intuition and 'gut feelings.' Then I began to realize that I always had an abstraction for what I did, only I rarely took it out and looked at it. When I became willing to clarify my abstractions consciously, I discovered my work was enriched and more coherent, for my conscious abstraction provided a framework for my intuitions and impressions. I felt more relaxed and sure of myself, which offered my clients clarity and safety for doing their work.

There is a subtle balance between, on the one hand, holding abstractions firmly, skillfully choosing interventions in line with them and, on the other hand, remaining disidentified from abstractions so that they can be readily given up if off target or premature. I have a tendency at times to interpret an individual's resistance to mean my abstraction is off target and to mistrust the intuition and experience which brought the abstraction to mind. It may be that perserverance and firmness in this case would offer my client an opportunity to confront significant issues. Yet pushing someone around so that he or she comes to my point of view, thereby 'proving' my wisdom, would obviously not contribute to the purpose of a session. Paradoxically, if I remain unattached to the abstraction and if my need for validation is kept out of the matter, it is far easier to remain steady in the face of resistance. I can take the chance of being wrong and test out the accuracy of my abstraction, willing to hold firm or let go as needed. Moreover, it is easier to see, from this perspective, when the abstraction is off base and to be open to a new understanding of what is going on.

What about discussing the guide's abstraction with the individual? This can be helpful and like any other intervention needs to be chosen with purpose. I might choose to discuss an abstraction on the basis of another abstraction that this particular person needs to develop his or her mind. I might hypothesize that the individual needs to disidentify and that discussing an abstraction would help this take place. I might share my abstraction after a process has taken place, to facilitate the individual's overall understanding of psychosynthesis principles and practices so that he or she can use them in working alone or with others.

On the other hand, I might choose not to discuss my abstraction if I believe the person to be too mentally identified and needful of direct experience. I might choose not to discuss it because I perceive the person to be too vulnerable to my 'authority' and authority is not the issue which needs to be resolved at the moment. And I might not share my abstraction if it has to do with resistance, because sharing it might only evoke more resistance and possibly result in a power struggle between us. As with any intervention, the guiding principle is what best serves the individual's growth process *in the moment*.

I find the concept of abstraction and intervention especially useful when evaluating my own guiding or supervising another's. It provides a framework for discussing what is going on, a short-hand to clarify one's inner process in guiding at any given moment of a session.

As we saw in the section on cycles, *grounding*, or bringing the learning and growth of a session into concrete terms of daily life, is an extremely important part of the plan of a session.

Grounding seeks to bring the energy and clarity released by self-discovery into the life of the individual and the community in concrete ways. The individual is encouraged to consider choices for specific situations in life, especially those mentioned as problems at the beginning of the session.

Grounding uses 'skillful will' as described by Assagioli (1974), applying his psychological laws in specific terms. These laws were outlined in Chapter 2. In the chart below, some of these laws are matched with specific examples of how they can be applied in grounding. Imagery, posture and movement, verbal affirmations, and practice of new behaviors can all contribute to grounding.

Psychological Law	Application in Grounding
I. Images or mental pictures and ideas tend to produce the physical conditions and the external acts correspond to them.	Client imagines him/herself carrying out choices of session in life situations.
II. Attitudes, movements, and actions tend to evoke corresponding images and ideas; these in turn evoke or intensify corresponding emotions or feelings.	Client may stand or move in ways expressing new quality or attitude about life and experience how this feels.
III. Ideas and images tend to awaken emotions and feelings that correspond to them.	Client uses mental images to evoke positive emotional states; i.e., peaceful scenes for serenity
VI. Attention, interest, affirmation, and repetitions reinforce the ideas, images, and psychological formations on which they are centered.	Client repeats key phrases or affirmations of choices at intervals during the day; selects pictures or artwork to vivify intentions.
VII. Repetition of actions intensifies the urge to further reiteration and renders their execution easier and better, until they come to be performed unconsciously.	Client practices chosen behaviors to express learning or change old habits.

After a particularly powerful session, it may be necessary to wait until the next session to consider specific ways of grounding, to allow time for the learning to be assimilated. The client may be urged to spend some time on his or her own, considering ways of applying what was learned. Each session can begin with some additional grounding of the previous one, a practice which unifies the work and augments the client's overall understanding of the process. In hindsight, the effects on daily life of the previous session can be seen, as well as the next step in the individual's overall growth.

The work of a psychosynthesis session, especially in guided imagery, goes on beyond the end of the session. Changes take place without the conscious involvement of the individual, and this is usually healthy and satisfying. It is not necessary for us to be conscious of everything that occurs in our growth process; besides being impossible, it is probably undesirable. Nevertheless, grounding brings the conscious mind and the will into this natural process as cooperative, facilitative agents. And the individual has the fulfilling experience of being at the center of his or her life and growth.

· MAPS, RECIPES, AND REALITY

At the risk of belaboring the point, I want to remind us all that the map is not the territory and the recipe is not the cake. The map helps us find our way through the territory and the recipe helps us include the necessary ingredients and balance the proportions of each. Yet there are always factors beyond the scope of either maps or recipes, having to do in both cases with the conditions of weather and of the individuals involved (not to mention the position of the planets, the season of the year, the phase of the moon, and who knows what else). My suggestion is to try out these formulations first in looking over past sessions, interventions, and interactions. Then begin to bring them into your work in 'real-time', always ready to set them aside if they seem to confuse instead of clarify. But give them a good strong chance to work, for they have proven very useful to many guides in many fields. They have also been useful to me and others in understanding and cooperating with our own processes.

7

THE WILL: CHOICE AND RESISTANCE

Only the development of his inner powers can offset the dangers inherent in man's losing control of the tremendous natural forces at his disposal and becoming the victim of his own achievements. . . . Fundamental among these inner powers, and the one to which priority should be given, is the tremendous, unrealized potency of man's own will. *Its training and use constitute the foundation of all endeavors. There are two reasons for this: the first is the will's central position in man's personality and its intimate connection with the core of his being—his very self. The second lies in the will's function in deciding what is to be done, in applying all the necessary means for its realization and in persisting in the task in the face of all obstacles and difficulties. (Assagioli, 1974, p. 6)*

The experience and development of the will is basic to psychosynthesis. Our will is what separates us from being the conditioned automatons envisioned in Huxley's *Brave New World*. True, we are subject to conditioning, but we can transcend it through the skillful and harmonious use of the will. That is why the will is identified closely with the self in psychosynthesis models; conditioning is what our environment imposes on us, but the self can still express itself and its inner direction through acts of will.

William James 'discovered' the will for Western psychology at the turn of the century, just before Assagioli began to develop psychosynthesis. Although James could not provide scientific proof of the will's existence, he found that it was useful and beneficial to human life to believe in free will and the responsibility for our choices. "Freedom's first deed should be to affirm itself" (1890, II, p. 573). James argued that we have an innate capacity to make real choices, both in our actions and in what we believe. He emphasized the importance of the *will to believe*, because when we act in accordance with our belief, we create the corresponding circumstances. "You make one or the other of two possible universes true by your trust or mistrust" (1896, p. 59). Thus the will is the foundation of our reality; can anything be more important? A few other psychologists have included the will in their thinking, notably Rollo May, Abraham Maslow, Carl Jung, and Victor Frankl, in addition to Assagioli.

Once again, I would like to suggest an exercise to provide an experience of our subject, before continuing to offer conceptual material about it. This is in keeping with Assagioli's approach to any aspect of human psychology: first discover its reality and nature through direct existential experience.

"[Life can be] a repetitious round, a treadmill of duty or a merry-go round of meaningless activity. Man is bound to the wheel of fate until consciousness of his God-given power of choice dawns upon him." (Frances Wickes, 1963, p. 2)

81

EXERCISE: EXPERIENCES OF THE WILL

Find a comfortable, relaxed and alert position and close your eyes. Allow awareness of your breath to calm and relax your body, feelings, and thoughts. Seek a place of receptivity and focus within yourself. . . .

Now recall a recent experience in which you acted *without much awareness or choice*, a time when you reacted automatically to a situation. Choose a time when you were *not comfortable* with your actions, when later you regretted what occurred. Take a few moments to relive that experience. . . . Notice the nature and scope of your perceptions at the time. . . . What were your feelings? . . . . How did your body feel? . . . What was your thought process like? . . . What was your self-image? . . . When you feel ready, open your eyes and make some notes about this experience. . . .

Now return again to your place of receptive awareness. Allow the previous experience to fade. . . . This time, recall a recent time when you acted without a lot of consciousness but the experience was *positive*; you felt good about what occurred and what you did. Relive this experience for a few moments. . . . Again, notice how you perceived the world and yourself. . . . Notice your feelings and body sensations. . . . Notice your thought processes. . . . What is your self-image in this experience? . . . When you are ready, open your eyes and make some notes about this experience and how it was different from the last. . . .

Again, take time to center your attention and allow the last memory to fade from the foreground. Relax and open to the next experience. . . . This time, recall a recent event when you acted *with a great deal of awareness* and *conscious choice*, when you really felt fully and consciously engaged in a situation or process. Relive this experience for a few moments. . . . Notice your perception of the world and of yourself. . . . How do you experience your body? . . . What is your emotional field? . . . Notice the nature of your thought processes. . . . Is there any resistance to your choices? . . . What is your sense of yourself? . . . Make some notes about this experience, too, and notice similarities and differences from the other two experiences. . . .

Return now to your receptive state for one last experience. Take a few moments to relax your body and feelings and open your mind to a memory from within. . . . Recall an experience of physical mastery, when you were able to perform a physical task or activity for the first time. . . . This may be recent or it may be from your childhood. . . . Recall such a time and relive the experience for a minute or two. . . . Remember what led up to that moment of mastery, how you approached the task. . . . Notice your feelings and body experience as you struggled and then gained mastery. . . . What thoughts moved through your mind? . . . What was your sense of yourself, your self-image during and after the whole experience? . . . How did the world look to you? . . . Take time to relive this experience in some detail, and then make notes about it, too. . . .

You may want to take another step with this and develop a gesture or series of movements to express your essential experience of your will in action. Experiment with moving your body in ways that express the qualities of the will you experienced and noticed in this exercise. If another form appeals to you more, capture an image of your experience in a drawing or a song. Expressing an essential experience like this artistically (whether or not you are an 'artist') can help bring its qualities more concretely into your life.

Now look back on your experiences and the ways you found to express them in writing and other forms. What qualities do you notice, qualities of your will? Is the will only determination, the stereotypical 'stiff upper lip,' or are there other aspects of it in your experience? Notice the stages you go through in the third and fourth memories, the steps you take in these willed actions or processes. It may enhance your understanding and use of the will if you take time to consider these questions before going on to read what Assagioli and other psychosynthesists have discovered.

WHAT IS THE WILL?

In *The Act of Will* (1974), Assagioli stresses that his observations are only the beginning of what we can discover about the will, a subject which has been sadly neglected. Many phenomenological studies can be made about how people experience the will, how it seems to operate, when it is conscious and when it is not, how it differs from impulse or instinct, and how it can harmonize these energies within us. I hope my outline here at least whets your appetite and sends you off to read, first Assagioli's book on the subject and then some of the other references in the bibliography.

Assagioli was concerned about the distortion of 'will power' which so many people associate with the will; the clenched jaw and stiff upper lip images. He underlines the value of strong will as *one* of the aspects of the will, providing the intensity or 'fire' to carry out a willed act. Strong will is often needed to change behavior patterns following a choice to do so in a session. But strength must be balanced by *skill*, "the ability to develop that strategy which is most effective and which entails the greatest economy of effort, rather than the strategy that is most direct and obvious." (1974, p. 47) "The most effective and satisfactory role of the will is not as a source of *direct* power or force, but as that function which, being at our command, can stimulate, regulate, and direct all the other functions and forces of our being so that they may lead us to our predetermined goal" (1974, p. 47). Skillful will would help the dieter replace the gratification of food with some other sensually or emotionally satisfying activity: warm baths, dance, or cuddling a teddy bear.

Even skillful will alone can lead to the distortions of manipulation and conflict if a third aspect of the will is not developed, the aspect of *good will*. Good will prompts us to choose "such aims as are consistent with the welfare of others and the common good of humanity" (p. 86). Good will arises from the recognition that we are each parts of the greater whole of family, community, humanity, and the planetary ecological system. Sometimes we act as if we can further our own welfare at the expense of others, but in the long run that proves to be untrue. Good will prompts us to act from a larger perspective of the welfare of the whole. A client might decide, for example, to take a much-needed vacation, but also to modify those plans to accommodate the schedules of other family members. In this way, conflict would be minimized and the vacation would provide deeper relaxation and companionship.

The union of these three aspects of the will—strength, skill, and goodness—is *loving will*, the expression of love through our willed acts. The loving will is personal will aligned with the will of the Higher Self or Transpersonal Will. Perhaps one of the experiences of will that you recalled in the exercise had qualities of the loving will.

All these aspects and dimensions of the will are involved in the individual psychosynthesis session. *Intention*, as discussed in the P-I-P recipe in the previous chapter, consists of strong will and skillful will with a healthy dash of good will as well. If we think of *purpose* as being

"True freedom consists in performing all actions . . . in accordance with right judgments and choice of will, not in being compelled by habits."
(Yogananda, 1968)

"Enlightenment therefore must involve the will as well as the intellect . . . The Will is man himself and Zen appeals to it."
(Suzuki, 1949, p. 115)

present for us to discover within a session, rather than a man-made construct to be imposed, the Transpersonal Will appears to be the source. *Loving will* is something we as guides aspire to bring to our work, with sufficient strength and skill to guide the individual toward that transpersonal purpose, in harmony with family and community. Most importantly, to experience the will *is* to experience being a self, which is a central purpose of psychosynthesis work.

DEVELOPING THE WILL

During individual psychosynthesis sessions, one of our primary aims is to facilitate the discovery, development, and use of the will in all its aspects. Self-awareness without conscious choice may prolong the time for moving forward with one's next step, and result in lengthy therapy without significant life change. Of course, individuals in therapy programs emphasizing insight do make choices and do change because the will is a natural human function. When this process of choice is specifically evoked and made conscious, however, individuals take the reins of their creative lives in hand sooner and more fully. They discover and own their power apart from their therapists earlier in the therapeutic program.

Opportunities for evoking choice abound in the very conduct of the session. As soon as a sense of purpose is established, the energy of intention to move towards that purpose needs to be mobilized, as discussed in the previous chapter. Depending on the individual's level of awareness and responsibility, various kinds of choices can be offered at any point during a session. Simple yes-or-no questions such as, "Are you willing to go into this, to explore this more deeply?" suggest the importance of the individual's responsibility at every step. At times it may be helpful to ask the person to take a moment to experience the willingness, or to inquire as to how the person knows he or she is willing. At other times, it may seem unnecessary to call that much attention to the experience. Every time the question is asked, however, it reinforces the message: "You are in charge of what happens here. You can choose."

"It is in intentionality and will that the human being experiences his identity . . . What happens in human experience is 'I conceive — I can — I will — I am.' The 'I can' and 'I will' are the essential experience of identity."
(May, 1969, p. 243)

Several levels of choice may be offered. When the guide has a strong sense that a certain method should be used, or a certain issue explored, he or she may not want to offer a broad range of choices and so simply asks, "Are you willing to take another step with this?" or, "Are you willing to try something?" This might be a level of choice most appropriate for someone who has little experience or skill in personal work, for whom a broad choice would simply be confusing. At times when the guide sees two possible directions, both may be suggested and the individual asked to choose between them. When the guide has no clear sense of what needs to happen, or when the individual seems to be relinquishing responsibility for the session, the guide may ask a broad question: "What do you want to do now? What's your choice about what happens next here?"

Disidentification is an important step in conscious choice, assuring that the choice is made from a perspective close to the self rather than from a disoriented subpersonality. The guide may ask to trade chairs with the individual, or at least have the person sit in the guide's chair. From this perspective, the individual may be able to observe what has been happening more dispassionately and see choices that he or she is unconsciously making within the session. Alternative ways of being may become obvious and the individual may be willing to make appropriate choices as a result. "Oh, I don't *have* to be that way! I don't have to feel that way!" expresses this realization.

A method for disidentification and choice I often use is to ask the individual to stand with me, looking down at the chair where she or he has been sitting. I ask the person to consult with me about 'my client's' needs. This is especially useful when working with people who are themselves counselors or therapists, and it is also often amusing, bringing in the leavening of humor.

Moving to a larger perspective may seem to be more an awareness process than one of choice, yet they are inseparable. The very act of moving to the larger perspective involves choice. Disidentification involves choice. We must choose to let go of our immediate limited identification, often in spite of strong emotions. It rarely just happens, spontaneously. Moreover, most of us find we cannot make choices if we do not know the alternatives, although we can choose to discover them. We need awareness to do that. Seeking that awareness is a step in the whole process of choice, an application of skillful will.

One way to seek the awareness of alternatives is through inner dialogue, as described in previous chapters, or through inner consultation with the Wise Person. An exercise introducing this process appears in the next chapter. The Wise Person exercise encourages the skillful and good aspects of will. We align our personal will with Transpersonal Will, the Will of the Higher Self, when we make choices from this perspective.

Silence offers one of the most powerful opportunities for making choices and taking responsibility. If I am struggling to make a choice, my guide's silent presence suggests patience and confidence, and leaves it all up to me. It gives me time and room to sort things out, to give expression to my resistances, and to discover my deeper willingness to carry through with my decision. As a guide, I sometimes curtail my client's experience of choice by too immediate an intervention, by jumping in too quickly to help. Silence with presence leaves the responsibility where it belongs, with the person working.

Beyond choice within a session, the will can be evoked and developed in relation to life issues, through the concerns that the individual brings to the session. As insight and awareness about the dynamics of behavior come, so also come opportunities for choice. Whenever an individual discovers a new perspective, the guide can ask what choices might be made as a result. This is the grounding process discussed and illustrated in the last chapter. The stages of the act of will as outlined by Assagioli (1974, pp. 135-196) can be used at this point to assure that all aspects of the will are included. The *purpose* behind the choice can be explored and explicated. Then various ways of realizing that purpose can be discussed in the *deliberation stage*, involving the psychological laws which skillful will can use (see Chapter 2). The individual can then *choose* which course of action or direction seems best. Ways of *affirming* that choice can be developed, including evocative word cards, drawings, and other methods (see Chapter 5). Next, a *plan* for carrying out the choice can be developed, again making use of skillful will in balancing all psychological needs and resources, and of good will in considering the impact of the plan on family, friends and community. Finally, the individual can *implement* the choice *and evaluate* the need for change in the plan or for new choices. This whole process can be done quite consciously in a session, or over a series of sessions, with further exploration and synthesis of issues which come up in the process. Or the sense of these stages may only be held in the background of the guide's mind, to be applied if needed.

Another area where choice can be experienced and practised is in guided imagery. Indeed, sometimes choices can be made there in relatively 'safe' symbolic terms and later carried over (consciously or not) into daily life. I have been amazed at the profound changes that have occurred in my life as an apparent result of choices made in guided imagery work. We can choose how to cope with various figures that appear in our imagery, to accept and include them, and how to move beyond the limitations they put on us. We can choose to symbolically meet the needs of subpersonalities and to use their gifts more constructively in the context of the imagined situation in which they appear. We can take symbolic steps and choose new directions and purposes for our lives.

In the following excerpt from Transcript C, the client faces a symbolic choice: to step across a chasm. This corresponds to a choice to identify more fully with the personal self and to some extent the Higher Self, owning the power and responsibility of that self-identification.

C: I'm starting to experience an anger and the energy of that anger. It's confronting that negativity again and saying, "No, not going to undermine me." (pause) The image is that I have to step across some kind of a chasm. And it's not a very broad step; I mean, I can step. It's not that there's any concern that I won't be able to actually physically do it. But, it feels like once I step across that chasm I can't go back, and I need to take everything that I want with me. So that I go across that chasm in the fullest manifestation of my being that I can. Maybe there's some parts I do want to leave behind. (pause)

G: What are you experiencing right now?

C: (pause) I'm experiencing a lot of breath inside. I'm experiencing a lot of sense of integrity, ah, individuality perhaps. Aloneness.

G: Aloneness?

C: But not loneliness, just aloneness. (pause) The Fool. . . the Tarot; the Tarot card, the Fool. (pause, sigh) I could stand here digging this forever, but I think I'll go on.

G: Stay there for a second. Does this feel familiar, being in that space?

C: No.

G: Describe it.

C: It's familiar only in the sense that I see the Tarot card and I know that that's representing the same feeling, experience. It's like I know about it from the culture, but it doesn't feel familiar in my personal experience.

G: Still experience yourself on the brink of this chasm?

C: Uh, huh. There aren't any. . . it's like that's all there is. There's just ground and there's this big jagged chasm and there's more ground and, ah, there's sunlight, but I'm not aware of trees or anything like that.

G: What does the chasm represent to you?

C: Obliteration, nothingness.

G: So it means to you to experience obliteration or the possibility of nothingness for you to take a step at this point. . . would you be willing to do that?

C: You're asking if I'm willing to die. (pause) Yeah, in the sense of this personality. . . I'm very fond of this personality, I have some pride in this personality. (pause) It's a fake chasm. This sounds mental but it's, it's more than mental. My personality is only, only exists because I create it and therefore it cannot. . . to talk about it's being obliterated is as if it had a life of its own and it doesn't.

G: That all may be true, but that's different than experiencing being on the brink and having to let go, which is a definite experience. There's a lot of other content you could introduce to assuage that experience.

C: Good old brain.

G: Good old feelings controlling brain.

As the session continues (see Transcript C) the guide counteracts a tendency of the client to leap ahead past the choice point by insisting that the client stay with the experience of the choice for a long time. Although the choice seems to be abstract, it is grounded in the imagery and in the intensity with which the guide focuses on the experience. It is nearly always possible to deepen an individual's experience of the will and of self in this way.

When a person makes a choice—about the course of a session, in imagery, or about an issue in life—that choice is an opportunity to deeply experience the will and the self. Sometimes we pause to do that quite consciously, especially when the choice is hard won. Interventions such as these can deepen the experience of choice: "Take a moment to really experience that choice. Who's making that choice? How do you experience yourself as you make that choice? Are you willing to make a statement about your choice? I choose to. . . . What do you experience as you say that?"

It is vital to consciously include *all* aspects of the will in the experience of choice. The individual needs to feel strong and committed in choice, and flexible in using many alternative paths to move towards its implementation, taking into account the various psychological, physical, and social needs and potentials involved. The guide's understanding of the will and his or her own experience of its power in life contribute essentially to his or her ability to facilitate growth in this area.

RESISTANCE AND THE WILL

Every therapeutic approach has to deal with resistance. It seems to be an inevitable aspect of growth. When we set about to evoke and develop the will, we face resistance from all our old patterns of habit and security, from all the ways in which we have protected ourselves from responsibility and freedom. Yet these old patterns, too, have their legitimacy and deserve honor. We can work *with* resistance, treating it with respect, just as we have learned to work *with* troublesome subpersonalities.

Resistance only erupts when something is about to happen. When we are set in our ways, just plodding along by conditioning and habit, there is nothing to resist; things feel safe. When we move towards new awareness and choice, however, all the parts of the personality which fear change come awake fighting. Resistance is a signal of change. It is a signal that idols are toppling, that a world view or identification is threatened. We need to understand this in our own process, as well as in those we guide. When resistance is seen in this way, it can be welcomed; it can be the source of a kind of motivating excitement for both the individual and the guide.

As we move toward a new paradigm of understanding about ourselves and our world, our old beliefs are challenged. They come to the forefront of our awareness in conflicting thoughts, emotions, and physical responses resisting new truths. We can misinterpret the symptoms to mean that we really shouldn't change, that the old truths were 'right.' If we do this, we usually find ourselves excluding something, limiting ourselves in some way, trying to stop the process of growth on which we have embarked. On the other hand, ignoring the resistance would only cause it to go underground from where it could sabotage our choices or erupt later with a vengeance. Somehow our resistance must be acknowledged as of value and included in our change. The old beliefs need to be embraced within the new paradigm, for they hold truth for us as well. Paradigm shift means movement towards an expanded belief system, not the substitution of one belief for another.

Resistance takes many forms in a session. We may change the subject, throw out a lot of distracting content, tell long and seemingly unrelated anecdotes, or give tangential 'illustrations' of the issues. We may get angry or project negative qualities onto the guide. Sometimes we become stubbornly identified with our feelings or with certain mental sets: "That's just the way I am!" Going blank, saying, "I don't know," is an extremely common form of resistance, and one that often catches up the guide as well. We may pretend that an issue has been resolved. We may cry, or, on the other hand, become emotionally paralyzed. We may use our intellect in arguing philosophical points to avoid facing a personal experience. We may feel like 'putting on the brakes,' with the kinesthetic image of digging our heels into the ground to resist being pulled forward. Our whole organism may seem to yell, 'Stop!' and can often succeed in stopping a process before we are even aware of it. Then it is time to take a look at what has happened.

How to respond? In some cases, the guide may simply focus on the insight or choice which evoked the resistance, continually reminding the client of what the storm is all about. Focusing on the emerging possibilities or qualities may mobilize sufficient energy to move through the resistance, especially if it is primarily based on habit or superficial beliefs. If resistance recurs several times within a process, the guide may call attention to the pattern and invite the client to make a simple choice between the old habit and the new possibility. For example, a man raised in a culture which devalues women may have acquired habits of thought and behavior which are really not based on a deep-seated problem with women, but have simply been imitations of behavior around him. In working through a problem with his wife, he might find these old habits reasserting themselves even as he attempts to move to an attitude of respect and cooperation. If his guide points these patterns out, he may notice them, a bit ruefully, and then reaffirm his vision of the relationship he wants to have and his specific choices to help create that relationship.

If focusing on the potential or evoking simple choice does not work, the resistance probably needs more attention. It may be based on deep hurts, angers and unfulfilled needs. In such situations, the guide may need to focus the work on the resistance itself, on the nature of its expression, on its reasons for being. Resistance may be the expression of a survival-oriented subpersonality, the 'will' of the subpersonality, so to speak. When we look at the resistance directly, when we work with the subpersonality involved, we have the opportunity to release the energy bound up in that part for use by the integrating self. The energy released may then flow *towards* the choice or awareness previously resisted.

Sometimes it is necessary to carry over a resistant issue from one session to the next; the time between may give the individual an opportunity to experience the pattern in daily life, to gain some perspective, and to develop the intention to change. Listening to an audiotape of a session can be extremely valuable homework in this process.

What is the source of resistance? Usually it is a healthy instinct which demands that we use our skillful will in making changes, that we honor the needs and potentials of all the facets of our personality. It keeps us from going off 'half-cocked' in the excitement of a new insight before we have had time to sort out all the implications and new balances we must establish in our living patterns. It forces us to take one step at a time and therefore is a response to be honored within ourselves and others.

At other times, resistance seems to originate in a tendency to keep ourselves confused and diminished; it could be called *psychological entropy*. This tendency is evident in our society's training in "the repression of the sublime" (Haronian, 1976), the denial of our creativity, wisdom, and love in the name of modesty and being 'realistic' about ourselves. It is a tendency against which we must skillfully and lovingly assert our will to meet a most basic responsibility to ourselves. One test of the nature of resistance is to ask ourselves where the direction of the resistance leads: "Where does that leave you?" When we perceive that the words in our minds and the fear in our hearts lead us only into a spiral of helplessness and despair, we are challenged to choose another path. We discover that we *can* choose to think and feel in another way, to step away from negative thoughts and feelings and to move toward growth in spite of them. At these times, awareness is secondary to will; we literally choose our awareness, opening to light and growth instead of darkness, hopelessness, and despair.

On the other hand, 'client resistance' can be a label for disagreement between guide and client, a way for the guide to avoid personal responsibility in his or her relationship with the client. To immediately assume that any conflict between guide and client is an expression of the client's resistance is prejudiced and irresponsible. When as guides we feel a client is resisting, we need to examine our own reactions; perhaps they are the source of that experience. We need to balance our firmness of vision with a readiness to notice when we are off the track or caught in countertransference. A client's calm and considered decision not to follow the guide's suggestions may indicate responsibility rather than resistance. We must honor our client's choices, at least provisionally, while together we evaluate their appropriateness and explore alternatives.

Sometimes the guide evokes resistance unintentionally by the manner of the interventions. If the guide is identified with a desire for the client to be a certain way, if he or she becomes attached to having a good session or performing brilliantly as a guide, the client's very integrity may resist a sensed manipulation. It is a healthy resistance, because the guide's will is not aligned with the Higher Will of the client. We can use resistance as feedback about our own process as guides: when resistance appears in a session, we can consciously let go of attachment to outcome. From this attitude, resistance can be optimally handled if it is not the guide's doing, and relieved at once if it is.

It seems to me that there is a natural resistance process in everyone as old patterns break down, making way for the new. As in most phenomena, a moderate amount is healthy and useful. It gives us feedback that change is taking place, offers us a chance to cooperate, lets us know that we are alive and responsible. We can think of resistance as friction; we need it in order to move! It gives us something to push against, to test ourselves against, to learn from about our strengths and the power of our will. It becomes a friend, pointing in a direction, guiding rather than limiting us, when we conceive of it in these terms and no longer believe we are helpless before its ponderous presence.

BALANCING LOVE AND WILL

In my conversations and work with people trained at various psychosynthesis centers, I notice that some people seem to emphasize *will* as central to psychosynthesis while others emphasize *love*. Nobody denies the importance of the other element, yet we do seem to 'specialize' in one or the other. Perhaps this is a natural result of our own personal development of these aspects, and it also seems that various centers tend to have distinctive styles in this respect. My training with Assagioli emphasized love, and good will, while my training in San Francisco focused more on the will, especially in the strong and skillful aspects. It has been an important part of my personal and professional work in psychosynthesis to balance and synthesize these two aspects of the self so that they complement each other and work together.

The danger of untempered will is that it lacks heart. We see, and used to see especially in Victorian times, the operation of a cold, stern, and even cruel will. On the other hand, love without will can make an individual weak, sentimental, overemotional, and ineffectual.

One of the principal causes of today's disorders is the lack of love on the part of those who have will and the lack of will in those who are good and loving. This points unmistakably to the urgent need for the integration, the unification, of love with will. (Assagioli, 1974, p. 91)

To facilitate this synthesis in others is an important aspect of guiding. We need to become aware first of our own predisposition and seek balance within ourselves. When guiding others, we need to appreciate their predisposition and work with them to develop the weaker aspect. Imagery can be quite effective in this process. We need to facilitate the awakening of higher aspects of each, for these higher aspects tend to blend naturally together. Higher levels of love, concerned with the growth and well-being of others, and higher levels of the will, directed toward purposes devoid of egotism, clearly are closer together and less prone to conflict than jealous, needy love and power-hungry will. Visualization and meditation are two common methods used to facilitate this awakening and 'transmutation.'

The synthesis of will and love allows us to accept ourselves and others just as we are while still moving toward growth and greater harmony within ourselves and in our relationships. It helps us have patience and serenity while working actively in the world to create more beauty, to alleviate suffering, and to evoke the inner potential of individuals and groups. It allows us optimal expression of the Higher Self. The synthesis of love and will is exemplified in all great religions, in the figures of Jesus, Buddha, Moses, Krishna, and Mohammed. The seeking of this synthesis is central to spiritual psychosynthesis, which is explored in the next chapter.

8
SPIRITUAL AWAKENING AND TRANSFORMATION

Spiritual development is a long and arduous journey, an adventure through strange lands full of surprises, joy and beauty, difficulties and even dangers. It involves the awakening of potentialities hitherto dormant, the raising of consciousness to new realms, a drastic transmutation of the 'normal' elements of the personality, and a functioning along a new inner dimension. (Assagioli, 1977, p. 148)

Recently a friend shared with me an experience she had several years ago which had a profound effect on her life, beginning a transformative process. In the midst of the crisis of her husband's emergency appendectomy, she suddenly knew that she was totally responsible for everything in her life. This realization did not come to her through teachings nor through logic; it was something she simply 'saw' in the depths of her inner knowing. She spoke of the pain of that knowing, the darkness of that moment, yet what she experienced was not guilt. It was a positive, almost ecstatic pain, allowing her to see at the same time her power to choose her life and the awesomeness of that task. She spoke, too, of the difficulty of finding someone with whom to share this experience, for most of her friends only warned her about going on a guilt trip or denied that she could be responsible in any way for someone else in her family getting sick. Realizing her ultimate responsibility for herself was a quantum leap in self-understanding, a leap beyond logic or rational deduction. Such a leap might best be understood by someone who had had a similar awakening. To others, her experience might be 'understood' as a possible pathology, a neurotic reaction at best. No doubt to these others, her experience was an uncomfortable suggestion that they, too, might be wholly responsible for their own lives.

Her story brought home to me both the power and the difficulties of spiritual awakening and transformative experiences. By their very nature, these experiences elude our comfortable concepts about the nature of reality, the world, and ourselves. They don't fit because our usual thought patterns or paradigms are not big enough for them. They demand that we change at a very basic level, which is unnerving and uncomfortable at best, to our friends and family as well as ourselves. We try desperately to 'stay in control' and keep the old balances and behavior patterns intact.

"The more one is conscious of one's positive impulses, of one's urge toward the sublime, the more shame one feels for one's failure to give expression to these impulses. There ensures a painful burning of the conscience, a sense of guilt at not being what one could be, of not doing what one could do. This is not superego guilt but rather the cry of the Self for its actualization."
(Haronian, 1967, p. 10)

Awakening and transformation move us to a more expansive context in which we can grow and learn for the next period of our lives. We are like snakes who must shed old skins of beliefs and habits from time to time in order to continue growing. But while we still remain within the old skin, the new experiences of awakening may be accompanied by a great deal of pain and confusion. We may need to face something about ourselves which we do not want to see because it is too awesome or because we fear the pain of seeing how inadequate we have been in the past compared to our potential. The pain of facing our failure, our denial of the divine in ourselves and in others, seems to be an important step for many of us on the road to becoming ourselves.

It is a complex challenge to address a process as subtle and deep as spiritual awakening and transformation. Many psychologists have avoided dealing with such experiences or have labeled and treated them as pathological. Religious organizations try to encompass these experiences, yet often fall prey to platitudes, formulas, and rhetoric which do not capture the richness and grandeur of them. Our institutions tend to reflect, after all, our psychological processes as individuals and as a society. If individual counselors and therapists have had no experiences of this nature, or have failed to integrate them into their own lives, this sort of experience as reported by another person will indeed appear to be pathological, or at least confusing or bizarre. Religious institutions are usually founded on the vision and experience of a religious figure in history; however, if the clergy who follow have not experienced their own transformations, they will tend to become attached to the *formulations* of the originator's teachings, rather than sharing the *spirit* and *process* behind the teaching. We are all vulnerable to both of these reactions: avoiding the discomfort of the challenge, or addressing it with pat formulas and glib platitudes.

Recently, there have been movements to better understand and integrate experiences of a spiritual nature, in psychology as well as in religious insitutions. The transpersonal psychology movement has begun to address the past limitations of Western psychology and to develop ways of integrating spiritual experience into daily life and psychological health. The Association for Transpersonal Psychology is one formal organization of this movement. Psychosynthesis thought and practice have been involved in this effort since Assagioli's earliest work.

To find descriptions of these kinds of experiences, we turn to religious and philosophical writings, to literature, and to the work of mavericks such as Aldous Huxley and William James. Besides these two, writers who have contributed to this field include Carlos Castaneda, Ralph Waldo Emerson, Reshad Feild, Kahlil Gibran, Herman Hesse, Laura Huxley, Carl Jung, Krishnamurti, Stephen Levine, Abraham Maslow, Michael Murphy, Ram Dass, David Spangler, Tarthang Tulku, Alan Watts. . . to take a few names off my own bookshelves. The list could go on and on. A few of them are psychologists who are willing to expand the limits of human science and to risk error and 'heresy' in the search for human truth.

RECOGNIZING THE AWAKENING PROCESS

In psychosynthesis, we assume that life is a process of Self-realization, at least potentially; that is, a process of bringing into expression in the world our spiritual Self. Every problem and crisis is an opportunity for spiritual growth. Yet much of our growth is not *consciously* spiritual, but more a matter of 'tuning up' the personality so that we function more effectively in the world and feel comfortable with ourselves. The integrated and effective personality needed for optimal Self-expression may require work on low self-esteem, negative conditioning, fears and constricting beliefs. While this 'tuning up' process is essential, it is qualitatively different from the quantum leap of a spiritual awakening which requires special understanding and skill on the part of the guide.

Because awakening experiences come in many different guises, neither the individual nor the guide may recognize what is happening at first. An awakening may seem more like a breakdown, an inexplicable change in energy level and motivation which can be misconstrued as a symptom of psychological malfunctioning. If we regard any issue or event in a person's life as *potentially* one of transformation, we are more likely to recognize such processes when they do occur.

Spiritual awakening and transformation are *experiences*, first and foremost. They are not something we can identify by objective, external measurements. Only the individual can 'diagnose' his or her experiences as 'spiritual' or 'transformational' although he or she may need the help of a guide to do so. The individual may prefer to use different words from these to name the experience. Nevertheless, a guide may come to recognize the symptoms and offer the suggestion that what is happening is something beyond normal interaction with the world.

Beyond the normal means supernormal, not subnormal, crazy or sick. Clients often ask, "Is it normal to feel this way?" The answer may be, "No, it's not normal; it's extraordinary and special." Einstein was not normal; nor was Bach. Spiritual awakening implies an opening of awareness to deeper and higher levels of both individual and collective unconscious, levels usually not available to 'normal' awareness.

Experiences have physical, emotional, mental, and perceptual components. Spiritual experiences are those which give us new expansive perceptions about our relationship to the cosmos, which allow us to glimpse a reality beyond the logical, rational, physically bound world we usually consider to be our home. These new perceptions are naturally accompanied by strong *emotions* of fear, joy, hope, and even despair. Our *thinking* may become confused, disjointed, and at the same time, expansive. We may create whole new patterns of understanding from this seemingly mental chaos. We may experience our *bodies* in new ways, such as becoming aware of how tense and bound-up they are, or finding new freedom and suppleness. We may experience leaving our bodies altogether for awhile.

When we undergo such experiences, our values change. We become more open to 'transpersonal' values: ethical, aesthetic, heroic, humanitarian, altruistic, and creative. "In this sense, 'spiritual' refers not only to experiences traditionally considered religious but to *all* the states of awareness, all the human functions and activities which have as their common denominator the possession of *values* higher than average." (Assagioli, 1977)

Forms of Transformation

Spiritual awakening takes many forms, compatible with the qualities and characteristics of the individual. It may be an artistic urge, a strong impulse to express one's self in color, shapes, textures, or music. It may come as a vision to create something of service to the world, such as an organization, an instrument or tool, or a new model for understanding a facet of our universe. Religious experiences of all kinds may be spiritual awakenings. So may be paranormal phenomena including out-of-body experiences, clairvoyance, mental telepathy, or receiving messages apparently from other beings. Spiritual awakening may begin in experiences in the waking state, or it may first nudge us in dreams. It may even express itself through unexpected behavior when we find ourselves acting with unusual effectiveness without conscious, logical thought. We may take whole courses of action and make major life decisions without

"I spoke of this to my teacher as we walked. 'Let me put it to you this way,' he answered. 'When we have the courage to realize that life itself is the teacher, the timeless truth lying within the moment can come forth from the knowledge written in the great books and preserved at sacred places. The difficulty is that, traveling or studying books, including the sacred scripture, is useless without your own inner experience.' "
(Feild, 19, p. 15)

fully realizing their significance until later. It just felt right. Many people speak of 'being guided' in their lives by a wisdom beyond their consciousness. As we come to trust and understand these experiences, our spiritual awakening progresses.

Sources of Transformation: Superconscious and the Higher Self

"Spiritual experiences can be limited to superconscious realms or can include the awareness of the Self" (Assagioli, 1977, p. 149). There may indeed be different 'levels' of spiritual awakening, which in no way implies a superiority of one level over another. There is, however, a qualitative difference between awakening which involves the influx of superconscious energies into the individual's awareness and an awakening which involves a direct experience of, and even identification with, the Higher Self. Let me describe in more detail what I mean by these terms and how I envision the corresponding experiences.

Superconscious Infusion

The superconscious, or higher unconscious, as described by Assagioli, is the realm of our unconscious which holds in trust our intuitions and inspirations before they dawn in consciousness. It is the source of feelings, motives, and ideas which move us toward harmony, cooperation, beauty, and service. When we challenge ourselves with creative problems, whether in science, art, or the humanities, the insight or new pattern which rushes into our conscious understanding arises from the superconscious.

Psychosynthesis sessions may focus on specific issues raised by the inflow of superconscious energies into the life and awareness of the individual. A person may feel an inner demand to do something indefinably different in life, experiencing a 'divine discontent'. Upon exploration, this demand may be found to be for musical or artistic expression, using a gift previously neglected or ignored. My father, for example, suffered deep depressions during his fifties and early sixties. When he began writing full time in his late sixties, the depressions disappeared. New levels of service or altruistic love may seem to be asked of an individual, although pragmatic parts of the personality may resist. New concepts and insights may require changes in the individual's value system and ways of thinking. These are all examples of superconscious energies which do not necessarily require the individual to take up meditation, prayer, or other 'spiritual' practices. Psychological work to integrate these energies may be far more helpful, especially at first. People may fully integrate transformative experiences through superconscious infusion without ever acknowledging their 'spiritual' nature.

Not so, however, a direct experience of the Higher Self. . . .

The Approach of the Higher Self

At times the Higher Self seems to approach awareness directly, as if demanding to be recognized as the true center of the individual's life. The individual may experience this approach as a kind of pressure or compelling energy from an unknown source within and may project the pressure onto others—therapist, spouse, parent. The experience is one of being asked to make a significant change and nothing seems to suffice until the change is made.

This demand may occur because of readiness, as an individual who has integrated personality and superconscious patterns chooses to be open to even higher realization. People may become conscious of the Self as the ultimate Source of being in times of personal crisis such as illness, external catastrophes, or death of a close friend or family member. The Biblical story of Job recounts this kind of awakening. Often the 'reason' for an experience of the Higher Self is beyond our present ability to explain. It just seems to happen. Perhaps as our understanding of the human life cycle deepens, we will be able to see distinct patterns for these kinds of experiences—during late adolescence, midlife and old age.

The following excerpt from a session transcript illustrates one person's struggle with a more or less direct experience of the Higher Self. Early in the session, the client says in regard to a friend's experience:

C: I don't want to suffer the pain she's suffering and there's something about the clarity of her vision; I want that! I don't seem to be able to have it; I seem to keep myself from that, the totality of that vision, of the things she was going through. So it's almost like I experience looking at it through some sort of invisible shield. I can see it but can't really get it.

Later, the guide says:

G: My sense is that this is an issue between you and your Self. I don't have any attachment to it. Now there's some kind of stuff I've been experiencing with us—

C: I don't know what it is but I know what it is (laughs).

G: Do you want to say what it is even though you don't know?

C: (Laughing) It's kind of embarrassing. It's like I'm playing out the gap with you. As long as I can keep on fooling you, I'm challenging you to do what I need to do for myself and being clever and elusive and withholding. "Well, I'll let you see this much today." It seems to be around the issue of control. The word Ego comes in, like there's a subpersonality named Ego, the Controller.

G: So from the level of trying to control what's going on, let's just make some statements.

C: What I'm trying to control?

G: Yeah: "Don't _____," whatever it is. "I'm trying to outsmart you. . ."

C: Don't see my imperfections. Only see one at a time.

G: Are you scared of me?

C: Yes. . . and I don't like to admit that.

G: Would you share what the fear is?

C: Projecting a lot of New Age Top Dog onto you. I'm afraid of your being disappointed in me, afraid of your disapproval.

G: So the fear stems from you wanting me to like you?

C: Hell, I don't want you just to like me, I want you to love me. (laugh) Not only love me and like me; I want you to enjoy me. Because then I feel good about myself. Somehow I need to find some new vocabulary: it's not my self, it's my personality.

G: So in some ways your resistance to your Self is from that place. All this stuff that's going on with me is going on with your Self.

C: (long pause) I'm experiencing a sense that I'm holding up different images between me and my Self. I hold you up there and I hold Roberto (Assagioli) up there and I hold. . . Roberto's a pretty safe image to hold up. . . sometimes I hold J. up there, not as much as I used to. I hold A. up there sometimes. The light is too bright. It's too bright not because it would be blinding, but because of the exposure. So I just keep holding up all these filters and some of the light comes through.

G: How meaningful is the light to you?

C: (pause) I have so much trouble with those questions.

G: Just tell the light what happened in relation to the question right now, exactly what happened, the process in relation to the question.

C: I had a flip answer about it was an irrelevant question, because the light's there whether it's meaningful or not.

G: Tell the light, talk to the light. Not just the quick answer, but about your response. Talk to the light.

C: My first response was to have a flip answer, to say it was a meaningless question. Then I went into my head and started thinking about what would be the proper response. (To light) And something inside craves you. It's this powerful desire and craving, and equally powerful avoidance.

G: Tell the light.

C: I find it very difficult to talk to you, can't look at you directly, feel like I want to shield my eyes. I want to go anywhere else, get away. And I feel ashamed. . . I feel. . . I can just taste it. . . inadequacy, a bitter taste in my mouth. And you don't waver, you just stay there.

G: Does this feel right what you're doing now?

C: I'm not allowing this as fully as I might.

G: Tell the light that.

C: I'm not allowing. . . I'm not allowing. . . I'm not allowing. . . it's a broken record. I'm not allowing this experience to be as full as I could. I'm kind of dipping my toe in and pulling it out again.

G: Is that okay?. Do you choose it?

C: I'm just getting to that, just getting to that it's okay. (to light/Higher Self) I experience you as being very patient, infinitely patient. I am a little child in relation to you. I accept myself that way. I'm experiencing compassion for myself. And that cosmic shiver is coming in again.

The client in this session projects her discomfort about her relationship with her Higher Self onto the guide, feeling afraid of his disapproval and embarrassed and nervous in his presence. The guide is able to redirect her projection readily because she is familiar with the concept of the Higher Self. This demonstrates the value of introducing concepts such as these to clients going through spiritual transformation; it provides a common language for guide and client to communicate about the process. The guide himself is alert to the possibility of a spiritual dimension to the work and correctly identifies the projection. Had he taken it at face value and spent time examining their relationship in great detail, the client's direct communication with her Higher Self would have been delayed if not derailed. That communication is of vital importance for the client to realize her own spiritual essence and her inner Source of wisdom, beauty and love.

Here the client is clearly working with a direct experience of the spiritual Self rather than with superconscious inflow. Yet, as the Self approaches awareness and the client opens to that vision, the superconscious is also energized. So the client may also experience a flood of new patterns, insights, emotions and perceptions. As the intensity of the experience subsides, there will be work to be done integrating these new patterns and energies into daily life and finding ways of expressing the vision in form (e.g., art, writing, service).

An opportunity for a more or less direct experience of the Higher Self is offered in the following exercise. This particular version was developed by Susan Farley in 1980.

EXERCISE: A LETTER FROM THE HIGHER SELF

Close your eyes and pay attention for a moment to your breathing. Just notice the breath as it comes and goes, without trying to change it in any way. . .

Now gently follow the breath inside your body. As you turn your attention inward, do you notice sensations of ease and pleasure anywhere in your body? Go to these places and enjoy the opening you find there. . . Now see if there are any parts of your body that feel tight or constricted and gradually move the sensations of ease and pleasure to those places of tension or discomfort. . . If you need to move and readjust your position to be more comfortable, do so. Allow the sense of looseness, openness, and pleasure to slowly permeate the tissues, the muscles, the cells. . .

You may have noticed certain feelings arising as you focused on the tightness and discomfort in your body. What are those feelings? What feelings are connected with the sensations of ease and pleasure? Let those feelings be as rich and full as they want to be, and enjoy them.

Thoughts may arise as you focus on your feelings. Just notice them; those that go with the discomfort, and those that go with the ease. Gently direct your attention to the thoughts that affirm your openness and pleasure and appreciate them. . .

These are all aspects of you—of who you are at this moment. Hold them all lightly; notice who it is that is holding them and who made the choices to direct attention to one aspect or another. . .

Now allow yourself to step back from all that you have been holding. Step as far back as you can so that you are moving to the widest perspective you can discover right now—to the deepest place that is available to you. . .

Let yourself imagine that you are the being who chose to be born into this lifetime, who chose to have this particular body, these feelings, this mind—who chose to be this person who is in the world. How would it be if you could remember making that choice? Go back to that moment and let yourself be in touch again with the purpose that brought you into the world, and with the love you as that being have for the particular form you chose . . . Go to the love and wisdom and clarity that are your birthright and claim them as fully as you can right now. . .

From that place of compassion and total acceptance, look at the person who is sitting here today, and at all the turnings and choices of a lifetime that have brought that person to this moment. . .

Is there anything you wish to say, anything you need to remind this person of? Write a letter to the person you chose to be in the world and let the letter be whatever it needs to be. . .

When you have finished the letter, put it in an envelope, seal it, and address it to yourself. Give it to a friend to mail later when it seems right to do so. It will arrive at the precise moment when your words are most needed and can be most clearly heard.

Clues

Certain clues indicate that the individual's struggle is of a transpersonal nature. The guide in the session above recognized the quality of the client's projections as clues. People may also express awe and wonder, their whole affect becoming enlivened by their inner experience. They may feel overwhelmed with the power and beauty of the Self they glimpse and be unable to verbalize their experience, although it may be expressed in tears, gestures, or through art or poetry. People sometimes experience a sense of personal inadequacy that is different in quality from low self-esteem and social inferiority. It is the humility of saints who see at once how far they have come along the road to truth, and how much farther they still have to go. Many express shame at their previous blandness, arrogance, and 'egotism'; this 'existential shame' (Firman, 1977) is motivating rather than debilitating and moves toward self-forgiveness, self-acceptance, and a new sense of freedom and choice.

Resistance, too, can be a clue to the approach of the Self, as the personality structure resists letting go its well-ordered world, established coping mechanisms, and power. The individual (identified with the personality) may fear death and annihilation as the experience surpasses anything previously known in life; themes of death in dreams or waking fantasies may indicate a transformation in the offing. In a confrontation between a fearful personality and the Higher Self, the individual may tend to project feelings of being pressured onto a guide, teacher, or friend. The true source of this pressure is the Higher Self.

PSYCHOLOGICAL PROBLEMS OF SPIRITUAL AWAKENING

Confrontations between the personality and the Higher Self are opportunities for people to choose to be who they truly are—to make a deep commitment to actualize superconscious potentials and patterns in the face of fear, embarrassment, and social pressure. Such a choice cannot be made lightly; we must see the implications of this step and wrestle with our various demons to be able to fully choose. The pressure on the personality from the Higher Self often forces our demons and neuroses into consciousness, allowing us an opportunity to see and understand more clearly than ever before what the central issues of our lives are, and what choices we must make about how to live with those issues. We see how past programming has limited us and how we can change in order to transcend those limits.

Lifestyle and Relationships

Superconscious energies may evoke fear and resistance because of their unfamiliar nature. This is especially true if we have centered our lives on the horizontal dimension of growth, paying attention only to a physical, emotional, intellectual reality. Demands for new creative expression or for increased service to the community may have a drastic effect on lifestyles and relationships, requiring disidentification from old roles and subpersonalities, a process which takes time and conscious work. Often there is no support from friends and family for the changes that an individual is undertaking; in fact, the social environment may actively oppose the process. As in the story of my friend at the beginning of this chapter, the people around the individual going through this experience may have no antecedents for understanding what is going on. Their concern for the person may be expressed in ways which subvert or complicate the process of healthy change. Even well-meaning counselors can block the process of transformation if they have no understanding of what is occurring. A previously social individual may withdraw, seeking the solitude needed to sort things out and attune to the changes from within; this withdrawal may itself be interpreted by a counselor or therapist as pathological.

When we undergo transformation in a non-supportive environment, we must struggle to maintain a mental grasp on the new insights and perspectives. We must protect ourselves from the fears and doubts of those around us. Sadly, we must sometimes choose between following our new truth and sense of right path, and remaining in old, beloved relationships.

Paradoxically, a struggle with our environment to remain true to our spiritual awakening often strengthens and clarifies our vision and our choices. We begin to discover secret companions in our search and to find ways of sharing our vision with those around us. Sometimes we can let go of old expectations about a relationship and accept a partner just the way he or she is, allowing the relationship to move into a new richness. This can occur even without the partner's conscious participation. I am convinced that it is possible, although far from easy, to transform a relationship by working on *my* perspective and behavior alone.

Going Crazy

Having no guidelines for understanding their experiences, however, people may think they are going crazy, a notion often fed by frightened and confused friends and relatives. Indeed, insanity is possible, if we are not able or willing to expand ourselves to integrate a spiritual experience. Such a time is truly a crisis; as the Chinese ideogram for *crisis* indicates, it is a 'dangerous opportunity.' The possibility of danger can become actual if professionals diagnose pathology and prescribe inappropriate drugs and invasive treatments. How many visionaries have gone insane, their insights lost to the world, because there was no one there to listen and give support?

Glamor

On the other hand, spiritual awakening experiences, or imitations of them, appear very glamorous in some circumstances and within some groups. Among people who value growth and spiritual or religious pursuits, transformative experiences may be sought after and encouraged. The problem is that this atmosphere may encourage pseudo-awakening experiences as well, or emphasize the emotional and dramatic aspects of genuine experiences disproportionately. People apparently undergoing such experiences may come to fancy themselves as gurus; they become identified with a subpersonality, perhaps a New Age Top Dog which becomes attached to the experience itself rather than allowing the process to continue and expand gently and naturally. Or such experiences may tempt a person to dramatize the suffering and confusion; going crazy is a good way to get attention, after all!

Escape

Without support, or even with it sometimes, people may seek refuge from the awakening process in various ways. We have probably all fled from the hounds of heaven at some time or another. We barricade ourselves behind rationality. We bury ourselves in work, claim we must 'survive' when survival is really not an issue. We drink. We use drugs, sleeping pills, tranquillizers, or nicotine. We lose ourselves in compulsive behaviors of various kinds, from extreme orderliness to wild abandon in 'play'. We overeat or put ourselves on stringent diets. We can see this kind of behavior in many of our well-known creative geniuses; in fact, a bizarre lifestyle has often been considered prerequisite to creativity. Perhaps such behavior is

"A mystical experience, however brief, is validating for those attracted to the spiritual search. The mind now knows what the heart had only hoped for. But the same experience can be deeply distressing to one unprepared for it, who must then try to fit it into an inadequate belief system."
(Ferguson, 1980, p. 362)

really only symptomatic of the intensity of the creative drive and the inability of the person to accept and integrate it fully into life. When creative people are able to cooperate with their superconscious energies, their lives are less chaotic and their genius finds even fuller expression.

Individual work with a guide can help with problems of spiritual awakening enabling recognition of the spiritual source of the difficulties and validating the individual's experience. When the valid motivation behind the fear, resistance, and escapist behaviors is brought to light, the individual can move beyond these reactions and make the necessary choices for outward transformation to match the inner awakening. When the true depth and reality of awakening is accepted and embraced, glamor and imitation give way to humility and surrender to the wisdom of the Higher Self.

THE ROLE OF THE GUIDE

To support others' growth during periods of spiritual awakening is to let them know that they are not alone, to communicate trust in the process they are going through, to recognize them as Higher Selves full of power, beauty and rightness. People often express tremendous relief and gratitude for such recognition. Sometimes a simple statement of understanding from a guide is all that is needed to facilitate an individual's wholehearted embrace of his or her unfolding destiny. Many people are willing to struggle with the most overwhelming pain and complexities if only someone near acknowledges the significance of what they are doing.

To work with someone in transformation requires close identification with one's own Higher Self. It requires full presence, trust and faith. These kinds of processes cannot be comprehended with the mind alone; the heart must be opened to faith and love as the other person is invited to do the same. Sharing feelings of joy and wonder helps create a context of openness, acceptance and trust.

People confronting the reality of the Higher Self and the choice to more fully identify with their spiritual being need their guides to demonstrate a delicate balance betwen firmness and non-involvement. The guide is needed to keep the choice to be a Self in the foreground, to prevent the temptation to get lost in content, glamor or resistance, losing sight of the central issue. On the other hand, a guide who attempts to influence the choice may dilute its power and effectiveness. The guide's role is not to intrude into issues between people and their Higher Selves, but to stand as a caring witness, in conscious alignment with his or her own Selfhood. The guide in the session excerpt above acts in this role.

The role and responsibility of guides in facilitating spiritual transformation is more a matter of intention than of form. I think it is essential for those of us who would guide others in this process to be committed to our own spiritual development, to be seeking our own path and practice. We need to be open to our own transpersonal experiences and to be consciously working on creating a coherent philosophy or world view which encompasses these experiences. In these ways we align our *intention* towards spiritual growth and can understand and facilitate similar alignment in others. We do not, however, impose our *forms* on others or insist that they use our metaphors. Stephen Levine, who works with the Hanuman Foundation's Dying Project, uses whatever spiritual metaphors a dying person suggests to support that person's growth and awakening. If the person is comfortable with Christian imagery, Stephen may talk about seeing Jesus or Mary waiting 'on the other side'. If the individual is not involved in a formal religion, the terms used to describe the experience may be of light, warmth, or radiance without form.

"When a therapist is identified as having a transpersonal orientation, we would assume that he/she thereby affirms the validity and importance of the spiritual quest, and supports the integration of spirit, mind, emotions and body. We would also assume that he/she has had some meaningful transpersonal experience which has experientially validated a transpersonal viewpoint. The therapist may also be assumed to be on his/her own path, regardless of whether he/she is formally identified with an organized religious group." (Vaughan-Clark, 1977, p. 80)

METHODS FOR SPIRITUAL PSYCHOSYNTHESIS

As is true for all levels of psychosynthesis guiding, the attitude and presence of the guide are of far greater importance than the particular methods used. A guide's acceptance of and attunement to an individual's process will facilitate selection of methods which best meet the individual's needs. Most of the methods suggested in Chapter 5 can be used. Dialogue, Gestalt techniques, dream work, guided imagery, affirmations, and meditation are all powerful tools for integrating spiritual experiences and opening to more. In my experience, most long-term psychosynthesis work eventually moves into spiritual psychosynthesis, sometimes right from the start. So it stands to reason that the typical psychosynthesis tool kit has many appropriate tools for guiding the process.

Imagery is certainly one of the most powerful tools because it allows unconscious material to come into consciousness past the barrier of our rational world views. Certain symbols can be suggested in guided daydreams or inner dialogue which will usually evoke transpersonal energies: the wise person; light, sun, or star; climbing a mountain; and water, especially from a spring or a fountain. People may spontaneously see personified images of spirit, perhaps after a climb to the top of a mountain; angels and images of Christ or Buddha are common forms. They may see an image of someone they have known who represents great wisdom and love to them, although it is wise to explore the qualities of such figures carefully. Sometimes the figure turns out to be a 'top dog' or judgmental figure, not one of acceptance and love which true images of transpersonal energies usually are.

Geometric figures may also occur spontaneously, in mental imagery and in drawings, or may be suggested by the guide for contemplation. The circle has been used for ages as a symbol of unity and wholeness, especially in the mandalas of Eastern religious art. An equal-armed cross may be used to symbolize our two dimensions: vertical alignment with spirit, and horizontal relationship to the world. The triangle may represent the three aspects of the personality—body, feelings, and mind—and serve as a symbol of synthesis. When we meditate on these three symbols, we practice concentration while opening ourselves on an unconscious level to the archetypal qualities associated with them. Assagioli (1976) suggests meditation on an equilateral triangle below a sun or star; the light above the triangle represents the Higher Self infusing the three-part personality below with its pure energies.

The following exercise uses transpersonal images in setting a scene which allows many people to tap their superconscious wisdom and strength. The Wise Person image may be a source of guidance and strength for making choices about a session or about an issue in life.

EXERCISE: THE WISE PERSON

Closing your eyes, relaxing your body, and seeking a quiet place within for a few moments, focus your awareness on your breathing. . .

Now imagine that you hold a candle before you in a candleholder. Imagine lighting the candle, watching the flame flicker and then grow strong. Watch the flame for a few moments, seeing how it burns stronger and brighter as you watch. . .

Notice the tiny blue flame at the heart of the larger yellow flame. Focus your attention there, looking deeper and deeper into the heart of it until that is all you see. . .

In the heart of the tiny blue flame appears the face of a very wise and loving person. Notice the wisdom and the love which are in the face and eyes of this person, wisdom and love which are there just for you now. . .

You may ask this person for advice about what is happening now, about where you need to go, what your next step might be. Ask any question you have and be receptive to whatever comes, in whatever form. . .

The Wise Person may have something to tell you besides what you have asked, a special message for you. If you are willing to receive it, tell the Wise Person that this is so and wait for a response. . .

Turn now and look at any issue in your life, with the Wise Person beside you. Allow yourself to see the situation as the Wise Person sees it . . . Perhaps you will want to make a choice about your role in the situation, about how you want to be . . . Tell the Wise Person about your choice . . .

Now imagine yourself carrying out your choice. See how you behave and feel and how others respond to you . . . Imagine yourself calling upon the wisdom and love of the Wise Person to help you sustain your choice . . .

Now take leave of the Wise Person, knowing you can return at any time to find guidance and strength. When you are ready, open your eyes and take time to make some notes about your experience.

This form of seeking the Wise Person may be longer than one used in a session. It is also primarily visual which might not be appropriate for an auditory or kinesthetic person. The dialogue with the Wise Person can be adapted to suit the specific needs of the individual in the moment. The Wise Person is an image for a sort of intermediary between the personal self and the Higher Self, a representative of this Source at a level we can comprehend and where we can feel comfortable. The Wise Person encourages the skillful and good aspects of the will. We align our will with Transpersonal Will when we make choices from this perspective.

This exercise is one of many forms which can be used to create an inner dialogue, an essential process in spiritual psychosynthesis. These are ways we seek within for wisdom and for personal truth, tapping our superconscious. It soon becomes a natural act to pause, ask a question, and wait for an inner response in imagery, words, or impressions. An image of a wise person need not be used every time, although I personally find it helpful when I am disoriented or in distress.

Writing can be useful in seeking answers from the superconscious and in opening ourselves to new perspectives. A letter *from* the Higher Self, presented above, is one approach. We can also write letters *to* our Higher Selves about issues and concerns, or requesting general guidance as described in Chapter 5 in the section on journal-keeping.

Assagioli (1976) developed a series of techniques for evoking and developing transpersonal qualities such as serenity. The exercise below is an adaptation of Assagioli's approach.

EXERCISE TO EVOKE AND DEVELOP DESIRED QUALITIES

The purpose of this exercise is to create inner and outer conditions through which one can foster and enhance a desired quality within one's self. In the following outline, the quality of serenity is used, but the exercise can be adapted for other qualities, such as courage, patience, joy, or compassion. It is important that the choice of such a quality and the decision to develop it come from within, not as a 'should' but as something chosen purposely and freely as a further step in growth.

1. Find a relaxed, comfortable position and take a few deep breaths . . . Now think about the idea of serenity—hold the concept 'serenity' in your mind and reflect on it. What is its quality, nature, meaning? . . . As you develop insights, ideas, or images associated with serenity, record them in your journal. . .

2. Open yourself to further ideas and images related to serenity that may emerge from your unconscious and write them down. . .

3. Realize the value of serenity, its purpose and use, especially in our turbulent modern world. *Praise* serenity in your mind. *Desire* it. . .

4. Assume a physical attitude of serenity. . . Relax all muscular and nervous tension. Breathe slowly and rhythmically. . . Allow serenity to express itself on your face. It may help to visualize yourself with that expression. . .

5. *Evoke* serenity directly. Imagine that you are in a place which makes you feel serene—a quiet beach, a temple, a cool green glade, perhaps a place where you have experienced serenity in the past. . . Repeat the word SERENITY several times. . . Let serenity permeate you until you seem to *become* serenity. . .

6. Imagine yourself in circumstances common to your daily life which in the past would have tended to upset or irritate you: perhaps being with a hostile person. . . facing a difficult problem . . . obliged to do many things rapidly. . . or in danger. . . and *see* and *feel* yourself calm and serene. . .

7. Resolve to bring serenity into your day increasingly. . . to be a living example of serenity. . . to radiate serenity. . .

8. Make a sign with the word SERENITY using the color and lettering that best conveys this quality to you. Place this sign where you can see it daily and if possible at the time when you need serenity the most. Whenever you look at it, recall within yourself the feeling of serenity.

This exercise to develop desired qualities can become the focus of a larger program. You can gather together poetry, symbols, music, drama, artwork, photography, dance, and biographical excerpts, all evoking or in some personal sense symbolizing serenity, and use them for a total experience. By surrounding yourself with these materials, you can evoke and develop a deep sense of serenity or of any other quality. You can use all that you find in your environment to foster a sense of serenity through your own creation of a synthesis of experiential forms.

(A possible contraindication: in a few cases, it is possible to experience a negative reaction to the exercise; attempting to evoke serenity may bring tension, restlessness, or anxiety. This is usually a sign that there is a core of negative emotions that block the development of the desired quality. Such a situation is most likely to be encountered during Step 6 above. If the negative reaction is strong, it is best to suspend the exercise while exploring the negative feelings and possibly releasing them through catharsis. After this, the exercise can be resumed and will then have particular value as a means of filling with a positive and desired quality the psychological 'space' left vacant by the release of the negative feelings.) (Assagioli, 1976, pp. 223-4)

Figure 9 offers a partial list of transpersonal qualities. You may want to add to the list or substitute other words for those suggested. These qualities may be used as seed thoughts for creative meditation as described in Chapter 5 and in more detail in Assagioli, 1976. Meditation on a quality increases our understanding and appreciation of it while bringing it into our lives through conscious and subconscious realignment.

Transpersonal Qualities

beauty	compassion	comprehension	courage
creativity	energy	power	enthusiasm
eternity	infinity	universality	freedom
liberation	non-attachment	cooperation	friendship
brotherhood	generosity	goodness	goodwill
gratitude	appreciation	admiration	wonder
harmony	humor	inclusiveness	receptivity
joy	bliss	light	love
order	patience	reality	being
truth	renewal	trust	faith
serenity	peace	service	silence
quiet	calm	simplicity	synthesis
wholeness	understanding	vitality	will
wisdom	responsibility		

Grounding

Perhaps one of the most valuable contributions we can make to each other's spiritual awakening is to help bring new vision and qualities into ordinary daily life, a process we have called 'grounding'. You may recall the importance of grounding in the map of the cycles of a session in Chapter 6. The purpose of a session is not merely to get 'high' but to bring something of value back to earth.

We can encourage people we guide to find practical ways to express their vision and transpersonal qualities and to make clear choices to do this. It is usually best to make choices which can be acted upon in the next few days, before the energy of the experience and the choice has dissipated. Perhaps the choice will be long-term, with specific steps chosen for immediate implementation. Assagioli's discussion (1974) of the stages of the willed act provides a useful framework for this process. I encourage the reader to refer to *The Act of Will* for that discussion; a brief outline of the stages appears in the previous chapter.

Affirmations are extremely useful in grounding spiritual experiences because they reprogram our thinking into more inclusive and expansive patterns. It is wise to create affirmations which are positive and in the present tense. Saying 'I will not worry' may only remind us of the possibility of things to worry about, while saying 'I am serene', or 'I am becoming more serene' introduces the image of the desired quality into here-and-now reality.

Another important element in grounding comes from the recognition of our interdependency. Because we need support from our environment, we need to seek out like-minded people and environments which inspire and sustain us as we struggle to understand and integrate spiritual experiences into life. Here is one area where a guide may act as advisor, sharing information about support groups and other resources. People may discover allies at hand within their own circles, friends or relatives who have been previously misunderstood or undervalued. They may identify a nearby natural setting or public place such as a museum or a church which is conducive to inspiration and attunement and choose to go there more regularly for renewal. We often need to recognize the value of a familiar situation or relationship and give ourselves permission to really make use of it. We need also to know that we deserve to be supported and sustained in our spiritual growth as much as in our personal life and career development.

SELF-EXPRESSION AND SERVICE

Very commonly, when we align with our Higher Self and open to superconscious energies, we experience two impulses. One is for Self-expression; that is, the direct and active expression of our special gifts and qualities in forms that are most compatible to our personalities. The other is for service, to contribute in some meaningful way to the evolution, health, and well-being of our friends, families, communities, and humanity in general. These two impulses complement one another, for we seek to serve the world in the manner most appropriate to our individual qualities and gifts.

When we know ourselves to be most essentially spiritual beings, Higher Selves acting through particular personalities and organisms, we are set free from the fear of selfishness which has plagued the good children of our culture for so long. We truly *can* trust ourselves! When we plunge deeply into who we are, we discover we are creatures of great potential who yearn to use our potential to serve humanity and to serve 'Gaia', the living being of the Earth. It is only when we identify with confused subpersonalities, or with material forms around us, that we become disharmonious. Then what we experience as our 'needs' may be distortions of our true needs and the pursuit of these distortions may lead to harm for others and ourselves. This is what we fear about 'selfishness'. To be truly Self-centered is to be a giver of gifts to the world.

As an experience in this splendid process of Self-discovery, Self-expression and service, let me suggest another exercise.

EXERCISE: QUALITIES, GIFTS, AND SERVICE

Looking back through your life, a few years at a time, recall things you have done which you believed *you did especially well* and which *you enjoyed doing.* You may think of them as achievements, accomplishments, or simply high points. Make a list of these events, leaving plenty of space beneath each for more notes . . . Be sure to include events from your childhood and adolescence . . .

Now looking over your list, note under each what it was that *you* yourself did, how you contributed to the venture . . .

Now note under each entry what your relationship to others seemed to be (i.e., team leader, team member, alone, or director) . . .

Next note under each entry what it was about the activity or venture which gave you satisfaction. What was the 'payoff' in your inner sense of satisfaction? Be as specific as possible . . .

Looking back over your notes, see if you can see any patterns emerging, patterns of skills or abilities, of relationship with others, and of satisfaction. Focus down the skills to around six and the relationship and satisfaction to one each, if possible . . .

Taking each area in turn (skills, relationship, satisfaction) move into a meditative state, relaxing your body, feelings, and mind. Hold what you have discovered gently in your conscious mind and wait to see if any synthesis occurs, if any new insight comes about yourself in this respect . . .

Make notes about any new understanding that occurs . . .

Still in quiet contemplation, ask yourself what qualities you seem to have expressed in all these activities, through these skills, in this relationship, and through this sense of satisfaction. What qualities has your Self sought to express through your endeavors? . . . Again, take time to make some notes.

Now imagine bringing this quality or qualities into even fuller expression in your life right now. In what ways are you already doing this? . . . In what new ways might you manifest these qualities even more richly? . . . How will the quality or qualities help your service in the world? . . . Visualize yourself in an activity expressing one of these qualities, noticing how others respond, what gets in the way, and how you move skillfully around or through the obstacles.

At this point, you may want to use some of the methods previously described to consult with a wise-person image, dialogue with a subpersonality, or whatever is needed. You may want to develop an affirmation about the quality you have identified and its manifestation in service. You may want to simply sit and experience this quality within. Remember to give yourself time to record your experiences in words or drawings.

(Ideas for this exercise come from Arthur Miller's "System for Identifying Motivated Abilities," from Bolles and Crystal's *What Color is Your Parachute* (1981), and from an exercise presented by Tom Yeomans at the Psychosynthesis Institute in San Francisco in 1978.)

When we inquire deeply into what gives us greatest satisfaction and happiness, it seems to be in expressing our highest qualities, which are also of value to the world! We no longer have to deny ourselves in order to serve the world, at least not in the sense of denying who we really are and what gives us deepest joy. We may need to discover that what we *thought* we wanted (ease, money, material goods, power over others) do not *in themselves* bring us the happiness we seek. Sometimes they facilitate our true fulfillment; at other times they frustrate and distract us from our search. The process of this continued discovery is psychosynthesis.

This whole issue of desires, wants, needs, and spiritual fulfillment is far from resolved for me. I still crave material abundance and I do not know if my reasoning— that wealth would make it easier for me to serve—is a rationalization or truth or somewhere in between. I see it as a basic issue for all of us in our culture who seek spiritual alignment; at least I know I am not alone in this struggle. We have lots of old programming to rid ourselves of, or to transform into more positive forms.

Our fear of ourselves may lead to a rather negative view of human nature in general. Some people seem to believe that we must vigilantly curb ourselves according to externally articulated rules in order to be not even holy, but barely saved from damnation. These people only express a fear *which we each have* within us; a fear of our own vast potential and of the awesome responsibility which accompanies that potential. I mention this phenomenon here because it is an issue for many who seek true Self-expression and service. We need to offer those in fear our understanding, our empathy, and compassion rather than our contempt. At the same time, we can affirm to ourselves the importance of trust in our basic goodness as Selves seeking expression in the world. We can seek ways of releasing ourselves from self-doubt and fear so that we can more fully share our gifts with the world.

Writing this book has been for me an enormous learning experience in my own Self-expression and service. At times I have felt presumptuous: how can I set myself up as any kind of authority on psychosynthesis and put forth a whole book on the subject? I know there are others who 'know' more than I do who should write this book. On the other hand, I feel called to write it. I perceive a great need for it. I have a gift with words and enjoy writing. So I began, and have discovered with increasing delight how deeply satisfying the writing is for me, and how much I continue to learn about my subject. As I write, I cannot yet know if and how my book will serve the world, yet I continue to feel a deep conviction within myself (is it only wishful thinking?) that the book will find its way into the world and into the hands of many people whom it will serve.

Spiritual awakening is an awakening to who we really are and a transformation in how we manifest our special qualities in the world. We discover that at the deepest levels, we can trust ourselves. Who we are is of value to the world. When we free ourselves of the inhibitions, distortions and fears which block our self-understanding, how rich and beautiful are our gifts, how joyful their expression, and how awesome the impact they can have upon the world!

The phenomenon of spiritual awakening and transformation in human life is an area long neglected by psychology and counseling. Symptoms of this process have often been labeled pathological and the individual experiencing them has been subjected to inappropriate and even destructive treatment. Indeed, there are some fairly serious problems associated with spiritual awakening, but these are best resolved with the help of a guide who recognizes the validity of the process and facilitates movement toward the potential rather than merely away from the symptoms. Although spiritual awakening takes many forms, from scientific discovery to artistic impulses to mystical experiences, the need to accept, cooperate with, and integrate the process into daily life remains the same. Those who work as counselors, therapists, and guides are challenged to open to their own spiritual dimensions as well as to develop methods and techniques for facilitating transformation in others. A vision of human potential which expands the conventional limitations we place on ourselves is invaluable. As we all awaken more to our spiritual dimensions and express our unique gifts, we will co-create a world of harmony, beauty and life.

9

THE LIFELONG PROCESS OF PSYCHOSYNTHESIS

There seems to be a way for things to happen which is intrinsically right for them: they become what they were meant to be. . . . Do human beings also tend to unfold according to such inner designs, or is our life wholly random? It seems a reasonable and useful hypothesis to believe that we are like the rest of creation. According to the Eastern doctrine of "dharma," we are each called upon to achieve a particular life-pattern. And while all patterns have equal dignity, each one of us should avail himself or herself of the possibility that is uniquely one's own and not someone else's. Each of us should try to discover the pattern and cooperate with its realization. . . . Our entire life's purpose is already present within us, and, furthermore, at each stage of our life there are subordinate purposes—steps along the way toward the fulfillment of our ideal pattern. (Ferrucci, 1982, p. 164)

The unfolding of Self in the world begins at birth, moves through the tremendous growth of infancy and childhood, the challenges of adulthood, and continues into old age and death. Each person's unique life purpose finds expression through interacting with the culture and its expectations and demands. It responds to the changing conditions and needs of our bodies and personalities. We may become conscious of our life purpose and pattern at some level, or it may remain entirely within the unconscious, guiding us without our conscious participation.

When we awaken in some way to our potential and to the possibility of cooperating consciously with our unfolding, we embark on an adventure of discovery, struggle and fulfillment. Any counseling or therapy we seek in the process needs to be seen as only a part of this long journey of a lifetime. We may seek help with a specific step we need to take, but the larger context must be honored, for our life purpose and pattern may require that our immediate plans be adapted to it.

Each of our lives is a mystery which we can only unravel for ourselves. None of us, including those in the helping professions, is an infallible judge of human process. We can understand models of human functioning and apply them to various situations. We may have overviews of the stages of life and growth which most of us go through. We can have insights into the problems and needs of others, sometimes quite accurate insights. But we cannot fathom the deepest purposes of others' lives; often we do not fathom our own. Each of us must take responsibility for unraveling the mystery of our own lives, leaving to others the final responsibility for unraveling theirs. This includes our spouses, children, and clients. We can share our search with each another, we can help each another, but we cannot presume to have ultimate knowledge of each other's purposes and right directions.

As guides we undertake to facilitate our clients' journeys of unfolding. If we can see our role as a tiny part of a larger mystery, we will approach our work with humility and with open minds. We will regard each step in the process in terms of its place in the whole. Individuals with outwardly similar 'symptoms' may be facing very different challenges, depending upon their life stage (adolescence, midlife, aging) or their progress through the whole process of psychosynthesis. Are they working with integrating personality elements or are they engaged in an experience of the Higher Self? The overviews offered below of the long-term process of psychosynthesis and the stages of human life may contribute to our ability as guides to understand where our clients are and what their next steps may be.

PHASES OF PSYCHOSYNTHESIS

Psychosynthesis often proceeds through similar phases. Although the content of those phases will differ from person to person, the dynamics frequently follow a pattern. The guide may play different roles and use different methods with clients in different phases. The description of these phases which follows should be taken only as a general indication of what may occur with various clients. Once again, the map is not the territory. Each of us is unique in our unfolding and should not be expected to fit any preconceived patterns or norms.

Imbedded Consciousness

When we operate with minimal self-awareness and choice, we are caught in what Duane Elkins (1979) calls "imbedded consciousness." In this state, we experience ourselves as buffeted by the winds of fortune, victims of circumstances with relatively little power to control our destinies. When we get sick, we believe our bodies have been invaded by 'germs' which must be destroyed by medical interventions. When we are injured, we think it's bad luck. We take our feelings and thoughts at face value and seldom question their source within us. "Anyone would feel this way in this situation!" is our protest if challenged. We are identified with our thoughts, our feelings, our sensations and desires. We think that's who we are, without choice or possibility for anything else unless the externals change. We are attached to our possessions, our opinions, and our roles, afraid that if we lose anything, we will lose ourselves.

We all spend a certain amount of time in this state of imbedded consciousness. Some spend their whole lives here; for what purpose we can only guess. When we guide people in this state, we work primarily for the most basic self-awareness and seek ways of facilitating experiences of choice. Biofeedback training may help establish a sense of control. We may be fairly directive in suggesting ways of resolving some conflicts in order to clear the way for self-discovery to begin.

Personal Psychosynthesis

When we are caught in imbedded consciousness, often something happens—a crisis, a life change, a peak experience—and we are eased or jolted into a process of growth, awareness, and choice. We begin to move towards what Elkins calls "self-reflective consciousness." Now we deliberately begin a process of self-discovery in one form or another, with the help of a guide, through a workshop or class, by reading, and/or by conversations with friends. We become increasingly responsible for and in control of our destinies. We become disidentified from the changing contents of our consciousness and detached from possessions, opinions, and roles, a process which allows us increasing power and freedom (Elkins, 1979). This is the first major phase in psychosynthesis: personal psychosynthesis.

The first step is usually the development of an Observer; a perspective from which we can observe ourselves, our feelings, thoughts, images, sensations, desires, and behaviors. From this perspective, we can become aware of ourselves and our patterns of reactions and behaviors *without judgment*, without attempting to improve ourselves or 'make it better.' We simply notice what is going on, inside and out. An exercise which is useful in building this perspective follows.

EXERCISE: THE EVENING REVIEW

This exercise is best done as the last thing in the day. Just before going to sleep, review your day in your mind, playing it back like a movie, only backwards, beginning with where you are right now, then the time of late evening, then the time of early evening, then the dinner hour, the afternoon, and so on until the morning when you awakened.

You may use this review to examine yourself, *without judgment*, and your life as a whole or you may focus on some aspect of yourself, on some pattern you would like to know more about, on some specific inner process you may want to explore. The *attitude* with which you do the review is most important. When you examine your day, do it as much as possible as a detached, non-judgmental observer, calmly and clearly registering each phase of what has happened. Then move on to the next phase without excitement, without becoming elated at an apparent success or depressed and down on yourself about an apparent failure or mistake. The aim is a *calm registering in consciousness of the meaning and patterns of the day*, rather than a reliving of it.

As you review the day, you also have the opportunity to observe your immediate reactions to the review: judgments, emotions, regrets, and hopes. Allow these responses to register calmly as well.

This exercise may be combined with the Identification Exercise found elsewhere in this book. It may be useful to write down your observations together with any insights or impressions that come, as part of your personal journal. By reviewing entries recorded over a period of time, you may observe patterns not otherwise apparent.

The Observer is an aspect of the self, but not synonymous with the self because it lacks *will*. It is a step on the path of deepening awareness, of learning to look upon one's personality with compassions and patience, in all its facets. In developing our Observer, we cultivate a receptive, non-judgmental attitude towards our experience and behavior. We learn to listen, really listen, to our various parts: body, feelings, and mind. We begin to disidentify from those parts, even as we notice them more keenly, for the Observer cannot be fully identified with what is observed. We must move a step away from the contents of our experience to notice what they are; that step is towards 'center,' towards the self.

With the Observer comes self-acceptance, the acceptance which is so vital to growth. This is a timeless paradox: unless I *accept* who, what, and where I am, I cannot change. Self-acceptance is far easier once we remove the self-judgment and begin to look at ourselves dispassionately. I had a powerful experience of this once, when I was feeling particularly depressed, worthless, and physically debilitated. I remembered a technique which had been suggested to me in a workshop: to think of myself in the third person. So I began to do so: "Molly is really feeling bad today," I observed out loud to myself. "She has a stomach ache, it's too hot, and she feels pretty worthless, too." Suddenly I was overwhelmed with a feeling of compassion and loving acceptance for this person I was observing, a feeling that I had previously reserved for my children. I knew for a moment that the person with all those feelings was indeed as a child in relation to my self, a child to be loved, sympathized with, occasionally directed firmly, and above all, accepted. For Molly is only my personality; in that moment I identified with my personal self.

Beneficial changes may spontaneously occur as a result of self-observation and acceptance alone. Many effective therapies, Carl Rogers' client-centered counseling in particular, are based on this phenomenon. Developing the Observer allows us to address the first major question in the process of psychosynthesis: where am I now in my life? (See the discussion of this in Chapter 6.) It may be the hardest task in overall personal psychosynthesis because it is such a basic shift in consciousness and perspective from imbedded consciousness. It opens the door for insight and the mobilization of the will.

The development of the Observer can be facilitated by active listening on the part of the guide, feeding back to the individual his expressed feelings and attitudes. The guide acts as a mirror, enabling the client to see his or her behavior and its undercurrents reflected back without judgment. Phrases such as 'notice what happens' or 'take a look at how you feel' or 'observe what comes up in response to this' encourage the Observer perspective. The use of the third person as mentioned above can be suggested in a session. The evening review can be assigned as homework between sessions. Probably most important in the development of the Observer in a client is the guide's own ability to model a non-judgmental, non-attached attitude towards him or herself as well as towards the client.

Once the Observer is operating, the second major step in personal psychosynthesis can begin: the various subpersonalities and aspects of the personality are balanced and harmonized around the personal self. Often this starts with our recognizing and working with a particularly troublesome subpersonality (as described in Chapters 3 and 5). Polarized subpersonalities emerge and are gradually integrated. We may begin to recognize patterns of emotional or mental behavior which can be transformed into more creative and constructive ways of functioning. An overly mental person may explore a greater range of emotional awareness and expression, while an emotionally identified person may begin to develop mental capacities. This phase continues on as the next stages begin. Clearly, personality integration is a long-term task, although we may reach a plateau from time to time when our level of integration is sufficient for awhile for our purpose and work. Then new challenges are encountered once again that demand new levels of integration of the personality. The clients in Transcripts A and B are confronting this kind of demand.

Personality integration is reflected in the remaining questions of the psychosynthesis process: what is my potential? what is getting in my way? what qualities do I need to develop? We take increasing responsibility for our life direction, for transforming our blocks into constructive energies, and for developing whatever qualities and patterns are needed for continued

"In the first stage of wakening . . . the client may need to get in touch with the body, with feelings, and with the deep intuitions which influence his/her choices. The process is essentially one of becoming self-conscious, of owning one's senses, emotions and thoughts, and taking responsibility for them. Initially it may be important to simply tune in to the inner awareness of sensations, feelings, and conditioned patterns of thought forms. At this stage, the work may focus on self-acceptance." (Vaughan-Clark, 1977, p.75) growth. We identify increasingly with the personal self and let go of our identifications with externals and with parts of ourselves.

At first, the process of psychosynthesis may focus on the *content* of personality change, on what we find uncomfortable or obstructive to our progress. Gradually, however, our attention may shift to *what is making the changes*, to our experience of the will and the personal self. We identify with the self and begin to 'train' our will, finding out how we have been inhibited and enslaved in the past and how to free ourselves now to take charge. We develop 'intentionality' and 'responsibility.' We discover a deeper sense of selfhood. This phase continues on also through the following phases, because we constantly learn more about the subtleties of will, such as moving ahead by letting go, the power of trust and belief, the interplay of strong will, skillful will, and good will, the synthesis of love and will.

The role of the guide in personality integration and the development of the will involve more than listening and mirroring. The whole range of active techniques described in Chapter 5 may be employed. The content of sessions will center on identifying desired changes, discovering and transforming blocks, and developing desired qualities. The dynamics will tend increasingly to evoke responsibility for the growth process from the client, both during and between sessions. The guide will move gradually from the role of teacher and leader of sessions to that of a resource and traveling companion.

As our personality becomes increasingly integrated and under the direction of the will, we can open ourselves more freely to superconscious energies and patterns which heretofore were too powerful for us to handle. Now they, too, can become integrated and expressed in our personalities. This phase, illustrated in Transcript B, is an interface between personal and spiritual psychosynthesis. During it, we become more conscious of our potential, discovering creative capacities, higher feelings, and wisdom we never before suspected we had. We have more frequent 'peak experiences.' We begin a process of spiritual awakening.

Spiritual Psychosynthesis

The phases of spiritual psychosynthesis overlap personal psychosynthesis. Each time we identify with the pure awareness and the will of the personal self, we are aligned with its Source, the Higher Self. Although we may not know it directly, our awareness is infused with its clarity and love. Our choices are more effective and harmonious, because they are aligned with the Transpersonal Will. The inflow of superconscious energies and patterns also open our eyes to a larger reality. We have glimpses of yet another level of consciousness, that which Elkins calls "unitive consciousness."

We begin, in small steps, to *use* our personality to express some of the qualities we experience in ourselves. Rather than seeing our personality as existing purely for itself, we recognize its value as an instrument for spiritual evolution in the world. We commit the personality to the expression of the highest potentials of the Self, and work to expand its capacity to fulfill this role. It is this commitment which the client undertakes in Transcript C.

Gradually and increasingly, we are able to identify ourselves with the Higher Self, to know Who we really are. Often we choose a religious form through which to celebrate this identification, but one of the characteristics of this phase is lack of dogmatism. We accept the value of other religious forms and see them all as expressions of the same Truth. We become increasingly dedicated to service of humanity and of the planet through whatever unique capacities we as Selves have chosen.

Assagioli (1977) describes this on-going phase in this way:

Thus one can anticipate and have an increasing foretaste of the state of consciousness of the Self-realized individual. It is a state of consciousness characterized by joy, serenity, inner security, a sense of calm power, clear understanding, and radiant love. In its highest aspects, it is the realization of essential Being, or communion and identification with the Universal Life (p. 171).

The role of the guide in spiritual psychosynthesis was discussed in the previous chapter. It is based upon an attitude of respect and trust in the process, and loving support for the client. It is enhanced by the guide's own work of spiritual unfolding.

These then are phases a person may pass through in the course of a lifetime or in the course of working with a guide. Actually, once an individual is committed to personal growth, he or she may experience repeating cycles of these phases, each time on a higher turn of the spiral of growth. So although it often seems that we go through the same kinds of problems and crises over and over again, closer examination may reveal that we are working through a higher level of those problems each time (unless, of course, we stubbornly refused to learn anything from the previous time around). I know from the often painful experiences of my own life how I must return again and again to developing my Observer, to integrating my subpersonalities and my body, feelings, and mind, to identifying once more with my personal self and exercising my will in more skillful and loving ways.

THE SEASONS OF LIFE

We also grow through interplay with our culture and the expectations which our culture has for us at different stages of our lives. Young people are expected to be engaged in education, for example, while 'old folks' are supposed to be content in rocking chairs. It is nearly impossible to resist these expectations; they influence (if not determine) how we grow and change throughout our lives. Yet individual needs may differ from this stereotyped pattern. Many retired people find a renewed interest in education and creative work and may have to struggle against the preconceptions of their families and communities to pursue these interests. On the other hand, young people may choose to find a sense of self-worth and purpose in the world through travel or work rather than through formal education. They may delay college or vocational school until they feel more confident of what they want to do, in spite of the protests of their families.

In recent years, there has been an upsurge of interest in the subtleties of adult development. Life stages previously lumped into 'adulthood' and 'aging' are being studied and described. We are expanding our understanding and appreciation of human life and growth. We are beginning to realize that life *is* growth, that learning continues throughout our lives, that we never 'arrive.' The various life stages are times of focused learning in one area or another. The so-called midlife crisis which now appears in the popular media is an example of such a time of focused learning. The reason it is often a crisis is because many people have become set in their ways and resist the inevitable demands of change. When we actively resist growing, we can create crisis and pain for ourselves and those around us.

Stages seem to occur, however, whether or not we cooperate with growth. When we do cooperate, they may be less painful and we may move through them more quickly. Then again, we may not, because our life purpose may require special attention to one developmental stage or another, to intensify our learning in that area.

A Map of Life Stages

In a training seminar in 1978, Tom Yeomans outlined the common developmental stages of life from a psychosynthesis perspective. Along with the phases of psychosynthesis outlined before, this map of life stages can guide our work with clients and help identify the challenges they may be facing because of their time of life.

From birth to age five, approximately, the personality moves from a state of undifferentiated unity with the Higher Self to separation and the beginnings of personal identity. At this stage, the body is the locus of identification; now more than at any time in our lives, what happens to our bodies happens to our most basic sense of self. We grapple with issues of sensation and movement, nurturance, survival, infant sexuality, and control.

During the rest of the first decade of life we cope with issues of coordination, subtle movement, and the beginnings of guilt and shame. We begin to move into identification with our feelings and lessen our identification with our bodies. We begin to experience mastery over at least some aspects of our world.

As we move into adolescence, the issues become more complex. In addition to concerns about guilt and shame, we begin to experience 'big' feelings, like love, hate, righteous indignation, and yearnings for a sense of meaning. Peer relations become paramount. Later we move toward the more subtle variations of the 'big' feelings we felt early on. Our mind becomes increasingly important to us and we move toward identification with it. During this time, the Higher Self may move to contact our consciousness and we may have religious or mystic experiences. We increasingly seek a sense of personal integrity and control, often rebelling openly against the values and demands of our parents.

Then we grow into young adulthood, in our late teens and early twenties. If we have lived in a nurturing, supportive atmosphere, we may readily integrate our body, feelings and mind into a balanced, effective personality. We develop a strong sense of 'I,' of personal identity. Our concrete and abstract thinking develops. We begin to experience true self-awareness, as opposed to the self-consciousness of adolescence. Our intuition may become an important function for us at this stage. As our Higher Self expands its influence upon us, we may experience a sense of its demands upon us in the form of strange yearnings and ambitions or religious promptings. In our later twenties we usually situate ourselves in a profession and with a long-term partner. We may also begin our families during this time.

During our thirties we continue to integrate our personalities around the personal self which becomes a stronger part of our conscious experience. We develop a sense of purpose. Our values become less rigid and yet at the same time stronger and clearer. As we move into our forties and fifties, the Higher Self increases its influence and our personality may become infused with superconscious energies. Because of this, the forties are often times of crisis as the personality struggles to encompass these powerful forces. This is the time of the existential crisis and the crisis of duality discussed in Chapter 2. If we are able to work through these dilemmas, we begin to truly express our Self in our lives and work.

Then we begin to experience the inexorable forces of aging. True, these forces are not so devastating as it used to be believed. We have found that attitude and beliefs about ourselves can either hurry or delay the outward signs of aging. Nevertheless, the latter third of life becomes a time of reflection upon the whole mystery of life, upon ultimate meanings and perennial truths. By now the Higher Self may be expressing fully through the personality, and the personal self may be experienced as an agent of that higher Source. As we move toward our time of death, we grapple with issues of acceptance and surrender. We increasingly experience our at-onement with the Higher Self and with all of creation.

Death, at whatever age it occurs, is our final stage of growth. Within the last decade, Americans have suddenly discovered that in death there is potential for growth and even for joy. This discovery has been guided by a few pioneers such as Elizabeth Kubler-Ross (1975) who through their work with dying patients have witnessed transformation at the very end of life and in the lives of those supporting the dying person. Death is our final opportunity to awaken to who we really are, to discover the rich Source of love, will, and joy within us. No matter at what age death occurs, it rounds out a whole life, complete and perfect unto itself, and allows those still living an opportunity to connect with their wholeness and perfection. Because others have written on this subject with beauty, power, and authority, I will not attempt to summarize their work, but refer interested readers to the bibliography at the end of the chapter. I urge anyone who works with others to read, study, and meditate on the meaning and potential of death and of the dying process.

Yeomans' outline of life stages considers the development and integration of the personality, the awakening of the self, and the increasing influence and infusion of the Higher Self. It is based more on relationships within the individual than on the relationships with family, job and community with which other outlines are concerned. Upon examination, however, there appear many parallels between the more popular models (referenced at the end of the chapter) and this one from psychosynthesis thought.

Each individual has unique challenges and purposes in life, yet all lives tend to follow some basic patterns, determined by biology, culture and the unconscious. When we look at an individual, descriptions such as the one above may provide a point of reference for the challenges the individual may be facing. It is often comforting for people to know that their crises are part of a larger, common pattern, and not purely the result of personal malfunction. They can see their problems as integral to life and growth and find support from others facing the same challenges. We must remember, however, to recognize the uniqueness of each individual side by side with his or her participation in cultural patterns and to honor each person's own process and time clock.

Patterns, Cycles and Evolution

In guiding others, we serve their ability to cooperate with their unfolding when we offer them ways to understanding the cycles and stages of growth. Here is a role for the mind: to observe one's own process in the light of basic principles.

One of these principles is that growth and change usually occur through cycles of disintegration (when old patterns of behavior cease to 'work'), expansion (when we seek new solutions, knowledge, alternatives), and integration (when we incorporate our new knowledge into a working system). Although there are degrees of intensity of this process, it seems necessary that we break down old forms (though not the value and truth within them) in order to move into new, expanded forms of thought and behavior. For example, a woman's image of herself as a perfect mother might have to be shaken before she can open to new ways of being with her children. She might come to understand that she does not have to reject all of her past mothering behavior and wisdom; one behavior, such as cuddling, will remain under new guidelines. She only needs to let go of a rigid form which does not allow for new possibilities. We must have an unstable system for energy to flow through, and unstable systems are prone to disintegration when sufficient energy shoots through them. But all is not lost. The parts are still there, albeit scattered and disorganized. They will come together into a new pattern, temporarily stable as it now can accommodate the demands upon it. Later this new pattern, too, will disintegrate in the face of other demands and stresses, in order to be able to reorganize once again. It is an unnerving process for all of us and can create fear and resistance in clients who do not understand it. We can help them make peace with this cyclical process as they look back over their lives and notice its recurrence. They may then develop an attitude of acceptance and learn skills for cooperating with the process.

Growth is cyclical and it is also spiral: each succeeding cycle moves to a higher level of integration and understanding, if growth has occurred. When clients are confronted again and again with the same issues, they may despair of ever learning. The truth is that we do learn; we have learned. Our previous learning is so integrated into our life that we are no longer immediately aware that we were ever any different. But we were, and each new cycle of learning is indeed a higher level of understanding of the same principle.

Throughout common life stages discussed above, we can see this spiral process at work. An example might be the struggle to find an inner locus of control which begins in the teens. We undertake this task in an environment of peer pressure and concern about what others think of us. We also have to cope with parental values and rules from which we strive to liberate ourselves without breaking the bond of nurturance we still need. Later, as adults in the workplace, we may find ourselves facing the same issue of self-determination and internal authority when we question the values of our supervisors or fellow workers. When we are sick we once again discover the need to rely on our inner knowledge of ourselves as we consult with physicians. Again and again, throughout life, we encounter situations in which we are tempted to let others lead us away from the path of our own values and inner purpose. Each time we encounter such a situation, however, we have the opportunity to strengthen our commitment to abide by our own authority.

Life transitions are always occurring; we are always progressing through a process of growth and learning. Crises are times of 'intensified' changes, often marked by an external shift: departures, moves, death, job changes, illness, marriage, divorce etc. They are times when many people seek counseling. 'External' changes are analogs for our internal emergence into ever-new patterns of living. Perhaps one of the most difficult principles to grasp in our own lives is that crises occur from within. No matter what happens outside, it is our *reaction* to events which determines whether they are crises. Illness and even accidents do not strike without some degree of receptivity or vulnerability on the part of the organism. Job change, marriage and divorce take place with considerable involvement of the individual, although we may have avoided noticing the early signs of an impending change so that it may seem to be totally unexpected. We may not have been conscious of the factors leading up to a crisis, but they were there all the same.

By exploring the images we hold, the actions we take, and our subtle communications and interactions with our environment, we can discover how we influence—even determine—what happens to us. We can see that changes in external situations reflect inner attitudes and changes. To the extent that we become conscious of this complex process and make choices about our participation, we can transcend conditioning from our past and from television, radio, advertising, social demands, and all the other environmental factors. We can create our lives and our realities. Helping others to do this is central to evolutionary guiding.

Just as we can regard dream figures as subpersonalities and work with them as such, we can discover different aspects of ourselves, of our conscious and unconscious personality in events and figures in our external lives. We can become aware of the significance and meaning of events in our lives, and use them to grow more whole and balanced. We can ask why we have drawn an event to us and what its message is. We can respond to and grow from life's events, rather than merely trying to survive them. By suggesting this perspective to clients, we help them to develop a sense of their own choice in what happens in their lives.

Teaching is a vital part of guiding. We can help our clients to discover these principles of life development for themselves by exploring their life experience with them. Books can also be helpful; the concepts encountered can be discussed and applied to specific situations during sessions. I believe that one of our major tasks as guides is to educate our communities in healthy attitudes toward the whole life process. We can do this one by one, for everyone has friends and family who will eventually notice changed behavior and discuss new ideas which emerge from the individual's work.

Recently a respected British plant physiologist, Rupert Sheldrake, proposed a hypothesis which could account for the rapid spread of new ideas and attitudes within a culture or a species. He suggests that all systems may be regulated not only by known energy and material factors, but also by invisible organizing fields. He calls these hidden 'blueprints' morphogenetic fields. An "M-field" is changed whenever a significant number of individuals in a species learn a new behavior. As the field changes, so do the members of the species regulated by it. Thus the M-field creates us and we can in turn create or at least transform our own M-field. As more and more people develop healthy attitudes toward the life process and put them into effect in their lives, what a transformation can result! So much human potential which now lies fallow for lack of appreciation and nurturance could become available for cooperative creation of a peaceful, prosperous, and harmonious world. If Sheldrake is right, we need only educate a critical number; then the whole species will be transformed.

GUIDING ONESELF

The process of Self-realization is ongoing, whether or not we are working with a guide or teacher. Working with a guide is helpful, sometimes essential, but not always. Psychosynthesis guiding seeks to place increasing responsibility for growth and transformation on the individual to the point when he or she no longer needs regular sessions. Psychosynthesis becomes a process in which an individual is consciously and constantly engaged. From time to time he or she may choose to have a session with one or another guide, or with some kind of therapist or teacher. The individual is the one making the 'diagnosis' and choosing the appropriate action. The individual is the real guide of his or her psychosynthesis.

I see this as one of my major responsibilities as a guide: to teach my clients to become their own guides, sharing with them specific tools and concepts they need to do this. Most of the methods and exercises suggested in this book can be used in just this way. Perhaps more important than the specific exercises, however, are the basic inner attitudes which facilitate self-guidance. Disidentification from the aspects of our personalities and identification with the self are essential. A sense of personal responsibility and power is another ingredient. An inner alignment and attunement to the Higher Self, and the Universal Self beyond, allows self-guidance to come from our highest wisdom and to be in harmony with planetary needs. Grounding that alignment in a sense of personal purpose and in appropriate choices and goals contributes to the tangible expression of Self-realization in daily life. With these attitudes and orientations, we can choose from various methods and exercises and create new ones as needed.

Some Personal Notes

Since my first intensive study of psychosynthesis in 1971, it has formed the framework of my personal life philosophy. It has also served as a base from which I can explore other philosophical and psychological perspectives. Far from limiting me to one point of view, psychosynthesis has challenged me to seek truth everywhere, in all systems and schools of thought. At the same time, I have been able to relate what I learn to the basic framework of psychosynthesis; often I find a direct correspondance in concept, model, and technique. At other times, a writer or teacher will stimulate me to expand some aspect of my basic framework, integrate new vocabulary, or seek a synthesis between what I consider 'standard psychosynthesis theory' and some new element. I have found very little in psychosynthesis thought which I need to discard altogether, although others may have. In my philosophical search for truth and understanding, psychosynthesis has enabled me to be my own guide.

On a more practical level, I use specific methods and general models of psychosynthesis to resolve my own life dilemmas and to guide my choices. When confused and upset, I use the Identification Exercise (Chapter 2) to calm and center myself. When in conflict, I often engage the inner combatants in dialogue, seeking their needs and potentials as subpersonalities. I use imagery, sometimes in the form of drawing, to discover answers to questions about what is going on in my life and how I can best respond. I use creative meditation on a daily basis. Far beyond the usefulness of psychosynthesis as a bag of tricks for counseling is its value for me as a unifying process which facilitates meaning, clarity, and joy in my daily life. Psychosynthesis has enabled me to guide my own life and growth in cooperation with my friends, guides, and colleagues.

At times I have skidded into True Believer behavior, advocating Psychosynthesis as the end-all and be-all for everyone. Psychosynthesis with a capital 'P' is not a panacea because its metaphors and language will not suit everyone nor facilitate growth for everyone. When I am a True Believer, I am identified with *form*, with a party line. That's a danger in any system of human endeavor, and Psychosynthesis is not exempt. At such times, something usually jostles me out of that identification, often painfully, kicking and screaming. After I let go, however, I find myself renewed at the *well-springs* of psychosynthesis: the essential, pre-verbal principles which underlie psychosynthesis and *every other* philosophical-psychological-religious system in the world. I appreciate on another level, then, the richness of psychosynthesis and its contribution to the evolution of humanity. I find myself wanting to share psychosynthesis with the many people who can learn and grow within this framework. At the same time, I experience unity with followers of other paths to the same truth, and am content to trust their choices.

Psychosynthesis is a description of the process of life when it is undertaken in conscious cooperation with growth and purpose. This process often proceeds through certain stages, from the development of the Observer to an identification with the Higher Self and a commitment to Self-expression and service. Psychosynthesis proceeds through the stages of our lives as well, from infancy and childhood through the challenges of adulthood, midlife, aging, and death.

As human beings we all share the common purpose of Self-realization, which also means the realization of our 'collective Self,' the group Self of humanity. As individual Higher Selves we create lives—bodies and personalities—through which to learn and evolve. As group Selves, we create families, societies, and cultures through which to learn and evolve. The same principles underlie all levels of our unfolding, individually and collectively. That which furthers the evolution of the individual furthers the evolution of family, community, society and ultimately humanity.

Psychosynthesis is a process we are all in together. In guiding, an appreciation of our partnership with one another in our collective evolution is essential. The roles of guide and client are seen as interchangeable from this perspective. Sometimes I seek guidance from another; sometimes I am able to offer guidance. Whichever role I assume, I am participating with another person in our mutual Self-realization and in the Self-realization of humanity. Moreover, from this same perspective we see that counseling is not only for somebody else—the troubled and disturbed or the affluent self-indulgent. Seeking guidance is a sign of responsible mental health for ourselves and for our families and communities. It is a contribution to planetary evolution. If we are to be effective in our work with others on this task, we must begin by transforming ourselves. None of the techniques or models described in this book are of any value if applied by a counselor or therapist who has not first used them for his or her own self-discovery. Let us begin with ourselves; then share with others, our clients, families and friends. The transformation will spread inevitably from our work, energized and guided by our collective Higher Self.

Psychosynthesis guiding is aligned with the larger movement in the world toward conscious evolution and planetary stewardship. If we are to survive as a species, we must recognize and act upon our interdependence with one another and with our planet. We must accept and develop our vast, unexpressed potential, individually and together. We must transform the patterns of fear and doubt which hold us back from being all we can be for ourselves and for our world. The task of transformation begins within the heart and mind of each one of us.

BIBLIOGRAPHY FOR LIFE STAGES

Bolles, F. *The three boxes of life*. Berkeley, Calif.: Ten Speed Press, 1978.

Bridges, W. *Transitions: making sense of life's changes*. Reading, Mass.: Addison-Wesley, 1980.

Erickson, E. *Childhood and society*. New York: W. W. Norton, 1950.

Gould, R. L. *Transformations*. New York: Simon and Shuster, 1978.

Kubler-Ross, E. *On death and dying*. New York: MacMillan, 1974.

Kubler-Ross, E. *Death—The final stage of growth*. Englewood Cliffs, NJ: Prentice Hall, 1975.

Levine, S. *Who dies?* Garden City, New York: Anchor/Doubleday, 1982.

Levinson, D. et al. *The seasons of a man's life*. New York: Ballentine, 1979.

McLeish, J. A. B. *The Ulyssean adult*. New York: McGraw-Hill Ryerson, 1976.

Sheehy, G. *Passages*. New York: E. P. Dutton, 1974.

Sheehy, G. *Pathfinders*. Toronto, New York: Bantam, 1981.

Washbourne, P. *Becoming woman: the quest for spiritual wholeness in female experience*. New York: Harper & Row, 1979.

Washbourne, P. *Seasons of woman*. New York: Harper & Row, 1979.

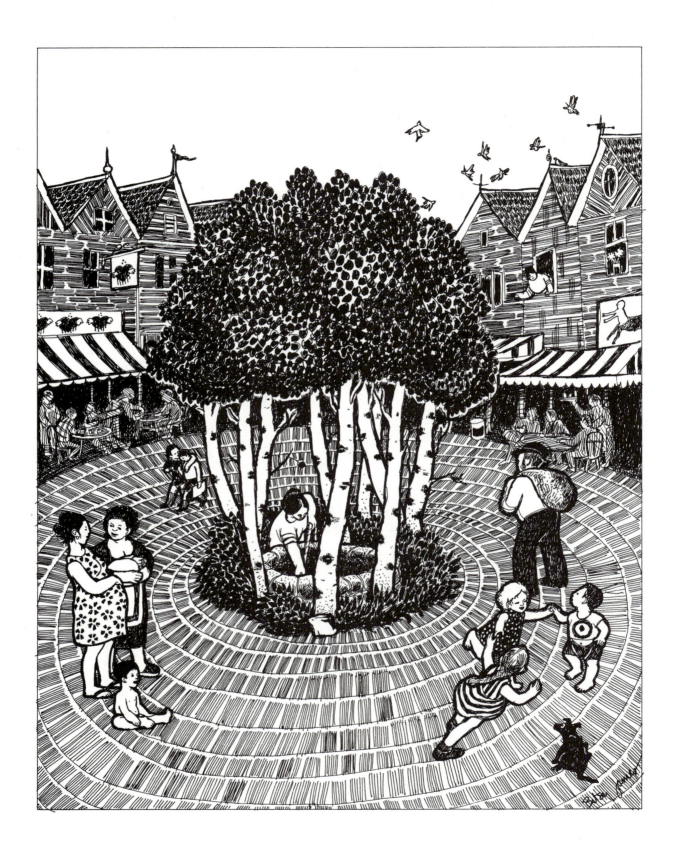

TRANSCRIPTS OF SESSIONS

These transcripts demonstrate the psychosynthesis approach with clients who have a relatively high degree of self-awareness and facility with imagery and inner dialogue. The sessions were chosen to illustrate optimal guiding; with many clients, the work would proceed more slowly.

The author is the guide in Transcripts A and B. Harry Sloan is the guide in Transcript C.

Comments in the margin indicate major steps in the process and suggest the guide's abstractions and plan. The four questions referenced are the four steps or cycles of a session discussed in Chapter 6.

TRANSCRIPT A

In this session the client explores her lack of direction and accomplishment, a self-evaluation based more on the imagined opinions of others than on objective facts. She would like to feel well-trained, competent, and successful in some specific field of healing. What seems to be holding her back is a sense of pushing against other people's imagined judgments. As she explores this experience, she discovers a needy subpersonality who seems to have much to offer her, and makes a commitment to spend more time with this part of herself.

C: I think if I told you a couple of experiences that happened to me last week, it would help clarify my feelings for me, too.

I met a woman again whom I had previously met who has moved out here from Los Angeles, as I did. I guess she must be around my age—I just met her on the street the other day. She was asking for directions and she is going around looking for a job. I had heard through a mutual friend of ours that she is really gung-ho about getting a well-paying, highly qualified job here. And I thought, more power to her. (laugh) And I met her and I talked with her a little bit and she said she spruced up her resume and she told me about the places she had been around to. I had this feeling I was really rooting for her and at the same time I was wondering why, somehow, I am comparing myself to her. And I fall very short in my eyes in terms of—oh—confidence, aggressiveness, and somehow financial earning ability. All this stuff is going around in my head. Why can't I be more like her? (pause)

Well, that is the main one that comes out.

Yeah, and the feeling that I am moving more in the direction of what I came here for, in terms of this job. I feel that I have learned a lot from these people just by osmosis and I can be a good liaison between them and the public. And yet, it is still survival and kind of—moan, groan—getting a job here and getting a job there and learning. I feel like there are two things: learning to relax into it and watch it all work out, because it always has in the past; but that voice seems to get drowned out by the other one that says— "Well, here I am, I have had blah, blah, blah education, and this, this, this experience. Why am I in the situation I'm in?"—maybe financially uncomfortable, but also I have a need for, I think, more authority and recognition in my work and more confidence and just room to move ahead.

exploring question #1: where am I now?

When I say that, it sounds like I really know what I want to do! But at the same time I feel like I don't. It's a real split.

G: Well, it sounds like you do know what you want to do in qualitative terms.

C: Yeah, but in detail no.

moving to question #2: what's my next step?

G: So what would you like to see happen?

C: Oh, other than that . . .

G: You said that there were a couple of things.

C: Yeah. The other thing is that I look around at some of these people that I will be working with, or even the people that are going to Canyon School and a few of my friends, and I see that we are all about the same age—some of them are a bit older.

Well, I look at where they are in their lives. I think in terms of them really being experts in their field, or so they claim to be and so people see them as being. And I don't feel like I have that expertise in a particular subject. I think my strengths lie, at this point—I have to see my strengths lying somewhere else, because I haven't trained in a particular discipline. You know, I am not up there teaching connective tissue polarity or doing acupuncture. Of course, then if I really stop to consider, a lot of them are ten or fifteen years older than I and in that time, you know . . .

G: You could have . . .

C: I perceive myself . . .

more on question 2

G: Decided to do that and gone ahead.

C: But, I feel like I am in this space here and they are in that space there. It is that kind of feeling of . . .

G: So you said you saw your strengths lying elsewhere. Where do you see your strengths?

emphasizing potential

C: Well, one example is that since I have come here I seem to have made many, many friends, and brought a lot of different groups of people together, either in my home or just through contacts. And that is something I enjoy, and it is something that just seems to come naturally. But that is like a quality. That is, right at this point, I am not earning a living by doing that (laugh) . . .

G: You could open a dating service! (joining in relieving laughter together)

C: Yeah, I've always had this kind of feeling of—What did they use to do, I guess it used to be a long time ago, where someone would open up their home or salon and they would have all these different people come and discuss things. Do you know what I mean?

G: Yeah.

C: That idea. That has always appealed to me. I really like that. I think I can carry some of that over into my job now.

G: It sounds like you can.

C: And build on that. But I feel like I somehow need to have more of an entrepreneur quality. Some people I have met here seem to look at an opportunity, or see a situation and they really can build upon it, expand it, and really make it work for them. And I feel like I am just learning those skills. Somewhere along the line, I came upon them kind of late. I don't know. Maybe . . .

G: At least later than you'd like to have. So you are comparing yourself to other people, seeing areas where you see yourself falling short in terms of having a well-paid, well-recognized type of job.

C: And really making conscious efforts to also recognize my strengths and those other qualities. I really, I *see* myself doing that right now.

G: There are questions coming up for me. One is, what's getting in the way? But it seems like before we get to that question we really should spend a little more time looking at what is the potential, that you see as possible for yourself—possible, but that you are not doing somehow.

margin: more on question 2 before exploring blocks

C: I just had another thought come up. I have been having acupuncture with this fellow and last time we did a little counseling session because I found that the acupuncture has really worked on my emotions a lot. It had a lot of expression of emotion, both anger and sadness. I went through a lot of crying and I talked with him about that. I had a feeling in my chest of tension and sadness. And I had an image come up for me which was in a dark foresty setting and it was a witch. I knew that she was a healing witch.

G: Huh!

C: Because she had something like a crystal ball or something in her hand. I couldn't really get a clear image of her or see her face at that time, but I know that she is part of me. She is a part I am not making contact with right now very well. I don't quite understand what she is, but at least I feel I have the image now and it is going to be easier to find out. I really have the feeling that it had to do with healing and somehow I'm not making use of that tool, or of that potential. But I am getting really racked up in judgments of myself that I could be up there studying at one of those schools. Why am I not? Or do I really need to be, even?

G: Is that the direction or path for you?

C: I came here with the expectation of studying at one of those schools and it didn't materialize. I made the choice not to so far. And I still think I am dealing with that original expectation that I came with, that I have come here to study at one of these schools.

I am studying from all the people that I have met. They have brought me all kinds of things that I didn't realize were here when I came. I think it's kind of giving up the idea that you have to be able to go to an institute in a building.

G: Where do you want to go from here?

margin: seeking purpose

C: Well, it is all kind of a mumble-jumble.

G: What is the strongest experience? What is the strongest feeling in this whole mumble-jumble?

(Pause)

C: Well, it is this feeling of "them" and "me" and the strongest right now is me. That's where I feel I am going to get my answers of what I need for myself—the image that I had of that healing witch. And just continuing to work through my process. It only exists in my mind. I am making up a lot of it in terms of my comparisons with other people.

intensifying awareness

G: When you said you have the experience of "me," what is that experience? What is that experiencing?

C: Well, how I am working on myself and growing through the training and psychosynthesis and through having the acupuncture done and exploring my dreams and I feel that that is the route that I am going to continue on and then my confidence and strength I think will come more and more as I understand.

trusting intuition

G: I heard you say "route that I will continue on" and I thought of the kind of "root" that a plant has. And then I thought, that's not what she said!

C: Oh, yeah. Hum.

G: The "root" of myself, instead of the path that I'm following.

C: Yeah, I like that, 'cause that's what it is like.

seeking purpose

G: Would you be willing to consult that root and see what needs to happen today in our session here?

C: (long pause, thinking, several hums)

question 3: what's in the way?

    What needs to happen in this session today? What do I need to find out? (pause) I just had this feeling that somehow I am pushing it, and I am not opening up enough to really hear what it is that I need to hear.

trusting experience

G: Would you be willing to go into that "pushing it" experience?

C: Uh-hum.

G: Allow yourself to really exaggerate that pushing.

C: I feel like I am pushing this rock, this huge boulder, and it is not going anywhere, and then it (cough) changed to a whole group of people.

G: How do you experience that with your body?

C: It's really a lot of effort, but it is not working. An obstacle or something is still there.

G: Are there any particular words that accompany that experience? What are you saying to them as you're trying to push them, push this group?

    (Pause)

C: Well, I get, "move," but that is not strong enough. It is not really that. It is almost like I am pushing them to give me space.

G: Okay. So maybe it wants to give you space.

C: "Give me space."

staying with experience

G: Allow yourself to sink into that experience. Really use the phrase "give me space," or anything else that comes. Really get into that experience.

C: Yeah, I feel like I want them to give me space but that I am pushing myself.

G: You are pushing yourself and using them as the . . .

C: Uh-huh. It is like somehow they're not really connected. I am the one that I have to deal with.

G: Keep experiencing that. Not only see yourself but really give yourself to doing that pushing. "Give me space."

encouraging conscious identification

(Pause)

C: Well, I get the feeling that it is really fruitless for me to keep doing this and I want to ask them for help.

G: Rather than asking for help, just yet, allow yourself to experience that fruitlessness. Really go into that frustration. How do you experience that?

deepening experience of subpersonality

C: I slump down. The boulder is there, or this mass of people. I'm slumped down by it.

G: What words come with that?

C: This is really hard, and I am about to give up.

G: I am about to give up?

C: Uh-hum.

G: It sounds like you haven't quite given up.

C: Unh-unh! (laugh) Not, it seems a little empty. Yeah, I feel like I am taking a rest. I am getting my second wind up. But I feel like I need to be a little bit more ingenious about how I am going to do it now. Because just pushing against this thing doesn't seem to be working.

G: What do you want? What is the want behind this pushing?

seeking the subpersonality motivation

(Pause)

C: I don't know. Am I pushing them away because I don't want them to judge me, or see me? I don't know.

G: Part of you is doing the pushing now. Allow yourself to sink into that experience. Answer directly *from that experience* Be the pushing part or the slumped-down discouraged part, either one. Allow yourself to feel your body. See what your arms are saying.

C: Well, I want to show them my strength.

G: You want them to see your strength?

C: Uh-hum.

G: And if they see your strength, then what?

C: Then I feel like they will accept me as an equal.

G: Okay. So what you are really after is acceptance.

what the subpersonality needs

C: Uh-hum. Yeah, that is how it fits.

G: Take a moment to really see if it feels like it fits. Can you imagine yourself saying to them—"I really want you to accept me" or does something else come?

C: No, it feels like there's something else there.

G: Okay.

C: Well, I got back up, and I am back with my hands against the rock and it seems to be moving now.

G: How does it feel for it to be moving?

recognition brings release

C: It feels good, it feels really . . . it's funny, it's really rolling all over the place now; it feels really like light-headed or something! It's (laugh) . . . I really see a lot of humor in it. It's like I'm not (groan) you know, really furiously pushing against this thing. And it really . . . I can feel it has a lot of energy of its own which I seem to have kind of let loose by moving it. Every once in awhile it stops and I move it again, but it seems like it is no (cough) big deal. I have this feeling that there is a very (deep-voiced) *serious* aspect of me that kind of sometimes gets in the way. But it is not real. It is not a true serious, it is a pseudo-. . .

G: Pseudo-serious.

another subpersonality

C: Pseudo-serious. And I see it coming up, or like a veil going down, or whatever. And I can almost feel it when it is happening and it's hard for me to break through that, at that moment. I can see it later, afterwards. An hour or so later, or a day or whatever. It really was kind of funny to see me with this rock (with enthusiasm)—Oh, and they changed the size of it! It became so much smaller!

G: Oh! (relief)

C: I mean it was . . . I forgot about that. There was this huge boulder I was looking at.

G: That's right. You were talking about it as a boulder. And then all of a sudden you started talking about it as a rock.

C: Then I was bigger than it! It was this thing I was pushing around real fast and I had this smile on my face. It was complete . . . something happened there in between.

guiding awareness of the process

G: Let's go back and replay it. See what made the difference.

C: I have a sense that it is when I said I wanted the acceptance from them and I wanted to see my strength—I wanted them to see my strength, too. That somehow it started to balance out in the right proportion. That I really have nothing to prove to them.

G: Somehow seeing what the motivation was, shifted that energy.

insight

C: I think it is important for me to remember that I know that that's okay. They will see me for who I am. And if I am satisfied and confident with how I am becoming, then that is all that really I need to have happen. And I don't have to . . .

grounding insight in experience

G: How do you experience that feeling, that sense of being satisfied with your own being?

C: That really feels like it needs support. (pause) I see myself sitting on that rock and I am thinking. It seems like a support, you know. If I sit on that rock, I can kind of get centered. It's funny, now it feels like it has turned almost into a friend. It has a personality whereas before it was this kind of giant.

seeking transpersonal qualities

G: Can you describe that personality? What are the qualities that it has?

C: It is where it is; it is not any place else, but right there. It has that sense of centeredness. And it is playful and relaxed and, well, 'nah!' (casually) And wise at the same time. Because I just have this feeling that if I make a connection with it, somehow the answers are going to come up through it and to me. But it definitely has . . . I really feel . . . and that was the part that surprised me the most . . . that playful quality, that kind of joyful quality that came through.

G: That's one of its most important aspects.

C: The other is there. The other strengths are there, the more solid stuff is there, but it is deeper and the quality that comes through more on the surface is the light one.

G: Would you like to sit on that rock and ask a question and see what answer comes up for you?

C: What do I need to do, to become more like you? . . . It says you are like me; you just don't see it!

question 4: what do I need to develop?

G: Would it be useful to take a few moments to experience those qualities more in yourself— the playfulness and the relaxedness and the "well, nay"?

C: Yeah.

(pause)

I have this feeling that there are part of me that are really having to make an effort to show themselves. And I don't feel that it really needs to be like that, that there should be more of a free-flowing. I am very concerned with all these other people and what they think, but they are not the ones who are going to be living my life. And somehow I shifted energy onto them that really belongs to me, to be working on my stuff. And I put it out there and it doesn't need to be out there.

insight

G: Would it be useful to imagine yourself doing that shift and see what happens when you do that, when that shift takes place-- what's going on?

exploring reactive pattern

(Pause)

C: I have this image of standing on the rock and I am reaching out to all these other people, but then I lose my balance and fall off the rock and then I am walking over to them. But the closer I get to them, the more this muddled confused feeling starts. It feels like I am losing the sureness that I had when I was back on the rock.

G: What is it that you are reaching out to them for? What is the energy of that reaching out?

C: It feels like for approval.

G: That experience of reaching out for approval, how do you feel that?

staying with experience

C: It feels very draining.

G: Where do you get the energy for that?

C: The energy to reach out for the approval?

G: Yes, or the impulse.

C: I can feel that feeling through here again and it is not deeply rooted. I can feel that band running across here (indicates chest).

G: Allow yourself to stay with that desire for approval. Stay with that experience. Describe what happened when you do that, with the bands across your chest.

another subpersonality

C: Part of it is kind of a whimpering, cowering—"oh, like me. See that I do the right things." And I don't like myself when I feel that. It is a kind of passivity that I don't like.

G: Can you allow yourself to suspend your reactivity to that feeling and really allow yourself to experience it? It may be necessary to take a look at the part that doesn't like it. But see if you can move directly into the experience—really cowering, whimpering.

C: It feels really sunken in here. And I don't know how anybody can like me when I am like that.

C: It is a little confusing now. But my feeling that is coming through is like sometimes when I do—when I am direct, or as direct as I feel I can be, I feel their discomfort and it is just uncomfortable all around. I can see through where they are. It feels like it is going bothways.

encouraging re-owning of projection

G: I grant you that we are talking about people that you know outside and we are also talking about some energy within yourself that is represented by those people. And so all that is true for that part of yourself: the insecurity behind the mask, the assertiveness and going ahead any way, the feeling a little contemptuous and impatient with you, the needful you. Not wanting to get involved and feeling a little uncomfortable with her needfulness. Does that sound familiar? Does that sound like part of yourself?

C: Yeah. It is difficult to really get into that needfulness and really acknowledge it and see it.

G: Because what will happen if you get into needfulness?

C: It feels like she is really going to take up a lot of my time. It is kind of like drowning in it. But I also feel like I haven't really acknowledged that.

G: What might happen if you acknowledged it?

C: I don't think there will be such a draw there.

hinting at the self

G: So there is another part of you that can see the value of acknowledging it. That's different from the group that feels they don't want to deal with it.

C: Yeah.

G: What is the value of acknowledging it? If I acknowledge it what might happen? What does it feel like to imagine acknowledging that? What is the part of you that wants to acknowledge that?

C: (with lots of pauses) It feels like comfort. It just feels like going real deep into a part of myself that I haven't gone into. I feel like I have been avoiding going into that. And I've been looking for other people to do it. I have the feeling that I don't really know what is there but if I can continue to keep in contact with that part, it will be really beneficial.

G: Would you be willing to somewhat formally acknowledge it now? And imagine how you would do that, how would you go about it?

C: Well, I feel like I need to go away and spend time with myself.

suggesting affirmation

G: What would you say to that part, to the needfulness, in order to acknowledge it, preliminarily?

C: Well, I feel like I have neglected you and I am not sure why, and it surprises me that I have. Because you seem to be asking for a lot all the time. You are the undercurrent. And I feel like you're a source. And I would really like to know you better and find out what you have to tell me.

G: How does that needful you respond to that?

C: It's like (heavy sigh), "finally!"

evoking experience of the self

G: Yeah (pause) Can you experience a part of you that is willing to acknowledge your needful part? How does that feel? What kind of qualities are in that experience?

the self

C: It is just standing and questioning, openness. And vulnerable.

G: I have a sense of there being either courage nor fearlessness. I am not sure which is the

G: But you say, I need to feed it or it will go out. Where did you get that idea?

C: Well, it is like feeding it oxygen, feeding it air. Right now I have the image of some of these other people who I feel are demanding and I am going to have to be able to feed this fire in me so that I can stand up to them. (pause) When I am feeling like this, I would like for it not to matter so much what they think of me.

G: How much does it matter?   *evoking meaning*

C: When I am like this it matters a lot. It feels like it matters a great deal.

G: Allow yourself to experience how much it matters, how important it is to this part. Per-   *seeking the value of this characteristic* haps get to the quality that is beneath that. And experience the energy beneath that. Maybe repeat the words, "It matters a lot."

C: It matters a lot. It matters a *lot*. I have the sense that they want me to see myself in another way. They don't want to see me like this and it is uncomfortable for me. They are trying to show me something. I don't think they like to see me like this either.

G: What do you want to say back to them when they don't want to see you the way you are?

C: What is it? Can you show me something about myself?   *identifying with conflicting subpersonality*

G: Could it be useful for you to become the people?

C: Uh-hum.

G: . . . looking back at sunken you?   *client still identified with first subpersonality*

C: I am getting a little mixed up in who they are, rather than what they can tell me. But what comes through are their feelings of insecurity behind the real strong front.

G: So, wait a minute. You have become the people now?

C: Yeah.

G: I am this group of people. And I . . .

C: I am feeling more where they are at rather than what they are telling me.

G: That is fine. Stay with where they are at for a few minutes. That's probably of value; the experience as the people. I am the people, and I feel insecure. What else? What else do you experience as one of the people, in the group? And try to keep it in the first person so that you own that experience.

C: I feel insecure but I feel there is a kind of assertiveness, going ahead anyway. There is an aggressiveness and a feeling that they are right.

G: So, as the people I am insecure, or we are insecure, but we also have a kind of assertiveness,   *modeling identification with group-of-people subpersonality* going ahead anyway, based on a feeling that we are really right. How do we feel toward this person who is reaching out to us for something, asking to be liked, begging to be liked?

C: Well, it really is a waste of time. Because she isn't going to have to go through all that   *now client identified with second subpersonality* stuff. And we don't really want to get involved in that kind of game.

G: How does she make us feel about ourselves?

C: A little uncomfortable sometimes.

G: Probably, *we* don't really want to go into that feeling of discomfort. But perhaps whoever is making choices in this session could go a little deeper into that feeling of discomfort.

C: It is a little confusing now. But my feeling that is coming through is like sometimes when I do—when I am direct, or as direct as I feel I can be, I feel their discomfort and it is just uncomfortable all around. I can see through where they are. It feels like it is going bothways.

encouraging re-owning of projection

G: I grant you that we are talking about people that you know outside and we are also talking about some energy within yourself that is represented by those people. And so all that is true for that part of yourself: the insecurity behind the mask, the assertiveness and going ahead any way, the feeling a little contemptuous and impatient with you, the needful you. Not wanting to get involved and feeling a little uncomfortable with her needfulness. Does that sound familiar? Does that sound like part of yourself?

C: Yeah. It is difficult to really get into that needfulness and really acknowledge it and see it.

G: Because what will happen if you get into needfulness?

C: It feels like she is really going to take up a lot of my time. It is kind of like drowning in it. But I also feel like I haven't really acknowledged that.

G: What might happen if you acknowledged it?

C: I don't think there will be such a draw there.

hinting at the self

G: So there is another part of you that can see the value of acknowledging it. That's different from the group that feels they don't want to deal with it.

C: Yeah.

G: What is the value of acknowledging it? If I acknowledge it what might happen? What does it feel like to imagine acknowledging that? What is the part of you that wants to acknowledge that?

C: (with lots of pauses) It feels like comfort. It just feels like going real deep into a part of myself that I haven't gone into. I feel like I have been avoiding going into that. And I've been looking for other people to do it. I have the feeling that I don't really know what is there but if I can continue to keep in contact with that part, it will be really beneficial.

G: Would you be willing to somewhat formally acknowledge it now? And imagine how you would do that, how would you go about it?

C: Well, I feel like I need to go away and spend time with myself.

G: What would you say to that part, to the needfulness, in order to acknowledge it, preliminarily?

suggesting affirmation

C: Well, I feel like I have neglected you and I am not sure why, and it surprises me that I have. Because you seem to be asking for a lot all the time. You are the undercurrent. And I feel like you're a source. And I would really like to know you better and find out what you have to tell me.

G: How does that needful you respond to that?

C: It's like (heavy sigh), "finally!"

evoking experience of the self

G: Yeah (pause) Can you experience a part of you that is willing to acknowledge your needful part? How does that feel? What kind of qualities are in that experience?

the self

C: It is just standing and questioning, openness. And vulnerable.

G: I have a sense of there being either courage nor fearlessness. I am not sure which is the right word. Or trust. There's some kind of strength there that allows you to stand there in openness. What is the quality of that strength?   question 4

C: The trust sounded . . .

G: What does this part know, the acknowledging part, standing and questioning openness? What do you know from that place? It's more a place than a part.   seeking inner widsom

C: I feel like if I go deep down into that other part of me I am really going to start to get to the core.

G: So from this place you know that there is a core down there?   affirming

C: Uh-hum.

G: What do you know about your ability to go into that place, to go into that?

C: I can see myself doing it. I might need some reminding and some support along the way, but I really feel like I am moving in that direction and it's like making friends in a sense, or getting to know someone.

G: So it doesn't feel terribly threatening to you?

C: No. I am just not exactly sure how I am going to do it.

G: What is your choice about going into this more deeply? Is that something you want to   evoking choice
do, work it now, or is that something you would like to do on your own?

C: Hmmm. Even though I am not sure how I am going to do it, I have a sense that I would like to try doing it on my own. There is a curiosity I have. There is a challenge and I feel like if I . . . if I can really succeed in doing this I will really have done something.

G: And if you can't?

C: No, I think I will.

G: Okay.

C: Wow.

G: Did the tears just come, just that moment? Would you let them come?

C: (crying) It is just a sense of surprise. It's really coming up against a sense that I have   tears signal release
carried with myself the surety that I have known myself, and now I really see this other part that I haven't acknowledged at all. It has been there forever asking for attention.

G: So it is a sense of humility, of, "Gee, I thought I knew myself so well and I find out . . ."

C: Yeah, wow. It is really coming up against this feeling of, well, you have it together, and you know yourself. It is just a feeling of awe. I don't know how else to describe it. And it feels like I am embarking on something.

G: Anticipation and excitement.

C: Yeah. It doesn't feel threatening. It may be, yeah, I really don't know what it holds, but whatever it is, I really feel like it is worth embarking on it. Just in that feeling of quest is just like (sound of release).

G: Opening up. Yeah. Relieving those bands.

C: Yeah, really. Just a funny feeling. It will take a while to just sit with it and get used to it. (laugh) When you said it's a sense of humility, there is a lot more than I have acknowledged and it is bigger than me and it unites me with all the rest.

Boy, I really feel . . . it is just amazing to me how that changes . . . comes and goes. I have the feeling that I have a lot to do and there is a lot will happen, but I don't have that feeling of pushing it.

G: (hearty laughter)

C: (laughter) It is like taking time to get to know a friend and that just goes along at its own pace and you can't force a friendship. It just happens. I really savor that feeling of taking that part of me and going and doing things with it. I really have this feeling of wanting to just go out on my own, maybe out into the woods, or out into nature, and . . .

G: Being with that part of yourself.

C: Yeah, and being with that part of myself. It almost feels like a kind of treat, just taking that time for myself and being that. Thank you!

G: Notice what you have. Appreciate what you have gotten to (pause). I want to share with you that I have been listening to a tape of a session that I did. It was getting in touch with a very similar needfulness and also the denial of it in myself. And it is different and it is the same. I think it is probably a universal phenomenon. I think we all have that. And it expresses itself differently and operates differently and comes from different experiences. But that is why you said you feel like it is bigger than you . . . I think that that is right on.

C: I really had that sense, and I haven't had that before. It's like all of this seems to have been brewing up and I have caught glimpses of it but I have not had that real experience feeling. I really feel it now! I can no longer not see it. I can't deny it, because I have felt it. It is really there, and it is much bigger than me.

G: The other aspect of guidance from that previous session is really going into the experience, not even just imaging it. Imagery is important, but it is only important as a doorway and I think we get skillful at using imagery as a way of keeping things at arm's length. To really experience it there seems to be some little key there.

The first time you were looking at that boulder . . . and then when you experienced it, all of a sudden it got smaller and you went through a transformation just spontaneously.

C: I am thinking of that part of me when I slumped down there. I just saw that. I just saw myself, I didn't feel it. But then later on when I had that feeling I could really put feeling into that slumped figure.

G: You could also see the parts of you that tried to keep you from having that experience, that felt judgmental about it, that said it seemed to look foreign.

C: That stood in the way of it, like making distance.

G: Anything to get away from that experience.

C: I felt before the end of the session that needful part has something very important to give to me or to tell me. And it is under the guise of whatever the character or the personality that it takes on, there's something of value to share.

G: Right.

C: And I am going to start finding out what it is.

validating client's experience with own

clarifying value of experience

TRANSCRIPT B

This client and guide have been working together in training and in sessions for four years. In this session the client is concerned about a conflict in her life between being responsible and impeccable on the one hand, and relaxing and having fun on the other. She discovers and works with two polarized subpersonalities through extensive imagery, culminating in a synthesis which reveals their combined purposes and power.

C: I thought over the past few weeks, got to places with various issues and I thought—I've got to have a session. And today I didn't have anything uppermost. I felt there was all this nebulous stuff ready to be called forth. I didn't know which one I would want to work with.

And just now closing my eyes I got a sort of survey of the various issues and I think they are all related. They all come down to one issue. I've been on one level with regard to my work—basically experiencing a lot of resistance both physically and emotionally, wanting to have fun and not be responsible all the time and not have to push myself.

And also I am still smarting under this most recent experience with the association meeting. The meeting was at 2:00. I hadn't had any time for myself. I hadn't had any lunch. I tried to meditate but my heart wasn't in it, and I finally just said "I am not really into doing this. And I don't even want to. I don't even care about the issue. I didn't want to be responsible for it. I want to go to the meeting and have a good time with my friends, talk to people." I just sort of threw in the towel.

As it turned out, the meeting was a fiasco. I didn't feel clear or centered, and ever since I have been down on myself because I see many ways in which had I been clearer or more centered I could have taken the leadership role and possibly turned the course of it.

So I feel like I lose either way. I'm either under the gun all the time and I have to be impeccable, or if I goof off then all hell breaks loose and I am miserable. Because I did have the potential. Maybe not to stem the whole course of the meeting; that's grandiose. But at least to have been clear about my own stand. To have kept some perspective on what was going on and to have spoken from that place.

I did speak but by the time I got it together to speak it was really too late.

I think in some ways what it all boils down to is the little child in me who still is demanding recognition and unconditional love— recognition for how much she is being asked to do all the time.

And what I got as the image for this session, my image was to just give her wings. I see her in the fetal position, curled up in some dark place, hiding out and trying to comfort and lift her. There is certainly a big part of me that does not want to do another session where I am trying to mollify the little child. Because it seems endless. It seems like it never changes. I've done it so many times and maybe it is never going to change.

If I go back to my viewpoint about a month or so ago, it was: this is it, right now. And you just endure the conflicts and there is nothing to change.

G: In what area does it seem like the sense of rebellion is the most distressful to you? Where you would most like to change that?

focusing on issue

C: With regard to my health, that is in some ways the biggest impediment to my just moving ahead. And yet I don't feel all that uncomfortable with that. It is very familiar to me and I see some value in, for instance, my having got sick when I did. I feel like I was just on the borderline of getting inflated when I noticed it in a lot of different ways. My impatience with N: if I could get myself together and move out into the world why can't she? That sort of thing. And so I see its value as a balance. It's humbling, it's grounding. It puts me back in touch with my humanness and my frailty.

G: Do you think there is some other way you could do that?

C: Yeah. I'm sure there are lots of better ways to do it. So I am kind of feeling torn.

question 1

G: Where are you right now in your life?

C: In big terms, in general?

G: What's the essence of where you are right now?

C: That's a good question! A whole lot of things going through my head. The first one is it seemed like such a great question and then I realized it is the 'first' question. (laughter)

G: It didn't come from there. (laughter) I know it's the 'first' question, but that's not where it came from. (joint laughter)

C: And then, you know, my initial impulse was: well, I am in a very expansive time.

G: Discourse about it.

C: I *am* in a very expansive and exciting time. I am coming into my work, or some aspect of it, which is something I've longed for these many years.

spontaneous image

Then the image I had was as if I had been a statue in the middle of a fountain, a pond. But I am at the edge of the pond. I've gotten off the pedestal and I'm a winged statue, and I am just about to lift off from the edge of this pond, so this circular pond of water is behind me. But then I notice that there are all these ponds in front of me too. There's a whole series of them, any one of which I might fall into in my initial flight.

G: So you are a little hesitant to take flight for fear you might fall into another pond?

C: Yeah. And maybe get stuck being a statue in the next pond.

G: That's quite an image. How does it feel?

C: I want to intervene, go up waving my arms and say, "Go ahead, you can do it. Do it." And then I see that this statue has a stone body. It does have wings that are alive. It has this very heavy stone sculpted body. So I see it is not just quite as easy as it might appear. It is going to take a little more encouragement.

encouraging initial identification and exploring subpersonality

G: Would you be the statue, have this stone body?

C: Well, these wings are not going to do it. They are very nice and they would be really more than adequate if I had a body that was just flesh and blood. But for a stone body they are not going to make it.

G: What's it like to have a stone body?

C: Well, it feels pretty safe, pretty impregnable and really solid, substantial, not exactly grounded but held down with gravity. Not really connected to the earth, but fixed on it.

G: Not likely to just float away?

C: It's like having an anchor. I don't know where these wings came from.

G: Are they stone too?

C: No, they are feathers. And they are . . . I know what they want. They want to just go up and up and up into the sun like Icarus. And we all know what comes of that.

G: Why have you gotten off your pedestal? You've gotten over to the side of the pond.

C: It was when I grew the wings. Up till then I'd been kind of paralyzed. I have a vague memory, I think I used to have water going through me. A real fountain that used to spray up into the air and fall down. I vaguely remember that. But that hasn't happened for a long, long time. And so I was just kind of stuck there and I couldn't make the water, I couldn't turn it on myself.

G: How did you feel when you were stuck there?

C: Really powerless, kind of safe and admired. You know, because I just had this one pose, that was it. Basically really powerless and constrained, restricted, imprisoned. And so you see those wings have done that already. I didn't really even choose to climb off of there. The next thing I knew here were these wings and . . .

G: They propelled you over to the edge of the pond?

C: Yeah, here I am beside the pond. It's all very exciting.

G: Would there be any value in having a conversation with the wings? Tell them how you feel about them.

initiating dialogue between subpersonalities

C: Interesting. There are sort of two. I was half getting into a crotchety sub-personality which I could get into further with the wings, but I also have a lot of feeling about the wings.

G: As a stone body? Perhaps it would be valuable to stay in the stone body and if that wants to be crotchety, let it be. Or it may have mixed feelings.

validating feelings

C: Well, I'm not too sure about you. I can't quite see you. I would like to take you off and look at you, but you are not detachable. I feel like I didn't ask for you, or maybe I did but I didn't know what I was asking for. And now all of a sudden here you are and you are attached to me, you are a part of me, and I can't even see what you really look like. I can feel you, but only from one part of my body. I feel like you have a mind of your own. You have some plans that I'm not even privy to, and I don't like that feeling.

G: You feel like they are sort of alien to you, not organically part of you somehow.

C: Well, I know they are attached. In a sense I grew them. I don't know how I grew living wings out of a stone body but they haven't been stuck on. Somehow I grew them. And that makes me feel like maybe the whole, all the rest of me, could change, and stop being stone.

G: And how do you feel when you are that way, when you see that possibility, that you could stop being stone, that you could change, become a living being with wings?

C: It really moves me, moves me and it scares me.

G: Can you be with those feelings for a few moments? Let them be there; let yourself experience it, the fear and the hope. If you could speak for the fear and the hope . . .?

staying with experience

C: I really want it. I think I'd be really beautiful.

G: You really want to be living?

C: I want all of me to be like the wings. It's not just living. It's luminous and radiant. But when I see it I see myself as sort of emerging. Somehow not that the stone would dissolve. That was what I first thought. More like the wings are a force that would pull the living essence of me out of the stone. Then there would be nothing holding me back. Then they would just rise up and fly.

G: And the fear? What does the fear say?

C: The fear says . . .

G: Icarus?

C: The fear says that's not it. Somehow it's not that any more because I see that when I, if I became all of the same substance as the wings, then there wouldn't be any danger. Then I could fly and I could go to those realms and I could move among them without danger. But I wouldn't be human. But then I'm not human now. I'm stone. And somehow there's something missing.

G: There's something that as the stone the wings offer you. That sense of vibrancy, aliveness and freedom. Why don't you become the wings for a moment and see what you can say to that stone body, why you've chosen that body to grow from?

C: Okay. We were always here. We've always been here. We've been waiting and waiting for an opportunity to unfold and we were captive in the stone, just as you are. You're not the stone. You're imprisoned in stone. And we had to wait. We had to wait very patiently for years till this slow erosion of the rain and the elements wore the stone away to the point where we could break through. And there is more there. You are right. We are, we do have a purpose and plan and that is to bring all of this living substance free of the stone.

So you are just a husk. You are just a protection that was necessary for a time and then you outgrew your usefulness but we were still imprisoned. Now the time has come for us to break free.

G: If that happens, will you be human?

C: No. The image has changed now and the image I have is of an eagle, with its claws pushing back fiercely, pushing itself out of the stone through the back.

need qualities of both subpersonalities

G: Good. Stay with that image. I have a sense, though, the stone still has something, a role to play. Something to offer you.

C: The stone is outraged.

G: Be the stone and express that.

C: What do you mean, just a husk? Who do you think you are?

G: What do you have to offer as the stone?

C: This is the thanks I get. I've been faithful to this bird for years and years, devoted my whole life to protecting him, to play a role, circumscribe my activity, movement, everything to protect him with everything I had. And what thanks do I get now? I'm just going to be discarded. My usefulness is over. So long. See you around . . . I did a damn good job. I did what I had to do. I did what was necessary.

G: What do you have to offer now to this eagle, this emerging life?

evoking recognition of value of statue

C: I don't know. I don't think that he needs or wants anything from me.

G: So you really are useless?

C: Well, I mean here I am stone. I am on the edge of a pond. The back of me is breaking open and he is an eagle and he is going to fly and do his eagle thing.

G: And what will be left?

C: Just a husk, just like he said, I guess.

G: Just for a moment imagine that that has happened. Don't actually allow it to happen, just imagine that it has happened. And just see what you experience. How you experience yourself as the stone, as the husk? What is that experience like?

C: I feel discarded, useless. I feel like I wasn't valued or appreciated. Even if somebody came along who could patch me up, you know, fix up the back of me — all I'd ever get to be is an old statue again. I don't want to be a statue.

G: What do you want to be?

C: I want to be a person.

G: Can you be a person without the eagle?

C: No.

G: Do you want the eagle to be a person?

C: He doesn't want to. What's in it for him to be a person? He's an eagle.

G: Talk to him. Tell him that you want him back, that you want him to be a person with you, that you need him. Let him know how much you need him.

dialogue between subpersonalities

C: I don't think he knows how to be a person either.

G: Can you tell him anyway, even though you don't think he will understand? Call out to him and grab hold of his foot or whatever you need to do to get his attention. He hasn't really freed himself from you, he just imagined that he did.

responding to intensity of feelings

C: Well, don't you be in such an all-fired hurry to get free of me! I don't want to be left cold and dead and empty. I want to be alive. I want to move. I want to be able to move.

G: Don't leave me!

C: I can see why you want to go. But I did a lot for you. I protected you for a long time, years and years. I gave up a lot to do that. I could have been a person if it weren't for you.

G: How is the eagle responding to this?

C: I don't know, but I am getting mad. Who does he think he is to just take off, you know?

strong feelings may indicate valuable perspective

G: What's the truth with your anger? What is the truth that you know?

C: That I am worth something. I wasn't always like this.

G: And you are still worth something?

C: Yeah, if I were given half a chance I would be. I can remember what it was like to move around, sing and all that stuff.

G: Does it feel like it would be useful to move to yet another perspective at this point?

C: Uh-huh.

disidentification for larger view

G: I would like to suggest that you become the pond.

C: Interesting. I am really sinking into it, the mass despair or something (sighing).

G: It's okay.

C: Okay. I'll become the pond. I mean this is all the 'me' that I adopted after those early visions. It is interesting.

G: The stone?

C: Uh-huh (long pause).

I don't know as the pond; I'm looking at this drama that is going on on the banks.

G: On your banks?

C: Yes. This empty pedestal here in the middle of me. And it looks to me like the eagle needs to break free from the statue.

G: If he does, if he flies off, where would that leave you?

C: I think I'll be all right. I just reflect what's there. And he'll fly over me and even come and perch sometimes on the pedestal. Perhaps drop some droppings into me. What I don't feel good about is this broken-down statue on my banks. I don't want to have to reflect that for the rest of my days.

G: So it will leave you with a broken-down statue?

C: Yeah. And then nobody will come to me. They will go to the other ponds. There's a whole chain of us.

G: Do you have anything you want to say to the stone statue that is so threatened and so miserable right now?

C: See, when I look at myself I am a prisoner, too, in a way. I mean, we are all in this formal arrangement, ornamental, and I am just water and I don't really particularly want to have to, to be bound in this concrete pool. I would enjoy . . . I didn't mind it too much when I was a fountain.

G: But you haven't been running lately?

C: Well, I haven't been running for a long time. I would like to just seep my way out of here and join some brook somewhere. Then I wouldn't care what happens to this broken-down statue.

G: And there would be an empty pond?

C: Yeah, an empty pedestal in the middle and this broken-down statue. It wouldn't be any skin off my neck.

G: You're not much help to that poor statue.

C: Well, I'm kind of sick of looking at it to tell you the truth.

G: Does it have any redeeming qualities?

C: It was okay when it was being the fountain. It did a pretty good job of that—adequate. Even then there was something really artificial about it, posed. I don't want to be, I don't like being posed. I'm posed myself. I'm sick of being posed, I don't like being very posed like that. I like a more formless existence. I feel really sorry for that bird being stuck in there all this time. More power to him if he can get free and fly away.

G: Interesting. When the bird flies away we have a broken-down statue left, which means that the statue is no longer posed; it somehow disintegrates.

C: Well, it is all broken at the back. So actually the front stays fixed. It comes out, you see, through the wings. So the front is still pretty rigid. I mean we could topple it into the pond and let it break.

G: I want to speak just for a moment to the statue, to the rock, to the stone. And I just want you, the stone, to know that I think you still have something very valuable to offer. And I really am determined to help that be discovered. There is something that you have to offer that has to do with humanity, with being a person, with being human, being whole. And the bird would like to fly away and leave that behind. And the pond would like to seep away and leave that behind. And yet somehow there is still something there. There is something that refuses to go away. You are something that refuses to go away and demands to be included.

validating the subpersonality

C: I appreciate the vote of confidence. I don't know, maybe it's too late for me. I mean really, I was a person. I was a kid and that's when I knew what it was about then, and I think about it and it's been so long . . .

G: That you became a statue.

C: Yeah, well I had to. I had to protect the bird. It's been so long. I've just been a statue for too long.

the value of this sub-personality

G: But you don't have to protect the bird any more.

C: I don't know how to move any more. I can't move. I'm just totally rigid.

G: So you were a person and then you became a statue to protect the bird?

appreciation of origin of subpersonality

C: Yeah. I was a kid you see and then I discovered I had this bird on my hands and . . .

G: When you were a kid were you rigid?

C: No.

G: What were you then?

C: No, I was just a kid. I was great. I was spontaneous, I laughed a lot.

G: What has happened to all those qualities?

C: Well, they have all just sort of shriveled up and . . .

G: Where are they now?

C: I don't know.

G: Are they somewhere in the stone?

qualities are still latent in the subpersonality

C: They are in my longing, I guess. I remember them.

G: Where is that longing? Where do you experience that longing in your stone body?

C: I guess it's here, in my throat. See, I can't speak.

G: If you could speak, would that make a difference?

C: Oh, that would make a huge difference.

G: And what prevents you from speaking?

C: Well, you see, if I ever spoke I might have given away the bird.

G: The bird is now free. Perhaps it is safe to speak now. What would you say if you were to speak now?

C: Now I am stone. What would I say?

G: If you could speak now, what would you say?

C: I'm here too.

G: What are you? Who are you?

C: I've been here all along. I just want to live. (Sigh)

recognizing potential for transformation

G: So the stone is not completely dead stone. There is still longing in it . . . There is still . . .

C: No, it's like fairy tales. I've turned to stone and I need someone to break the spell. I need the prince to come.

G: And who is that prince?

C: And then I will turn into a woman.

bringing in the other subpersonality

G: Can the eagle do it?

C: It feels like the eagle should be able to.

G: How could the eagle release you? To reverse that process?

C: He can't do it as an eagle. He has to do it as a prince.

seeking key to transformation

G: And what does he need in order to become a prince?

C: He needs to fall in love with me.

G: How that can happen? How could he fall in love with you?

C: I'm calling to him. And he's broken free and he's flying in the sky straight past me. Flying and flying. And I'm saying, "Wait, wait. Don't leave me." And he looks around. And he sees how lovely I am. And he falls in love with me and he starts falling. And he's turning into a prince in the air and he's falling. And he lands on the ground and he's quite a long way away. And he has to find me.

G: Keep calling to him . . .

beginning of synthesis

C: (very long pause) He found me. The fountain's on again, too.

G: How did you turn on the fountain?

C: Well, it's easy to do if you are human. Just find where it turns on. Just when it comes up through the pedestal. But still it's kind of nice.

G: Are you still stone?

transformation

C: No, I turned into a young woman. And my back part all came together, but it didn't come together quite straight. That's okay.

G: Is your prince loving you?

C: That's what helped me remember who I am.

G: And what you've been through.

C: Uh-huh. We're going to leave this place now. He has a horse.

G: Ask him if he is content to be a human—the prince—and stay with you? Is that what he chooses?

potential for transcendence

C: (long pause) He says that he will always long for flight, but that he wouldn't wish to be an eagle without me. And that some day we will fly together. And now we're riding to his kingdom.

They've been waiting for him there for a long, long time. He was taken away as a young child. He was kidnapped.

G: He came into your care and your keeping, your protection?

C: Uh-huh. There will be much rejoicing because he's returned. His father is dying, the old king. The prince will be able to take over and he will have a bride already. Then we'll be the king and queen. I don't know if I am ready to be a queen. I haven't had much practice being anything but a statue.

G: Is he ready to begin?

C: He's kind of scared too.

G: Take a moment to just step back and allow yourself to be some encompassing awareness, something that encompasses both the prince and the princess or the king and queen in the kingdom. Speak to each of them.

identifying with the self

C: When I became a tree, a really old venerable tree, and then I looked at them and they were trotting along this country road in the valley where the kingdom was. And I wanted to talk to the horse that was carrying them. I don't know quite what I want to say. Just that they should know, as they undertake this task and these roles, that they are not just alone, that they are supported and carried and moved along in a very tangible way. That the kingdom is very fertile, an abundance there, much nourishment: animals and grain.

G: It can be heavy to be a king or a queen. A sense of responsibility. It can get very heavy and you can be resented. Say more about that.

balancing positive and negative aspects

C: This is clearly their destiny but that doesn't mean that they can't have any fun, enjoy themselves, enjoy life. They are going to a kingdom which is very orderly and at peace and prosperous. There will be great rejoicing when they arrive. The only real sorrow in the kingdom is that the king is dying and the old queen will still be there and she can give guidance. And they can bring more happiness to the kingdom and declare feast days and holidays and dancing and singing and festivals. It doesn't have to all be serious. That's an important part of their role. They should be creating rituals and festivals, occasions for community rejoicing.

key to synthesis between responsibility and fun

G: So their role and their purpose in the kingdom is what?

clarifying purpose of synthesis

C: To be a focus, a focal point for all the people there, to stand for peace and prosperity and abundance, and fairness and wisdom. Stability. And also to be a catalyst for joy and rejoicing.

G: Just take a moment to see how it would feel to affirm that by moving back into a sense of yourself now and saying, "I am a catalyst for joy" or any of the other phrases.

affirmation

C: In my being I represent stability and order. I am an organizing principal. And I rule over my subjects with wisdom and with fairness . . . with gentleness. And I am also a catalyst for joy. I encourage rejoicing. And in this position I know that I am not alone. That I stand on the earth and the earth provides for me, as it does for everyone. And that there is vast abundance. What I need to do to bring this into myself is to bring the prince and princess and the whole kingdom into my heart.

owning the synthesis

They are standing on the balcony of the palace just after their wedding and all the people below are shouting and throwing confetti.

(long pause)

It feels like an important piece of work. I don't know quite how to translate it.

G: Perhaps just look at some of those issues that we were talking about before. Just take a look at them and see if you see any difference. And if you don't, it's all right because it hasn't cooked yet.

grounding

Client and guide now ground the session by looking at various issues in the light of the imagery, noticing the correspondence between various images and aspects of her life. The conflict between responsibility and relaxation which began the session has been resolved in the synthesis of the king and queen, whose responsibilities encompass stability and order, and acting as a catalyst for joy and celebration in the kingdom.

TRANSCRIPT C

This session takes place about three-quarters through a year of psychosynthesis training for the client, and is the sixth or seventh session with this guide. The previous session, about a month before, helped the client to allow her sexuality greater expression in beauty and joy. Since then, the client has begun to feel that she is still holding back from her potential and has chosen to focus on that now. Through imagery, she explores the implication of the choice to step into her power and identify with her Higher Self, and eventually is able to take that symbolic step in full consciousness, integrating the resistance that has come up along the way.

This session begins with a review of the last session five weeks before and its effects in the client's life since. Then the client indicates readiness for this day's work.

C: I'm ready to take the next step (chuckle). I'm really aware that I have some subpersonalities, attitudes, energies, ways of being, patterns, whatever, that get in the way of my expressing my power and my love in the world. It's come up in supervision. A. had listened to a tape I did and she said, "Look, here there's this moment when you put out this very clear statement. You say, 'Oh, I see blah-blah.' And it's a very clear statement. It's on and it's clear. And then you giggle. And the giggle goes: dilute, dilute. 'You don't have to take me seriously.' " That was an example of the kind of things that happen. I experience that giggle within myself. Even if I don't giggle, there's still some part of me that's saying, "Oh, don't confront me with what I've just said. Maybe I'm wrong." And it really undermines me, gets in my way. We were working with it in the supervision a bit. And she said, "Maybe it's time to give that one up." That really felt right. It's time for me to grow up. It's time for me to stop being insecure and "Oh, dear, am I doing the right thing." It's a whole child subpersonality that it's time for me to give up. It's just time. (Client gives other examples of this pattern.)

Another thing is I have this really big thing that says, "I must not be dependent." That's a cardinal sin, to ask people for things. (Gives example of asking a friend a favor.) There is some relationship between those two phenomena: the phenomenon on the one hand of backing down and diluting things that I say and do, and this other thing of denying and not allowing myself to be needy and dependent, or to have those feelings. And of course it comes out, anyway. It comes out in ways that are destructive to my effectiveness. And what I got this morning was: the first thing is some kind of fear of my own power. Real fear. I don't get any catastrophic fantasies or anything, it just feels like fear. Something about the fear of being wrong. I might be wrong. I put something out—what if somebody challenges me, what if I'm wrong? Even if I'm right and somebody challenges me, maybe I'm wrong. That's another no-no, to be wrong. And what the common factor is seems to be some kind of fear of rejection.

G: Rejection from?

C: From other people. If I put out myself real powerfully and somebody contradicts me, then I get rejected by that person because they say, "No, you're wrong." And if I ask for something, and I'm dependent, I can get rejected, too. People can say, "No, I don't want to give that to you. Go away." That seems to be the common pattern.

G: What's the tie-in to power? I don't see the connection.

focusing on issue

C: Well, if I really allow my power to be out there, it might create some conflicts; it might bump up against somebody else's idea of what's right and that person might not like me and reject me and so on.

147

G: Say more about that other stuff, the issues that you had, and so on.

C: There's something about embarrassment. "Don't notice me too much." Not wanting to be too noticeable. And that I connect with the fact that almost always when I talk about something I've accomplished I use "we." Usually what I have accomplished is done by "we" but it is hard for me to say "I did that" and easy to say "We did that." That fear of standing out, of really being out there. I want to blend a little more into the background. I want to still be able to do my thing and be noticed and matter and make a difference, but not too much. There's a certain point when it becomes uncomfortable. (Gives another example of this discomfort.) Maybe it goes back to trusting myself. Just being who I am is okay. It's a whole constellation of stuff. But I want to get it out of the way because I want to start being everything I can be. I'm tired of being a half-assed version of myself. I look at myself fairly objectively and it seems to me I'm an exceptional person. I've always been. I've stood out from my peers. But I've never really done as much as I could have, never really expressed that completely. I haven't used my power and my wisdom.

giving client responsibility for session

G: If you were me, what would you suggest you do right now?

C: I don't know what I would do if I were you. I'm asking my inner Buddha.

G: Okay, what's your inner Buddha say?

C: It feels appropriate to tune into my inner Buddha and then from there look at any one of these, doesn't matter which—sort of become it, identify with it, do all that stuff . . .

seeking basic issue

G: As the Buddha—what would be a pertinent question to ask in relation to all this stuff?

C: It seems fairly obvious: What's the purpose of all this? I feel real strongly about my purpose. My purpose is to be able to express more fully. It isn't just for me. The world out there needs me (laughs). And ah . . . oh, see, there it was. That was hard. "The world out there needs me"—I reacted to that statement. That's embarrassing, presumptuous.

G: What are you experiencing now?

C: The embarrassment and presumptuousness?

G: And the stuff behind it, your emotions?

C: It feels like some old childhood stuff. (pause) I think I just need to get kind of. . . I'm feeling. . . . What's presumptuous? I'm embarrassed to say that. . . . (pause) The fear came in that you would say that I was conceited, that I was arrogant, that I had an inflated opinion of myself. That feels like somebody said that to me sometime, long time ago.

G: It sounds like you don't step into this bigger sense of yourself. It's there, but when you step into it your personality reacts to it, makes it less.

C: I don't really step into it. It comes out through my personality, but I'm not really in it.

G: Right.

C: It's like I am the personality; I have this source of deeper wisdom within me but I am not that source. I can tap into it, but I'm not really there.

G: Which keeps the personality in control.

C: Yeah. And it kind of allows a little bit out every now and then because it gets off on it. It's kind of an ego trip. Yeah, it's tied up with the ego trip, it's tied up with a fear of being arrogant and conceited! (laughs) It's irrelevant. I feel real resistant to really believing that is *me*, that I am that wisdom and power. No! I'm just this little old personality, in pretty good shape; I do pretty well.

G: So what do you want to do?

giving client responsibility

C: Who? What does who want to do?

G: Like the caterpillar in Alice in Wonderland . . .? "*Who* are you?"

C: (Thoughtfully) Okay, the personality is afraid of letting go the identification because then I might neglect it and become—it's a real distortion—a disembodied spirit that doesn't have any juice or anything.

G: I hear all the stuff. So what do you choose? You see the pattern, you have the awareness, what do you choose? (Client laughs) One of the things that comes in, is that you're going to be juiceless, right? Another thing is you're going to be arrogant. What do you choose?

C: I don't choose to be juiceless and I don't choose to be arrogant.

G: Those are the fears that come in, that doesn't allow you to move towards that.

C: Right.

G: So what do you choose?

C: (long pause) Whew.

evoking the will

(After long pause) I'm getting images of mythological, warrior-type things, slaying dragons and such. It has epic proportions, that choice does.

G: Allow yourself to stay with the images, but *experience* experientially the epic proportions.

evoking intention

C: I am.

G: I mean, suddenly you're at the brink.

C: Yeah. I need to be a warrior and I need to be . . . I need to use my sword, my sword and my clarity and my will.

G: What do you choose?

choice

C: I know what I'm choosing.

G: What are you choosing?

C: I'm choosing to become my power, to be my power, and the reason I'm taking so long is because . . .

G: It's okay to take long . . .

C: Because I really want to do it, I don't want to just say it . . .

intensifying awareness of the process of choice

G: It's okay . . . you don't have to push past it. Just share with us what's going on all the time with your process.

C: What's going on is I'm looking at it and stuff comes up and I put that aside and I'm looking at it and some more stuff comes up and it's like: and that too, and that too, and that too . . .

G: Uh-huh. See that? That's the brink of the choice.

C: Uh-huh. I have to see all that stuff and I have to know all that stuff and own all that stuff in order for the choice to be real. Otherwise it's just an imitation choice. (pause)

I'm starting to experience an anger and the energy of that anger. It's confronting that negativity again and saying, "No, not going to undermine me." (pause) The image is that I have to step across some kind of a chasm. And it's not a very broad step; I mean, I can step. It's not that there's any concern that I won't be able to actually physically do it. But it feels like once I step across that chasm I can't go back, and I need to take everything that I want with me. So that I go across that chasm in the fullest manifestation of my being that I can. Maybe there's some parts I do want to leave behind. (pause)

image for choice

G: What are you experiencing right now?

C: (Pause) I'm experiencing a lot of breath inside. I'm experiencing a lot of sense of integrity, ah, individuality perhaps. Aloneness.

G: Aloneness?

C: But not loneliness, just aloneness. (pause) The Fool . . . the Tarot; the Tarot card, the Fool. (pause, sigh) I could stand here digging this forever, but I think I'll go on.

G: Stay there for a second. Does this feel familiar being in that space?

C: No.

G: Describe it.

C: It's familiar only in the sense that I see the Tarot card and I know that that's representing the same feeling, experience. It's like I know about it from the culture, but it doesn't feel familiar in my personal experience.

G: Still experience yourself on the brink of this chasm?

C: Uh-huh. There aren't any . . . it's like that's all there is. There's just ground and there's this big jagged chasm and there's more ground , and, ah, there's sunlight, but I'm not aware of trees or anything like that.

evoking meaning

G: What does the chasm represent to you?

C: Obliteration, nothingness.

raising the stakes to clarify choice

G: So it means to you to experience obliteration or the possibility of nothingness for you to take a step at this point . . . would you be willing to do that?

client identifies with a pseudo-self

C: You're asking if I'm willing to die. (pause) Yeah, in the sense of this personality . . . I'm very fond of this personality, I have some pride in this personality. (pause) It's a fake chasm. This sounds mental but it's, it's more than mental. My personality is only, only exists because I create it and therefore it cannot . . . to talk about it's being obliterated is as if it had a life of its own, and it doesn't.

cutting through content to experience

G: That all may be true, but that's different than experiencing being on the brink and having to let go, which is a definite experience. There's a lot of other content you could introduce to assuage that experience.

C: Good old brain.

mentally identified client controlled by feelings

G: Good old feelings controlling brain.

C: (big laugh, pause) When you asked if I was willing to risk that, to let go . . .

G: To move forward . . .

C: What came was "No."

G: Good.

C: "I'm *not* willing." And that doesn't mean I'm still not going to choose to do that. The willingness feels more like, do you want to, that kind of thing. Is that your preference, is that your . . . yeah. And the answer is no, that's what came, but I'm not willing to accept that as my final answer.

G: The question, to put it in a larger context: If it means for you to really experience and own your power, and own your death and, it sounds like, your willingness to serve . . .

continuing to clarify and intensify choice

C: Uh-huh.

G: And all that up front; are you willing to experience nothingness or the sense of death or whatever, to go forward toward that?

C: What I experienced, and then I told you that my answer had been no; I experienced a sense of "I must. I must go forward. I must take that step."

G: If it means for you to choose to take that step, to experience embarrassment or your death, are you willing to experience death or embarrassment and still . . .

C: Yes.

G: And still move beyond the embarrassment?

C: Yes, I'm willing to do that. And there is that sense of mustness, of being compelled by some, some very deep, ah, oh, what's the word I want? (sigh) It's real . . . I, I don't know if I've experienced this before. I know what the word is, but I can't . . . It's kind of like a natural law or something that says, "This is what you must do, this is your dharma; this is your. . ."

G: You have a sense of that experience, of that . . .

C: Yeah. And that is part of that willingness. Carlos Casteneda is standing on the brink. (pause) I must do it and I choose to do it. (pause) I choose to identify myself with Buddha, with power (pause), with wisdom. . . . I am having a familiar sensation . . . familiar and yet unfamiliar. It's a sensation I've had occasionally in my life. It's very unpleasant and yet it somehow accompanies expansion. And I feel literally expanded; I feel like I'm this enormous balloon. The way my fingers fit together, they feel like they're just *huge*! Like they're filling up this whole room, just my fingers are filling up this room. Just *huge*. Really unpleasant. And there's a difference this time because this time I'm experiencing a seed in the middle, at the center. And what I'm experiencing is a sense that I am that seed at the center and this puffing up stuff is, is the peripherals.

getting lost in experience: 'tripping out'

G: I'm curious; did you choose before?

C: Did I choose?

G: Choose to take that step?

C: Yes.

G: You did?

C: Yes. This feels like . . .

G: And when you chose to take that step, this stuff came in?

C: Right. (tape change)

G: Experience your willingness to take that step, in lieu of any of this stuff; experience your willingness to take a step.

'trip' a form of resistance

C: Okay.

G: Tell us what happens when you experience your willingness.

evoking intention

C: When I experience my willingness, my experience is of that decision to align with that . . . I wish I could think of that damn word; I'll think of it sooner or later. That mustness, that sense of this is what you must do.

G: Good. Let's go a step further, okay?

C: And that's the willingness; the willingness has to do with aligning with that.

G: Right. Are you willing now to choose the mustness? Experience yourself choosing that?

client notices resistance

C: (pause) I just went on a little side trip that I think is relevant. It's just a oh-that's-how-I-do-that, a little self-observation. I started thinking about what's that damn word, what's that word that I want, and I realized that my mind was withholding the word from me so that I would stew and worry about what the word was and wouldn't get on with what I was trying to do here. So that's just a side thing, okay? Choosing the mustness, choosing the something . . . there's a lot of rebellion in my personality and I choose that.

exploring resistance; using skillful will

G: Don't push past the rebellion. Are you willing to experience the rebellion? See, it's really important not to repress the rebellion. Describe that experience. What are the voices saying?

C: The voice is saying I want to play; I want to have fun; I want to relax; I don't want to have to be all serious and warrior-like and I want to just enjoy . . . ah . . .

G: Okay. Are you willing to experience all that pulls and still choose; allow it to be there and choose in the face of it?

C: Yes, that's what I was doing before, but I want to modify that now. I want to include, somehow just bring it all along, not as resistance, but as part of me. See, when you talk about choosing in the face of it, I experience it as sort of, as pushing it aside, as . . .

G: Exactly.

C: And I, ah . . .

G: That's being included within the choice, that's there and I'm still choosing to go on and it's there.

choice is made from integrating self, repressing and excluding nothing

C: And it's still there.

G: Right. And it's still there, right?

C: Right. It's still here.

G: What you do is, my experience is that you 'strong-will' it . . .

C: Yeah, yeah.

G: Which represses it . . .

C: Right.

G: And then there's a backlash if you 'strong-will' it. If you 'skillful-will' it, that allows it to be there, experience it, include it within your choice.

C: Right. (pause) I choose to bring the playfulness and joy and warmth and relax and have fun. I choose to bring that into that alignment with what I must do.

G: Good. How do you know you can?

C: I know it, I know I can.

G: How do you know you can?

C: I know I can (laughs). I know I can, because I have a skillful will and . . .

G: If that means to you, let's assume, hypothetically, to choose the mustness, that that's not going to be present, are you still willing to choose it . . . the playfulness and the warm stuff . . .?

raising the stakes again

C: It's not going to be present if I choose, that's the assumption?

G: Yeah, hypothetical.

C: (sigh) No.

G: Where does that leave you, then?

looking at consequences of choice

C: On this side of the chasm? But it leaves me with my playfulness. I don't believe it, though. I don't believe that's necessary. It's a hypothetical thing and it just doesn't . . .

G: But, pay attention: In terms of — it's hypothetical — but in terms of escalating the terms, you see what your priorities are. And, within the context of that choice, you would choose the playfulness over . . .

C: No, I wouldn't; no, I wouldn't.

G: Well, you just did right now.

C: I know it (laughs). That was just a momentary thing.

G: Oh, I see.

C: (sigh) Because the playfulness is really attractive to me.

There's a real trap there, because if I start to think in terms of *making*, you know, if I *had* to, that energizes a part of me that says (deep voice), "Yes, you must!" you know, and gets very stern and very exclusive.

exploring patterns of resistance

G: Then it evokes your Top Dog . . .

a common subpersonality

C: Yeah.

G: So when your Top Dog takes over, then what happens?

understanding the process

C: Well, then I do exclude . . .

G: Exactly. And then you're not really choosing.

C: Right. I'm doing what I "should" do . . .

G: And there's backlash later.

C: Yeah.

G: Right. Let's stay at that point, then. There's your Top Dog there; can you see the playfulness, can you see all the other stuff?

C: Uh-huh.

G: Are you still willing to choose, to go toward the mustness, what you must do?

C: (pause) I have to get real quiet to do that. (pause) Yes.

clarifying meaning of choice

G: What is the "must do"? What does it represent to you?

G: What does it represent to me?

G: Yeah. What are you choosing?

C: I'm choosing to express my Self and bring that into manifestation, to . . . I'm having a little trouble now because I know the "I" isn't supposed to have any qualities and all that stuff, but . . . I experience this sense of power and wisdom and love and compassion, a constellation of manifestations or energy that comes from the Self.

G: How important is it to bring that into your life?

C: What does it mean to bring . . .

G: How important is it?

C: It feels . . . that's why I say there's this sense of mustness . . . it feels like it's at center, it feels like it's at center of importance.

G: So how important is it?

C: It's the central importance; it's *the* meaning.

G: So if you had to choose between the playfulness and, and the step on the brink, what would you choose?

C: I know I *have* to choose the expression of my Self, because the other is only a . . . it's like one means, it's like . . .

G: Are you willing to choose the expression of your Self?

C: Yes.

G: How do you experience yourself when you experience the willingness, the willingness to choose it . . .?

C: I feel strong; I feel joyful and I also feel solid.

G: Do you want to make a choice?

C: I feel courageous.

G: Are you ready to make the choice? What do you think?

C: (laugh) Well, we're taking little baby steps and I didn't know which baby step we were at.

G: Are you willing to make a choice now? To choose the wisdom and power, all of the above, what you must do?

C: Yes.

G: Experience that choice.

C: What I'm experiencing right now is that it's gotten very quiet. Somehow, the stuff that was . . .

G: Did you experience the choice? I hear it's gotten quiet . . . did you experience the choice?

C: I'm not sure.

G: Right. Take a moment to slow that down to where you experience that choice. Don't push past it.

C: (sigh) I'm not used to experiencing choices without experiencing things that are clamoring against it. That's what the quiet is; I'm not getting any resistance right now.

G: Just experience the choice. Slow it down; experience "I'm choosing; I'm choosing the mustness."

C: (pause) I'm choosing to know who I am. (long pause) I don't experience a lot of continuity; I experience a lot of little 'puh, puh, puh.'

G: Okay, just stay with what is. Don't look for what's not. Describe what is.

C: Little 'puh,' little glimpses, little brief moments of light.

G: Are you willing to express what you're experiencing now in the face of embarrassment, in the face of whatever?

testing choice

C: I'm not sure what you're asking. I'm not sure if you're asking me to literally just verbalize or just asking about my willingness.

G: I'm asking you rhetorically about your willingness.

C: I'm willing to and what it feels like is I'm willing to take the risk of being embarrassed.

G: What else?

C: Being wrong.

G: What else?

C: Being rejected . . .

G: What else?

C: Being clumsy and awkward.

G: Allow yourself to move toward that embarrassment, awkwardness, being alone, clumsiness, rejection. See if you can allow yourself to experience that.

C: Experience the embarrassment and all that stuff?

G: Experience all that stuff.

C: Okay.

G: All those patterns; being alone, being rejected; all that stuff.

C: What I'm experiencing now is a sense that it happens out here—the embarrassment and stuff like that.

G: Uh-huh. It happens when you come out?

C: It happens out here but I'm in here.

identifying with the self

G: Right. Okay. Are you still willing to experience all that?

C: Yeah, because I'm in here.

G: And you still choose to express yourself in the face of it?

C: Yes.

G: Okay, experience that choice. Are you willing to choose to express yourself in the face of being rejected and alone, being clumsy, being awkward, being embarrassed?

C: Absolutely. I mean, I feel a very energetic choice

choice is inclusive and strong

G: Okay, experience that choice. Really feel that choice. "I'm willing to choose to express myself in the face of all that." (pause) Allow this.

C: Yes.

G: What do you experience now as you choose this?

C: Right now I experience a very strong identification. I am in this center place. The embarrassment and that sort of stuff is out here.

strong experience of self through choice

G: Good. Do you see that? What do you need to do to see that it's out there and you're there? What do you need to do?

C: Just choose to be.

G: Right.

C: It's the identification (pause) I feel very strong, quiet, quietly strong. Resistance is coming in the form of a caricature of myself. I'm not going to choose that.

further choice

G: Allow it to be there and still choose.

C: Yes. (very long pause) I don't have anything else to say.

G: What do you need to do?

C: That's what I was aware of. I don't know. It feels like I don't need to do anything, not *do* anything. Part of it is just affirming the experience for itself, and not doing any particular numbers around it, because I have a number that I might do which is getting into a distortion of it, doing a kind of imitation of it.

G: Right. What do you have to hold consciously, not *do*?

C: Who I am.

G: The question is, are you willing to be ready to do battle with the parts of your personality which are going to pull you away and make you less? And still choose in the face of this?

C: Choose them, and also . . . I mean choose to be who I am in the face of them and also choose to be in relationship with them.

G: Uh-huh. That would mean you would do this session and not get stuck bumping up against someone or being rejected, or that other stuff. Are you willing to take that risk, to incur the risk of being rejected, being alone, being awkward and clumsy?

C: Yes, because . . . I'm extremely willing to do that and the willingness is kind of *resident* in what I feel, where I am right now. It doesn't even take a conscious movement; it's right here, the willingness is, and it seems to be because all that stuff I'm risking is trivial . . .

G: Are you willing to do this now?

affirming inclusive nature of choice

C: Yes. It's like saying are you willing to learn to ice skate even though you might fall down a few times, or to ski. Sure you will, you're bound to fall down if you're skiing. That doesn't bother me; it's that kind of feeling about it. Yeah, I'm willing to be wrong, I'm willing to be embarrassed; I'm willing to make mistakes; I'm willing to be challenged; I'm willing to be rejected; that's all sort of like practicing.

G: In fact all those things could help move you towards . . .

C: Exactly. It's all part of the learning.

deepening experience of the self

G: Right. Let's just go a step further, okay? Now get a sense of who you are in that choice. What comes up in that moment? (pause) And ask yourself what's most meaningful to you in that moment, who you are right now?

C: (pause) I'm getting a lot of words that are sort of pointing to something, some phenomena. Love and purpose and harmony and at-one-ment.

seeking deep source of experience: the Self

G: Okay, let's go a step further. See what comes up when you ask yourself the purpose of love and harmony and at-one-ment.

C: I thought there were no words for it and then I said to myself if I did have words for it, what would they be? (pause) Being, an expression of being.

G: Stay with that; keep on penetrating into that. What's the purpose of love and harmony and at-one-ment? What is the purpose of love?

C: Expression. Identification. Creation.

G: Really experiencing that.

C: I'm experiencing the words I was just saying. I'm experiencing myself as part of that.

G: Do you have a sense of that? Shall we go a step further?

C: Uh-huh.

G: From this place of experiencing yourself as part of that, look out on the world, see how the world looks to you.

grounding in the world

C: I see out the window, the spires of the city.

G: Can you see the city there?

C: It seems very multi-faceted, incredibly rich, teeming with, with complexities, interrelations. I see a lot of pain and I see a lot of joy and I see a lot of growth and I see a lot of death and I see a lot of everything.

It seems a mystery and yet it isn't the kind of mystery that means I can't know about it. It just means that my intellect can't know about it.

G: How do you experience yourself now in relation to all that?

C: Part of it. And yet there's . . . I'm part of it and yet there's something that I'm in touch with that transcends it.

G: Experience both; part of it and also the transcending at the same time.

C: There's a, there's like a big circle; I became part of it and transcended it, became part of it and transcended it. It's like a . . . (pause) When I think in terms of . . . when I'm in touch with the transcendent part of the cycle, there's a sense of wanting to serve and then in the process of doing that, I go back and become part of it again.

integration of service and transcendence

G: Okay, stay with that.

C: And every now and then I have to come up out of it in order to be able to see what needs to be done.

G: Right. But see, there's a big impulse to serve.

C: Um.

G: So let's just follow this . . . step back for a moment. As you made the choice to express yourself in the face of all those risks, from that place, I said what's most meaningful to you and you said love, harmony, at-one-ment, purpose. And I said go with the purpose of all that stuff and you moved towards this experience which gave you a sense of transcendent qualities which come with the impulse to serve. So for you to make that choice . . . brings you closer to the impulse to serve. Make sense?

clarifying process, making it more conscious

C: Uh-huh. In fact, the impulse to serve seems to be part of that mustness, part of that compelling energy.

G: Now let's go a step further. Just allow yourself as much as is appropriate to experience the energy of this transcendence and still have the connection with people. Just energetically, experience the energy of this.

C: (pause) I feel the light coming down through the top of my head. And somewhere inside of me, I'm saying "Oh! That's what it is, that's what it's all about."

G: Let's go a little deeper. Every time a pattern comes in, when you see a pattern, whatever guiding away from form to source

it be light or anything, let go of the pattern and experience the energy the pattern is holding. Whether it be thought or an image or . . . focus on the energy; that's the essence of the pattern.

C: (very long pause) I'm seeing some things and I'm still experiencing; it's like I'm seeing from this place. One of the things that I'm seeing is that the fear or arrogance that I was experiencing before was a fear of transcendence. That's where that "Oh!" was coming from.

G: Stay with the energy.

C: I will.

G: The transcendence you're experiencing, remember, is in relation to people.

C: I know. It's part of a cycle; it isn't a separate sort of immovable spot.

G: Without the connection to people, what would happen then?

C: I become arrogant.

G: Exactly, see that? Which removes you. What grounds you is to have that connection.

C: That's a big part of it. (pause) The world needs me and I need the world.

G: Right. Exactly. Saying the second part, that I need the world, takes care of the arrogance. The arrogance is a reactive thing that removes you, removes itself. When you see what the meaning is, you experience both the transcendence and what's behind the arrogance, and it keeps that connection.

C: All right. (chuckles, sigh) I have an image of being in that cycle of trancendence and being part of it and I was seeing you in the same cycle and I was seeing us meeting each other at different points in our cycles. So sometimes you're transcendent and in a position to serve and I'm down there in all the muck. Sometimes it's the other way around and sometimes we're both halfway or . . . it feels like a very adequate model. (laughs) I feel finished.

The margin notes read:

guiding away from form to source

understanding the balance

summarizing

GLOSSARY

Terms used in this paper and in psychosynthesis practice are defined here as they are commonly used in that context. Words common to other psychological approaches are not included unless they have a special psychosynthesis meaning.

abstraction: The guide's working hypothesis of what is emerging in the client's process. Also, the models and concepts used to understand the client's process.

alignment: Congruence between one's personal will and choices and Transpersonal Will.

attachment: A desire to acquire and/or keep something perceived as external to one's essential being, be it object, role, identity, relationship, or circumstances.

awareness: The most basic experience of consciousness. It includes but is not dependent on perception, comprehension, analysis, and understanding. Awareness is considered to exist even without sensory input; it is the apprehension of being.

balance: To bring parts of oneself into equal awareness and value so that each is used without any being in control.

causal: Consciously choosing one's actions and attitudes based on values rather than purely on external circumstances.

center: As in a wheel, the hub of power and balance; the personal experience of being non-attached and non-identified with an particular object, event, or personality aspect.

chairwork: The Gestalt therapy technique of using an empty chair to represent an aspect of the client or another person with whom the client then dialogues.

choice: Conscious or unconscious selection of attitude or action; the essential act of *will*.

client: The person being guided. Synonyms are patient (may imply sickness), and traveler (not understood in common parlance).

content: The specific ideas, words, situations, feelings, and images contained in awareness or in a client's verbal description of process.

disidentification: The process of removing one's sense of 'I' from an external role, attitude, subpersonality, or limited aspect of oneself.

dynamics: The forces which produce motion and change in a system or process.

emerging: Coming into manifestation from the unconscious.

emotionally identified: Perceiving oneself primarily in terms of one's feelings.

evoke: Bring forth an idea, insight, or choice by careful questioning, suggestion, or non-verbal communication.

facilitate: To cooperate with and assist in developing.

grounding: Creative and practical integration of insights and choices made during a session into one's daily life.

group Self: A source of purpose and energy for a group which is the union of the Higher Selves of the group members.

growth: Development to a more inclusive, integrated, and effective whole person.

guide: One who helps others discover and travel their own life paths; synonomous with counselor or therapist in the broadest sense of those terms.

guided daydream: A coherent imaginary inner 'story' with suggestions for proceeding offered by a guide.

guided fantasy: A guided daydream.

guided imagery: The use of symbols and imaginary situations to explore feelings and life patterns, either briefly or at length. May include visual, auditory, tactile, and kinesthetic imagery.

guiding: Counseling which focuses on cooperating with and enhancing the client's natural growth process and fullest potentials.

Higher Self: "A deep and all-inclusive center of identity and of being" within each person "where individuality and universality blend" ("What is Psychosynthesis?", *Synthesis 1*, 1974, p. 113).

higher unconscious: The realm of the unconscious from which originate more highly evolved impulses: altruistic love and will, humanitarian action, artistic and scientific inspiration, philosophic and spiritual insight, and the drive for purpose and meaning in life. Also called the superconscious.

161

homework: Activities which the client does between sessions to continue, develop, and ground work done in a session.

I: 1) Traditionally, a synonym for the personal self, a sense of unchanging identity beneath transitory feelings, thoughts, and physical actions. 2) Recently, Doug Russell has proposed the 'I' be considered a moveable point of identity which may reside in the self or be temporarily identified with a subpersonality or personality aspect (personal communication, 1979).

identification (with): The act or process of including an experience or quality in one's sense of who one is. This can be a re-owning of a previously denied part of oneself, or it can be a limiting self-definition which excludes a larger reality. One can also identify with the self.

identity: Self-concept; who one thinks and feels one is.

inner dialogue: A conversation between various symbols, figures, or voices within one's imagination.

inner wisdom: The deep knowledge and integrative faculty of the superconscious; although usually unconscious, can be reached through meditation and other techniques.

intention: Energetic willingness to move towards a purpose; within a session, the motivation to learn and grow in a specific area.

intervention: A response of the guide to the client's process, including verbal and nonverbal communication.

intuition: A wholistic, syntnetic apprehension of truth without reasoning or outer experience. Intuitive knowledge is in harmony with universal principles and originates in the superconscious.

knowing: Besides the traditional meaning, can also refer to inner conviction, similar to inner wisdom and intuition.

love: Used here in the sense of impersonal, altruistic love which appreciates and desires to serve the highest and best in other people

lower unconscious: The realm of the unconscious from which originate biological drives and instincts, and which is the repository for repressed past experiences.

manifest: To bring into conscious, visible expression a pattern which heretofore has been unconscious and latent.

meditation: Quiet, inward awareness used in many forms for the purpose of reaching a relatively pure experience of the self and opening to superconscious patterns and techniques.

mentally identified: Perceiving oneself primarily in terms of thoughts and intellectual capabilities.

mind: In psychosynthesis, mind usually refers to the faculty of reasoning and other intellectual activities.

model: An intellectual construct which is useful for presenting a concept which helps the mind to comprehend something indirectly, but should not be mistaken for reality itself.

next step: The new, larger whole towards which the natural process of growth is leading; implies a conscious choice to embrace and integrate this new pattern in one's daily life.

pattern: A constellation of interrelated energies. On the personality level, a pattern may manifest as behaviors, feelings, thoughts, intuition, and/or physical states.

peak experience: Periods of intensified perception, heightened emotion of an esctatic, pleasurable quality, and increased mental receptivity and apprehension, often including a sense of union and harmony with all Being—with one's highest conception of God.

personal psychosynthesis: The process of growth leading to the integration of the personality around the personal self, a center of awareness and will.

plan: In a session, the overall sense of direction and of appropriate methods which the guide develops and modifies as the session unfolds.

presence: The totality of the guide's personality, consciousness and will as it is focussed in a session on the client and the client's process.

process: The totality of interactions and changing relationships between the various psychological and physiological energies of an individual or a group.

projection: The attributing of one's internal characteristics or conflicts onto external people, objects, or events.

psychological entropy: The tendency to avoid responsibility and choice, to lose identity in passive mass consciousness, to avoid pain even at the cost of personal integrity and purpose.

psychosynthesis: The natural growth process of human beings towards coherence, wholeness, and harmony, on the level of the personality and the individual as well as within relationships, groups, communities, and the whole of humanity.

purpose: In an individual session, the sense of what is to be enhanced or facilitated by the session; the reason for doing the session on the deepest level of the client's growth process.

quality: Usually, a transpersonal quality; attributes of character which reflect universal principles, such as love, strength, clarity, or harmony.

reactive: Unconscious, automatic response to a stimulus, as opposed to consciously chosen response.

resistance: Energy opposing the bringing of something to consciousness or expression; also, behavior having this effect.

responsibility: The conscious recognition and acceptance of one's capacity to choose the various aspects of one's life.

Self: The source of individual awareness and will of which the personal self is a partial reflection; one's deepest and most essential identity which unites the individual with universal Being.

self: The personal self, the center of awareness and will which directs and harmonizes the personality; a reflection of the Higher Self.

Self-expression: The bringing into form through the personality of qualities and patterns originating from the Self.

Self-realization: Awakening to one's true nature as a Self and the expression of that Self in one's life.

service: Activities which contribute to the growth and expansion of life; for each individual, service may take a specific form, such as humanitarian activities, teaching, healing, artistic or musical expression, ecological enhancement, etc.

session: A period of focused work with a guide and client (the latter may be an individual, couple, family, or group).

spiritual: Pertaining to the realm of human experience involving values, meaning, purpose, and the unification with universal principles, patterns, and energies.

spiritual psychosynthesis: The alignment of the personal self and the personality with the Higher Self through a gradual assimilation of superconscious energies and their integration in the personality; a natural process which can be enhanced by conscious choice.

subpersonality: A semi-autonomous "structured constellation of attitudes, drives, habit patterns, logical elements which is organized in adaptation to forces in the internal and external environment" (Crampton, 1977).

superconscious: The higher unconscious.

synthesis: The transformation into a larger, inclusive whole of two or more previously disparate or conflicting elements; the effect of syntropy in psychological process.

transformation: A holistic, all-at-once change in nature or form to a higher order.

transpersonal: Pertaining to experience which transcends or goes beyond personal, individual identity and meaning; involves values, meaning, purpose, and unification with universal principles; synonomous with spiritual.

Transpersonal Self: The Self or Higher Self; the source of individual identity and will which unites with the universal.

Transpersonal Will: The will of the Higher Self; a unifying, synergistic force which brings the individual's life into harmony with universal principles.

transcend: To rise above, to raise one's consciousness and choice above the control of forces at a lower level.

traveler: One who is consciously engaged in the process of growth and seeks assistance from a guide; a client or patient seen in a broad perspective.

two dimensions of growth: The concept that human growth occurs along two dimensions: the personal (horizontal) and the transpersonal (vertical). (Firman and Vargiu, 1977)

Universal Being: The totality of essential Reality.

Universal Will: The essential intentionality expressed in all movement and relationship in the universe.

vision: An ideal image of purpose and direction to be brought into manifestation in one's life.

will: The primary psychological function of the self through which every aspect of one's life is chosen and integrated; the capacity to choose and direct one's actions and destiny.

ILLUSTRATOR'S NOTES

The inner eye and the outer eye: the illustrator shuttles between them. The inner eye has the visions, but the outer eye must pull them to earth and find them clothing in the metaphors of ordinary sight. Here is a series of visions on psychosynthesis.

CHAPTER 1
Two youths rest on a wall, on the brink of new territory. Are they boys or girls? Who is the guided, who is the guide?

CHAPTER 2
Suddenly there is no weight, no drag: the plant is whole, root and leaf, but it floats free.

CHAPTER 3
The subpersonalities and guides are too many to name! But you may look for Daniel and the Healer, the Master and the Welshwoman, the Centaur and a cloud of nameless fear—that should get you started.

CHAPTER 4
Equals around the growing tree, both women nurture it as they nurture each other.

CHAPTER 5
In the tree, the seasons coexist in time, from winter to summer back to winter again and rest.

CHAPTER 6
Remember the white stag of European folktale: the idea, the theme, the quarry that wills itself to be caught.

CHAPTER 7
The waterfall flows onward effortlessly, with fluidity and power, easing itself around obstacles and slowly wearing them away, adapting rather than resisting.

CHAPTER 8
The light! The light! But it comes from within.

CHAPTER 9
Old, a little worn, lovely, grieving, wise: she has turned her back on the clutter, dear though it is, and she will talk instead to the cat and to the open window.

THE WELL
The source of life and nourishment lies in the middle of the town square, and the community radiates out around it.

Betsy James
Santa Fe, 1983

REFERENCES

Assagioli, R. *Jung and psychosynthesis*. New York: Psychosynthesis Research Foundation, 1967.

Assagioli, R. *The act of will*. New York: Penguin, 1974.

Assagioli, R. *Psychosynthesis*. New York: Penguin, 1976.

Assagioli, R. *Self-realization and psychological disturbances*. Synthesis 3-4, 1977, 148-171.

Bandler, R. & Grinder, J. *The structure of magic*, Vols. I & II. Palo Alto: Science and Behavior Books, 1975 & 1976.

Berne, E. *Games people play*. New York: Grove Press, 1964.

Bolles, R. *What color is your parachute?* Berkeley, Calif.: Ten Speed Press, 1981.

Bugental, J. F. T. *The search for authenticity*. New York: Holt, Rinehart & Winston, 1965.

Bugental, J. F. T., Ed. *Challenges of humanistic psychology*. New York: McGraw-Hill, 1967.

Bugental, J. F. T. *Psychotherapy and process*. Reading, Mass.: Addison-Wesley, 1978.

Carkhuff, R. & Berenson, B. G. *Beyond counseling and therapy*. New York: Holt, Rinehart & Winston, 1976.

Carter-Harr, B. Identity and personal freedom. *Synthesis 2*, 1975, pp. 56-91.

Castenada, C. *The teachings of don Juan*. Berkeley: University of California, 1968.

Chaudhuri, H. Yoga psychology. *Transpersonal psychologies*, C. Tart, ed. New York: Harper & Row, 1975.

Crampton, M. The use of mental imagery in psychosynthesis. *Journal of Humanistic Psychology*, Fall, 1969.

Crampton, M. Answers from the unconscious. *Synthesis 2*, 1975, pp. 140-152.

Crampton, M. *Psychosynthesis: some key aspects of theory and practice*. Montreal: Canadian Institute of Psychosynthesis, 1977.

Deatherage, G. The clinical use of 'mindfulness' meditation techniques in short-term psychotherapy. *Journal of Transpersonal Psychology*, 1975, 7, 133-140.

Deikman, A. J. The observing self: Mysticism and psychotherapy. Boston: Beacon Press, 1982.

de Ropp, R. S. *The master game*. New York: Delacorte, 1968.

Desoille, R. *The directed daydream*. New York: Psychosynthesis Research Foundation, 1966.

Emmons, M. *The inner source*. San Luis Obispo: Impact, 1978.

Erhard, W. & Fadiman, J. Some aspects of *est* training and transpersonal psychology: a conversation. *Journal of Transpersonal Psychology*, 1977, 9, 27-42.

Fadiman, J. & Frager, R. *Personality and personal growth*. New York: Harper & Row, 1976.

Ferguson, M. *The aquarian conspiracy*. Los Angeles: Tarcher, 1980.

Ferrucci, P. *What we may be*. Los Angeles: Tarcher, 1982.

Field, R. *The invisible way*. San Francisco: Harper & Row, 1979.

Firman, J. & Vargiu, J. Dimensions of growth. *Synthesis 3-4*, 1977, 59-120.

Frankl, V. *The will to meaning*. New York: New American Library, 1970.

Fromm, E. Psychoanalysis and Zen Buddhism. *Zen Buddhism and psychoanalysis*, Susuki, Fromm & DeMartino. New York: Grove Press, 1960.

Gendlin, E. *Focusing*. New York: Everest House, 1978.

Gibran, K. *The prophet*. New York: Alfred A. Knopf, 1960.

Goleman, D. Meditation as meta-therapy; hypothesis toward a proposed fifth state of consciousness. *Journal of Transpersonal Psychology*, 1971, 3, 1-8.

Haronian, F. *Repression of the sublime*. Psychosynthesis Research Foundation, 1967.

Haronian, F. A psychosynthetic model of personality and its implications for psychotherapy. *Journal of Humanistic Psychology*, 1975, 15, 25-51.

Hillman, J. *Re-visioning psychology*. New York: Harper & Row, 1975.

Hughes, A. & Hughes, N. In *Third annual symposium report west*. Meditation Group for the New Age, Ojai, Calif., May 20, 1978.

James W. *The principles of psychology*. 2 Vols. Dover, New York: Henry Holt & Co., 1890. Unaltered republication, New York: Dover, 1950.

James, W. *The varieties of religious experience*. New York: New American Library, 1958.

Jourard, S. *The transparent self*. New York: Van Nostrand Reinhold, 1964.

Jung, C. G. *Psychological types*. New York: Harcourt, Brace & World, 1933.

Jung, C. G. Conscious, unconscious, and inviduation. *Collected works,* Vol. 9, Part 1. Princeton: Princeton University Press. (First published, 1939).

Jung, C. G. Foreword. *The I Ching,* R. Wilhelm Translation. Princeton: Princeton University Press, 1950.

Jung, C. G. Aion: Contributions to the symbolism of the Self. *Psyche and symbol,* V. S. de Laszlo, ed. Garden City: Doubleday, 1958.

Jung, C. G., ed. *Man and his symbols.* Garden City: Doubleday, 1964.

Jung, C. G. *Analytic psychology: its theory and practice.* New York: Pantheon, 1973.

Jung, C. G. *Letters.* G. Adler, ed. Princeton: Princeton University Press, 1973.

Keen, S. The golden mean of Roberto Assagioli. *Psychology Today,* December, 1974.

Kennett, J. (Roshi), Radha (Swami), & Frager, R. How to be a transpersonal teacher without becoming a guru. *Journal of Transpersonal Psychology,* 1975, 7(1), 48-65.

Kubler-Ross, E. *On death and dying.* New York: MacMillan, 1974.

Leonard, G. *The silent pulse.* New York: E. P. Dutton, 1978.

Leonard, G. *Education and ecstacy.* New York: Delacorte, 1968.

Leuner, H. Guided affective imagery (GAI). *American Journal of Psychotherapy,* 1969, 23(1), 4-22.

Maslow, A. H. *Motivation and personality.* New York: Harper & Bros., 1954.

Maslow, A. H. *Toward a psychology of being.* 2nd ed. New York: Van Nostrand, 1968.

Maslow, A. H. *The further reaches of human nature.* New York: Viking, 1971.

May, R. *Man's search for himself.* New York: Norton, 1953.

May, R. *Love and will.* New York: Norton, 1969.

Miller, S. Dialogue with the higher Self. *Synthesis 2,* 1975, 122-139.

Moreno, J. *Psychodrama,* 3 Vols. Scranton, Penn.: Beacon Press.

Nelson, Alan. The profession's role in peace facilitation. *Winter Newsletter,* Association for Transpersonal Psychology, 1982-3.

Perls, F, *Gestalt therapy verbatim.* Lafayette, Calif.: Real People Press, 1969.

Perls, F., Hefferline, R., & Goodman, P. *Gestalt therapy.* New York: Dell, 1951.

Pribam, K. What the fuss is all about. *Re-Vision,* 1978, *1,* 14-18.

Progoff, I. *At a journal workshop.* New York: Dialogue House, 1975.

Rama (Swami), Ballentine, R. & Ajaya (Swami). *Yoga psychotherapy.* Glenview, Ill.: Himalayan Institute, 1976.

Ram Dass. Advise to a psychotherapist. *Journal of Transpersonal Psychology,* 1975, 7,(1), 84-92.

Ram Dass. *Grist for the mill.* Santa Cruz, Calif.: Unity Press, 1977.

Riordan, K. Gurdjieff. *Transpersonal psychologies,* C. Tart, ed. New York: Harper & Row, 1975.

Rogers, C. R. *Counseling and psychotherapy.* Cambridge: Riverside, 1942.

Rogers, C. R. *On becoming a person.* Boston: Houghton Mifflin, 1961.

Rogers, C. R. In retrospect: forty-six years. *The American Psychologist,* 1974, 29, 115-123.

Rogers, C. R. *Carl Rogers on personal power.* New York: Delacorte, 1978.

Russell, D. Seven basic constructs of psychosynthesis. *Psychosynthesis Digest,* 1, (2), 1982, 67-68.

Shapiro, S. B. Myself as an instrument. *Challenges of humanistic psychology,* J. Bugental, ed. New York: McGraw-Hill, 1967.

Sheehy, G. *Passages.* New York: E. P. Dutton, 1974.

Shorr, J. E. *Psycho-imagination therapy.* New York: Intercontinental Medical Book Corp., 1972.

Shultz, J. V. Stages on the spiritual path: a Buddhist perspective. *Journal of Transpersonal Psychology,* 1975, 7(1), 14-28.

Singer, J. *Boundaries of the soul.* New York: Anchor, 1973.

Spangler, D. *Revelation: the birth of a new age.* Findhorn: Findhorn Foundation, 1977.

Sutich, A. J. Transpersonal therapy. *Journal of Transpersonal Psychology,* 1973, 5(1), 1-6.

Suzuki, D. T. *Introduction to Zen Buddhism.* London: Rider, 1949.

Suzuki, D. T., Fromm, E. & DeMartino, R. *Zen Buddhism and psychoanalysis.* New York: Grove Press, 1960.

Tart, C., ed. *Transpersonal psychologies.* New York: Harper & Row, 1975.

Taylor, G. C. *The essentials of psychosynthesis.* New York: Psychosynthesis Research Foundation, 1968.

Vargiu, J. Subpersonalities. *Synthesis 1,* 1974, 52-90.

Vargiu, J. Lecture delivered at the Psychosynthesis Institute, Redwood City, Calif., August, 1974.

Vargiu, J. Creativity. *Synthesis 3-4,* 1977, 17-53.

Vaughan, F. *Awakening intuition.* Garden City: Anchor, 1979.

Vaughan-Clark, F. Exploring intuition: prospects and possibilities. *Journal of Humanistic Psychology,* 1973, 5, 156-166.

Vaughan-Clark, F. Transpersonal perspectives in psychotherapy. *Journal of Humanistic Psychology,* Spring, 1977, *17,* 69-81.

von Franz, M.-L. The process of individuation. *Man and his symbols.* C. G. Jung, ed. Garden City: Doubleday, 1964.

Walsh, R. N. Initial meditative experiences: part II. *Journal of Transpersonal Psychology,* 1973, 5(1), 7-14.

What is psychosynthesis? *Synthesis 1,* 1975, 112-115.

Wickes, F. G. *The inner world of choice.* New York: Harper & Row, 1963.

Wilber, K. *The spectrum of consciousness.* Wheaton, Ill.: Theosophical Publishing House, 1977.

Yeomans, A. Psychosynthesis: a personal experience with a holistic system. *New Realities,* 1977, 9-13.

Yogananda, P. *Sayings of Yogananda.* Los Angeles: Self-Realization Fellowship, 1968.

REFERENCE NOTES

Elkins, D. Talk at conference of Association for Humanistic Psychology, Princeton, N.J., 1979.

Yeomans, T. Seminar at the Psychosynthesis Institute, San Francisco, CA, 1978.

INDEX

Available early in 1993:

A new book by Molly Young Brown

GROWING WHOLE:
SELF-REALIZATION ON AN ENDANGERED PLANET

Offering simple, direct access to the powerful tools of psychosynthesis, this self-study guide is for people seeking to live more creative and meaningful lives and to contribute to an Earth-saving transformation of consciousness.

Order from:

Hazelden Educational Materials
P.O. Box 176
Center City MN 55012
(612) 257-4010

or through your local bookstore